全国高职高专院校商务英语规划系列教材

新编国际商务礼仪

An English Course for International Business Etiquette

主　编　陆　恩

副主编　周福娟

编　者　（按姓氏笔画排序）

李长江　李琰艳　吴芳方

何剑霞　张晓红　陈　瑛

徐秋萍　龚　琳　潘莉莉

魏敏华

顾　问　Ross Patrick Deecke

策　划　汤定军

苏州大学出版社

图书在版编目(CIP)数据

新编国际商务礼仪/陆恩主编. —苏州：苏州大学出版社,2013.4
全国高职高专院校商务英语规划系列教材
ISBN 978-7-5672-0460-7

Ⅰ.①新… Ⅱ.①陆… Ⅲ.①国际商务-礼仪-英语-高等职业教育-教材 Ⅳ.①H31

中国版本图书馆CIP数据核字(2013)第063258号

书　　名：新编国际商务礼仪
An English Course for International Business Etiquette
作　　者：陆　恩　主编
责任编辑：汤定军
策　　划：汤定军
装帧设计：刘　俊
出版发行：苏州大学出版社(Soochow University Press)
社　　址：苏州市十梓街1号　邮编：215006
印　　刷：常熟高专印刷有限公司
网　　址：www.sudapress.com
E - mail：tangdingjun@suda.edu.cn
邮购热线：0512-67480030
销售热线：0512-65225020
开　　本：787mm×960mm　1/16　印张：18.5　字数：333千
版　　次：2013年4月第1版
印　　次：2013年4月第1次印刷
书　　号：ISBN 978-7-5672-0460-7
定　　价：38.00元

前言

随着经济全球化和网络信息时代的到来，国际商务往来越来越频繁、越来越便利。世界各国的社会制度、文化背景不同，礼仪习俗也存在着一定程度的差异。中国自古以来一直有“礼仪之邦”之美誉。俗话说，国无礼则无兴，事无礼则无成，人无礼则无立。国际商务礼仪是商务人员在国际商务交往活动中应该遵守的礼仪规范，是体现相互尊重的行为准则，是人际交往的艺术。中国时尚礼仪教母周思敏老师认为，人的礼仪价值百万，有礼可以走天下。礼仪是企业形象、企业文化、员工修养素质的综合体现。因此，商务人士必须了解言谈举止、谈判沟通、迎客送往、接听电话、餐饮等方面的礼仪，在涉外贸易中应当了解出口地商人的风俗，做到“入乡随俗”，从而在国际贸易中处于不败之地。

《新编国际商务礼仪》是针对高等职业技术学院培养外贸企业、进出口业务公司、涉外服务性行业、各类企事业单位等从事外贸业务、行政文职、营销和涉外接待等岗位工作的应用型人才而编写的教材。本着“以就业为导向，以能力为本位 ”的人才培养目标，其教学模式突出职业能力的训练与培养。教材采用项目编排方式，以工作任务为核心，同时突出“情景模拟”，注重听说能力的训练，让学生在模仿实践中通过完成具体项目来构建相关知识框架，发展职业能力。

《新编国际商务礼仪》适合高职高专院校商务英语、国际贸易、国际商务、应用英语、旅游英语、文秘、旅游服务与管理等专业使用，也可供涉外从业人员参考阅读。

《新编国际商务礼仪》共分为十一个项目，涵盖服饰仪表礼仪、办公室礼仪、沟通礼仪、电话礼仪、商务接待礼仪、餐饮礼仪、面试礼仪、商务谈判礼仪、商务馈赠礼仪、商务旅行礼仪等方面，让学生学习跨文化交际中的基本礼仪常识。在编写本教材时，紧跟时代步伐，反映最新语言知识，充分吸收国内外最新的成果，同时不忘常规内容，内容上做到注重基础性、实用性，大多数材料主要选自互联网最新英文资料，充分体现了“必须”、“够用”的高职特色。本教材是为数不多的高职高专国际商务礼仪英文教材之一。在编写过程中，吸收行业企业人员参加，以工作过程为顺序，对接职业标准和岗位要求，教材内容增加了利用互联网学习的部分，使学生学到原汁原味的英语，保证了语言的正确性。

本教材的编写人员均来自高职高专教学第一线，有多年的教学实际经验。他们了解高职教学，了解企业对高职人才的岗位职业能力的需求。本教材配有练习参考答案，使用者可以和主编陆恩联系，联系方式为 luen123@126.com。

陆　恩

2013 年 3 月

Contents

Project One
Introduction to International Business Etiquette

Learning Objectives

After completing this project, you will be able to:

* identify the definitions of etiquette and international business etiquette.

➡ Warming-Up

Discuss the following questions with your peers.

❑ What is etiquette?

❑ Can you give some examples of etiquette?

▶ Listening

http://www.unsv.com/voanews/business-etiquette/lessons/001/

Listen to the recording and fill in the blanks.

Introduction on Etiquette

(*Office ambience*)

C:Excuse me, Mary, 请问通知上这个词是什么意思呀? E-t-i-q-u-e-t-t-e。

M:Oh, etiquette, 原来是法文,意思是礼节。

C:噢,原来是要我去参加礼节训练班。Mary,这词是怎么发音的?

M:E-ti-ket。Q-u 是发 k 的音,而不是发 q 的音,e-ti-ket。

C:我们来公司工作,又不是来社交,为什么要讲礼节呀?

M:____。

一个公司的雇员对客户是不是很客气、有礼貌,这对经营有很大关系。

C:具体地说,这儿说的 etiquette 指些什么呢?

M:____

____。

C:以文明的方式对待别人的一些原则。

M:具体地说就是

____

____。

C:嗯,(若有所思地) 对人要有礼貌,要尊敬别人,还要让人觉得和你在一起很自如。这没问题,

____。

M:但是,训练班讲的是西方礼节——Western etiquette,和中国的礼节还不完全一样,因为两国有文化差异。

C:这礼节还有文化差异?我得去训练班听听再说。

C:嗨, Mary,我的训练班结束了,你那天说的文化差异一点也没错。

M:听起来训练班好像让你开窍啦?

C:是啊。我那天跟会计室的那金发女郎聊天,聊得很愉快。结果我问她多大年纪了,她一下子就变得很不高兴,支支吾吾没有回答就走了。

M:____。

C:参加了训练班才知道不能问美国人年龄的。

M:你办公室里的小王今天早上突然问年薪有多少。美国人认为打听这种私人的事是不礼貌的。我想对有些中国人来说也是不礼貌的。

C:没错。

M:既然你训练班已经结束,我来考考你:Tell me what is etiquette?

C:我来试试。

____

____。

M:____

____。

C：Mary，以后我有问题还会来请教你哟！

M：No problem.

▶ Reading

Task One

What Is Etiquette?

When we talk about etiquette, we often say that China is a country with a time-honored civilization and with a long history of ritual and etiquette. China is known as "the nation of rites", "a country of etiquette and ceremonies". Then what is etiquette? *Merriam-Webster Collegiate Dictionary* defines it as "the forms, manners and ceremonies established by convention as acceptable or required in social relations, in a profession, or in official life". According to *Collins COBUILD Advanced Learner's English-Chinese Dictionary*, Etiquette is a set of customs and rules for polite behavior, especially among a particular class of people or in a particular profession. From Wikipedia, the free encyclopedia, we can see that etiquette is a code of behavior that delineates expectations for social behavior according to contemporary conventional norms within a society, social class, or group. It refers to conventional requirements as to social behavior; proprieties of conduct as established in any class or community or for any occasion. It also refers to a prescribed or accepted code of usage in matters of ceremony, as at a court or in official or other formal observances. To some of us, the word "etiquette" simply means "good manners". To others, it means so much more. While both of these concepts involve rules of behavior, they are slightly different, and they involve different types of skills. The primary distinction between etiquette and manners is that the first includes specific rules of conduct, while the other is more generalized. Manners involve general behaviorial guidelines, such as treating the elderly with respect and courtesy. Etiquette is a specific code of behavior, with an example of etiquette being knowledge of the proper mode of address for a queen.

Etiquette is derived from the French word "étiquet", meaning "sign". The French word "étiquette" used to mean "keep off the grass". Louis XIV's gardener noticed that the aristocrats were walking through his gardens and put up signs, or étiquets, to ward them off. The dukes and duchesses walked right past these signs. Due to this blatant disregard, the King of Versailles decreed that no individual was to go beyond the bounds of the étiquets. The meaning of etiquette later expanded to include the ticket to court functions that listed the instructions on all rules and regulations regarding what to do and where to stand at all court functions. The meaning of etiquette has evolved over time, but in a sense it still means "keep off the grass".

In business today, we hear the term "protocol" used more than "etiquette" because it sounds more professional and official. Most companies have established their own set of rules of protocol as part of their culture to ensure smooth daily operations. The term "protocol" is derived from two Greek words: "protos", meaning "the first", and "kola", meaning "glue". By the 19th century, the French term "protocole diplomatique" or "protcole de la chancellerie" referred to ceremonial rules to be observed in all written or personal interaction between heads of different states or their ministers. Today, protocol serves as the code of international politeness that blends diplomatic form, ceremony, and etiquette. Protocols are forms of ceremony and etiquette observed by diplomats and heads of state. In short, protocol is the science of rules and regulations while etiquette is the way you handle any given situation and how you make others feel.

New Words and Expressions

etiquette	[ˈetiket]	*n.*	礼仪,礼节,礼貌;规矩
time-honored	[ˈtaimˈɔnəd]	*adj.*	历史悠久的
civilization	[ˌsivilaiˈzeiʃən]	*n.*	文明;文化
ritual	[ˈritjuəl]	*n.*	仪式;惯例;礼制
		adj.	仪式的;例行的;礼节性的
ceremony	[ˈseriməni]	*n.*	典礼,仪式;礼节,礼仪,礼貌
convention	[kənˈvenʃən]	*n.*	习惯,习俗;集会,(正式)会议,(定期)大会

encyclopedia	[inˌsaikləu'piːdiə]	*n.*	(encyclopaedia)百科全书
delineate	[di'linieit]	*vt.*	描写,描述;叙述
contemporary	[kən'temprəri]	*adj.*	现代的,当代的,同时代存在的
norm	[nɔːm]	*n.*	标准,规范,准则
propriety	[prə'praiəti]	*n.*	适当,适宜;正当的行为;礼貌,礼节,礼仪
community	[kə'mjuːnəti]	*n.*	社区;社会;社团;团体
prescribe	[pri'skraib]	*vt.*	命令,指示;规定;限制,限定
observance	[əb'zəːvəns]	*n.*	遵守,奉行;纪念,庆祝;程序;仪式,礼仪
distinction	[di'stiŋkʃən]	*n.*	辨别,识别,区别,鉴别;差异,不同
encounter	[in'kauntə]	*vt.*	受到,遭遇,遭到(困难、麻烦、反对等)
aristocrat	['æristəkræt;ə'ristə-]	*n.*	贵族阶层的成员;(一个)贵族
duke	[djuːk]	*n.*	公爵,(公国的)君主
duchess	['dʌtʃis]	*n.*	公爵夫人,女公爵
blatant	['bleitənt]	*adj.*	露骨的,公然的;炫耀的;显眼的
disregard	[ˌdisri'gɑːd]	*vt./n.*	不顾;不理会;不注意,不考虑
decree	[di'kriː]	*vt.*	颁布(法令、政令),发布(命令);命令;任命
evolve	[i'vɔlv]	*vi.*	渐进,演化,演进
protocol	['prəutəkɔl]	*n.*	礼仪;外交礼节;议定书;协议

Task Two

What Is International Business Etiquette?

Etiquette is dependent on culture; what is excellent etiquette in one society may shock another. Etiquette evolves within culture. For example, men don't remove their hats when they enter a building and men don't open doors for women much anymore nowadays. As standards of conduct are heavily based on cultural tradition and heritage, etiquette varies from culture to culture or nation to nation. China has a rich culture developed over a long history. That history has helped shape standards of etiquette much different from Western norms. In China, a person who takes the last item of food from a common plate or bowl without first offering it to others at the table may be seen as a glutton and insulting the generosity of the host. In America a guest is expected to eat all of the food given to them, as a compliment to the quality of the cooking. In Bulgaria and Albania, the gestures are so confusing that they could make your head spin：nodding your head means no, while shaking it means yes.

Modern business is global and demands people travel to foreign countries and mix with foreign clients, colleagues or customers. Business etiquette varies from region to region and country to country, that is international business etiquette which manifests in many aspects. Throughout the world people from different cultures have varying etiquette rules around areas such as personal space, communication, gift giving, food, business meetings and much more. Etiquette, manners, and cross-cultural or intercultural communication have become critical elements required for all international and global business executives, managers, and employees. Bad business etiquette can ruin a company and business relationships. International business etiquette is in essence about building good relationships with people from different cultures or nations. International business etiquette is simply a means of maximizing one's business potential.

As global business continues to expand and bring everyone closer, the critical element of a successful business outcome may be the appreciation and respect for regional, country, and cultural differences and requiring good intercultural communication. Analyzing, understanding and implementing the etiquette rules of different cultures will help you recognize what business etiquette is and how it should be employed within the business world. Remember the famous saying：“When in Rome, do as the Romans do.”

New Words and Expressions

heritage	[ˈheritidʒ]	*n.*	遗产;继承物;遗留物;传统;文化遗产
shape	[ʃeip]	*vt.*	使形成;使成形;塑造;计划;设计;想出
glutton	[ˈglʌtən]	*n.*	贪吃者,好食者

insult [inˈsʌlt] *n.* 侮辱;辱骂;损害;危害
blend [blend] *vt.* 使混合,掺和;使混杂;使交隔;融合
generosity [ˌdʒenəˈrɔsəti] *n.* 大度;豪爽;慷慨,大方
compliment [ˈkɔmplimənt] *n.* 恭维话,赞美词,颂辞;谦恭有礼,敬意
spin [spin] *vi.* 旋转;纺线,纺纱;疾驰,飞跑
essence [ˈesəns] *n.* 本质,实质;要素;实体,本体

Exercises

I. Read the statements below and decide whether the statements are true or false. Write T for true and F for false.

1. Etiquette is derived from the French word "étiquet", meaning "sign".
2. The French word "protocole" used to mean "keep off the grass".
3. Etiquette and culture are inseparable from each other.
4. The primary distinction between manners and etiquette is that the first includes specific rules of conduct, while the other is more generalized.
5. In Bulgaria and Albania, nodding your head means yes, while shaking it means no.

II. Match each of the following words in Column A to the phrase or definition that is most closely related in Column B.

Column A	Column B
1. manifest	A. the final result of a process, meeting, activity, etc.; the possible or likely result of something
2. implement	B. pleasure in understanding something that is good or beautiful; the feeling you have when you are grateful to someone
3. outcome	C. obvious and easy to notice or understand; to show something such as a feeling or ability, so that it is easy to notice

4. appreciation — D. the most important part of something, usually the part that gives it its general character; a liquid that contains the strong taste or smell of the plant that it is taken from

5. potential — E. to destroy or severely damage something; to spoil something; to make someone lose all their money or power

6. essence — F. to make something such as an idea, plan, system, or law start to work and be used

7. ruin — G. possible or likely in the future; the possibility to develop or achieve something in the future

8. aspect — H. a particular part, feature, or quality of something; the appearance of someone or something

9. colleague — I. kindness, especially in giving things to people

10. generosity — J. sb. who works in the same organization or department as you

III. Put the following sentences into Chinese or vice versa.

1. Graduates are often wet behind the ears and they fail to observe even the very basic business etiquette.
2. The culture of a nation has a set of etiquette patterns that distinguishes it from those of other cultures.
3. Kissing a lady's hand is the general etiquette used to show respect to honorable women in Western countries.
4. Learning proper international business etiquette can be one of the most daunting tasks in the professional world.
5. 还有哪些商务礼仪是你应该记住的?
6. 这位政客常常遵守外交礼节。
7. 当今的全球经济时代,学习和掌握国际礼仪是必不可少的。
8. 大家应该要注意旅行的礼仪。

▶ Speaking

1. Read the text loudly, and try to recite the following paragraph.

Business etiquette varies from region to region and country to country, that is international business etiquette which manifests in many aspects. Throughout the world people from different cultures have varying etiquette rules around areas such as personal space, communication, gift giving, food, business meetings and much more. Etiquette, manners, and cross-cultural or intercultural communication have become critical elements required for all international and global business executives, managers, and employees. Bad business etiquette can ruin a company and business relationships. International business etiquette is in essence about building good relationships with people from different cultures or nations. International business etiquette is simply a means of maximizing one's business potential.

▶ Supplementary Listening

Business Etiquette (008 Protocol)

http://www.51voa.com/Business_Etiquette_1.html

Listen to the dialogues and dictate down the key points.

▶ Supplementary Reading

International Business Etiquette

Rachel Zupek

In Spain, a business dinner will last well into the early morning hours—many restaurants don't even open until 9 p.m. and don't get busy until 10 or 11 p.m.

Australians aren't impressed by a title or status—they expect your work to speak for itself.

The Japanese aren't afraid to ask how much money you earn or how large your home is.

These are only three out of thousands of different customs, business protocols and social mores throughout the world. International business can be tricky; if you aren't prepared, your business deal can go down in flames.

Dana Persia, owner of DP Image Consulting, offers the following lessons in international business etiquette.

Before you go

- Prepare. Do plenty of research on the business and personal etiquette of the particular country you are planning to visit. Purchase a travel book for the country you are going to visit and remember: The Internet is your friend.
- Learn key phrases. It's always a smart move to learn several key phrases in the language of the country you'll visit. It's a nice way to bridge the gap between cultures—and natives will appreciate the attempt.
- Leave the attitude at home. Americans sometimes assume superior attitudes when interacting with foreign cultures—for them it is "our way is the best way". Ditch this stance quickly—you could be ignored or met with disapproval.
- Blend in. In general, Americans dress differently, speak loudly and have distinct accents—so it's best to try not to stand out more than you already will.

Jet lag: Affecting your business?

The last place you want jet lag to take its toll is during an important meeting or business outing. Persia offers these five tricks to deal with jet lag and still do business effectively.

- Try to arrive a few days early to give your body a chance to adjust before important meetings or conferences.
- Get plenty of rest before your trip. Jet lag is worse if you start out sleep-deprived.
- Dehydration doesn't actually cause jet lag, but it does make symptoms worse. Drink plenty of water before, during and after your flight to counteract the dehydrating effects of dry cabin air. Avoid caffeine and alcohol for further dehydration.
- Sleep on the plane if it's nighttime at your destination. Resist the urge if it's

daytime there.

- Set your watch to the new time before you leave. Once you reach your destination, try not to sleep until nighttime, no matter how tired you are. If you must sleep, take a short, one-hour "cat nap".

Different countries, different customs

It's common knowledge that etiquettes differ from person to city to country to continent; keeping all the customs straight can be a headache.

Persia offers these tips to deal with various traditions:

- **Gender roles**

Gender etiquette plays a significant role not only in business, but overall in foreign travel. In some countries, where gender is rooted in the tenets of a particular religion, faux pas are often considered unforgivable.

For example, in the Arab world, shaking hands is mandatory in a business setting; but touching women in traditional, western dress is forbidden. In India, men and women shouldn't make physical contact in public other than handshaking. In Japan, older generations may not be comfortable shaking hands with Westerners and it's important that you don't get too close to them. In Argentina, women should initiate handshakes with men.

- **Talking business**

If you're on business in Germany, leave the trade talk at the boardroom door. Business matters are usually discussed before or after the meal, never during.

Conversely, in China, it's OK to discuss business as long as it's not the main topic of conversation. Personal exchanges about children, spouses or other personal information are encouraged and welcomed.

- **Business cards**

The business card exchange is extremely important in Japan—almost ceremonial. Always give business cards with two hands and make a point to admire and examine the card. The more time you spend looking at it indicates the more respect you have for the person. In Italy, do not exchange business cards at social occasions; it is the norm at business functions and meetings.

• **Alcohol at meals**

In Australia, alcohol is discouraged at business luncheons. Drinking moderately at business meals is acceptable in Germany; in Russia, you are expected to drink to establish closer relationships—though again, in moderation. In France, avoid drinking hard liquor before meals or smoking cigars between courses—the French feel it compromises the taste of the meal.

• **Gifts**

A standard to keep in mind for any gift you select is quality. If you give gifts with your company logo, it's better if the logo is discreet. Never give company logo gifts in Greece, Spain or Portugal. In general, be safe rather sorry and choose non-logo gifts. In China, it's considered rude to open a gift in front of the person who gave it. In Africa, gifts are opened immediately upon receipt.

(http://msn.careerbuilder.com/Article/MSN-1050-Workplace-Issues-International-Business-Etiquette-101/)

Answer the following question:

What are the tips that Dana Persia gives in international business etiquette?

Project Two Business Dressing Etiquette and Grooming

Learning Objectives

After completing this project, you will be able to:

* follow the basic guidelines when preparing to meet with people;
* list the grooming checklist;
* explain the principles of dress etiquette and the differences between a traditional or formal business dress and a business casual;
* apply good or correct posture at workplaces.

Warming-Up

Discuss the following questions with your peers.

❑ Did you ever wear make-up? If yes, who did for you?

❑ What do you think is appropriate attire for work or for a job interview?

❑ What's the difference between business casual and business formal?

Listening

http://www.unsv.com/voanews/business-etiquette/lessons/002/

Listen to the recording and fill in the blanks.

First Impression

陈豪在北京的一家美国公司工作了一个月。今天下午他有机会见到公司总裁。第一次见面怎么才能给美国老板留下一个好印象呢？他决定去和 Mary 谈谈。

(*Office ambience*)

陈：Mary，我下午会见总裁，这是第一次见面，你说我要注意些什么事呀？

M：第一次的印象，first impression，是很重要。美国人说，

____。

最初的印象只有一次，绝没有第二次机会。

陈：第一次印象的重要性我知道，问题是怎么才能给人留下好印象。

M：根据一项研究，人们在初次见面时对一个人的评价有 55% 是根据他所看到的。

陈：这不是只看表面嘛？打扮漂亮就行了吗？

M：不是打扮漂亮，而是打扮得体。你今天不是会见总裁吗？我们就来看看你有什么地方需要改进的吧。

* * * * * *

M：首先，____。

嗯，你的头发梳得很整齐美观。有的人既不洗头，也不梳头，那是非常不礼貌的。

陈：对了，我注意到我们办公室里的美国男同事好像天天剃胡子。我不是天天剃胡子的。我年纪轻，没多少胡子，人家看不出来。

M：我就看出来你今天没有剃胡子。

____。

对了，我早上看你戴着领带，怎么没有啦？你要去见总裁，领带一定要戴。

陈：噢，我到了办公室，把它取下来了。

M：在办公室里放松一会儿是可以的，但是要去见某人或出去办事，

____。

你一会儿千万别忘了把领带戴上。

陈：行，行，我一会儿剃一下胡子，戴上领带就齐了。

M：等等，一般人还会看你的腿和鞋子。哎，你的裤子太长，裤腿都拖在地上了。

____。

陈：啊呀，我知道，可我妈没时间给我改短嘛。

M：你这双鞋是新的吧，很干净，擦得很亮。

____。

陈:哟,那我裤子太长,怎么办哪?

M:别着急,你不是下午才见总裁吗?赶快回家去换条裤子。还有,千万把白袜子给换了。

____。

陈:啊呀,还不让穿白袜子,规矩还真多。你看,我一紧张把你刚才说的都忘了。快,再说一遍。

M:____

____

____。

▶ Reading

Task One

Personal Grooming

Most of us have heard the expression, "A picture is worth a thousand words." Our appearance speaks louder than our words. First impressions really matter; first impressions really are crucial. Giving a bad first impression can make you lose the confidence of prospective employers, customers and clients, and even cost your business. The first impressions you give a customer or client will set the tone for your future business relationship and shows that you are professional and prepared. Your appearance is important and impacts how others perceive you. Remember this when preparing to meet with a prospective employers, customers and clients. Some basic guidelines to follow are:

- Be clean and neat, including your fingernails, teeth, shoes, hair and face
- Conservative two-piece business suit in a basic color
- Empty pockets—no bulges or tinkling coins, keys, etc.
- No gum, candy or cigarettes
- Light briefcase or portfolio case if needed
- No visible body piercing (nose, eyebrow, tongue, etc.)—wear minimum jewelry and cologne

- When going for a job interview, arrive ten minutes early and arrive alone, take resumés and/or other pertinent information
- Smile and be friendly
- Demonstrate a positive attitude
- Use good eye contact
- Shake hands firmly
- Use good manners
- Don't chew gum

From the above guidelines we can see that our dress and grooming are two key elements. Dressing appropriately is very important in first impressions. Appropriate dress shows that you respect your business and your customers. If you look successful and confident, then others will have more confidence in you as well. When you are dressed properly, there is also nothing to distract others from your message. Personal grooming is just as important as what you wear. Personal grooming, also referred to as personal hygiene, is the act of taking care of your body through proper cleanliness and self-care. You may select the right clothes, but neglecting personal hygiene can ruin the image you wish to present. Showing up to a meeting poorly groomed shows the other person that you do not care enough about the meeting to bother making an effort. Review the following grooming checklist before meeting with the employers, customers and clients.

ITEM	GROOMING
Hair	Clean, trimmed, and neatly combed or arranged. Men's hair must be off the face and cut above the collar. Women's hair may not be more than three inches higher or wider than the head.
Facial Hair (Men)	Freshly shaved; be clean-shaven; mustache or beard neatly groomed. Mustaches must be trimmed and even with the corners of the mouth and may not extend over the top lip. Beards are allowed if medically necessary and must be kept well trimmed. Sideburns may not extend past the inner ear.
Hands and Fingernails	Clean hands. Neat, clean, and neatly manicured and trimmed within 1/2 inch of the fingertip. Conservative nail polish colors are permitted.
Teeth	Brushed and fresh breath.
Breath	Beware of foods which may leave breath odor. Beware of tobacco, alcohol and coffee odor. Use a breath mint if needed.

(continued)

Body	Freshly bathed/showered; use deodorant. Excessive jewelry or erotic/subculture jewelry will not be allowed. Two small rings plus a wedding ring on each hand is acceptable. Women may wear a small matching set of earrings in their ear lobes. Remove body piercings, tongue rings, and cover tattoos if possible.
Make-Up (Women)	Use sparingly and be natural looking. Naturalness is emphasized. Excessive make-up is unacceptable. Blush, eye make-up, and lipstick in conservative colors may be used.
Perfumes/Colognes/After Shave	Use sparingly or none at all. Your "scent" should not linger after you leave.

The primary goals of appropriate dress and grooming is to "feel good" about the way you look and project a positive image. When you feel good about yourself, you naturally convey confidence and a positive attitude. These nonverbal messages are as important as the verbal skills you use in business meetings.

New Words and Expressions

groom	[gruːm]	*v.*	擦洗,刷洗;修饰,打扮
crucial	[ˈkruːʃəl]	*adj.*	决定性的,关键性的;极重要的
prospective	[prəˈspektiv]	*adj.*	未来的,将来的;可能的;预期的
client	[ˈklaiənt]	*n.*	客户,主顾,顾客
impact	[imˈpækt]	*vt.*	(对某事物)有影响,有作用;冲击;撞击
	[ˈimpækt]	*n.*	巨大影响;强大作用;撞击;冲击力
perceive	[pəˈsiːv]	*vt.*	察觉;发觉;感知;领会;理解;认识
conservative	[kənˈsəːvətiv]	*adj.*	保守的;传统标准的
bulge	[bʌldʒ]	*n.*	膨胀,肿胀;鼓起,隆起,突出;装满,塞满
tinkle	[ˈtiŋkl]	*vi.*	发叮当声,叮当作响
		n.	叮当声;清脆的金属声
portfolio	[pɔːtˈfəuliəu]	*n.*	(皮制)公文包;文件夹;纸夹
pierce	[piəs]	*vt.*	刺穿;刺破;穿过;在(鼻、耳等身体部位)上穿孔

cologne	[kəˈləun]	*n.*	古龙香水
resumé	[ˈrezjumei]	*n.*	摘要;履历,简历
pertinent	[ˈpəːtinənt]	*adj.*	恰当的,适当的,贴切的;中肯的;有关的
demonstrate	[ˈdemənstreit]	*vt.*	证明;展示;论证
		vi.	示威
hygiene	[ˈhaidʒiːn]	*n.*	卫生
trim	[trim]	*vt.*	修剪;整理;装点;整齐
sideburns	[ˈsaidbəːnz]	*n.*	[复数][主美国英语](下巴无须的)短连鬓胡子;鬓角
manicure	[ˈmænikjuə]	*v./n.*	修指甲
deodorant	[diˈəudərənt]	*adj.*	解臭的,除臭的,脱臭的
		n.	解臭剂,除臭剂,脱臭剂
erotic	[iˈrɔtik]	*adj.*	(引起)性爱(或性欲)的;与性爱有关的;色情的
subculture	[ˈsʌbkʌltʃə]	*n.*	亚文化
tattoo	[təˈtuː; tæˈtuː]	*n.*	纹身
		vt.	刺花纹于
		vi.	刺花样
excessive	[ikˈsesiv]	*adj*	过多的,极度的;过分的
make-up	[ˈmeɪkʌp]	*n.*	化妆;化妆品;性格;构造
sparing	[ˈspɛəriŋ]	*adj.*	有节制的,有保留的;谨慎的;节约的
linger	[ˈliŋgə]	*vi.*	缓慢消失;继续逗留;流连;闲荡

Task Two

Dressing Etiquette

Whether you're headed to an interview for a new job, or you're getting ready for your first day in a new position, or you're going to the business meeting, knowing the right way to dress for any type of office and occasion can help give you a step up in your career. Dressing or clothing etiquette is the way we communicate with our clothing and dress. Be professional in your dressing at all times according to the company's level of "professional appearance". The professional image of a company is reflected on your professional dress. The way you dress communicates to everyone around you, your clients, coworkers and boss. It says how you feel about yourself and how you want them to feel about you. Most people do pass some sort of judgment based on your clothing and the way you look, so be sure to put your best foot forward, no matter what field your work is in and the office policies concerning dress. Whatever you do must reflect your professional status. Professional dress guidelines are as follows:

- Clean, neat, wrinkle free clothes
- Minimal perfume
- Appropriate length of skirt
- Depends on the industry you work in
- Never go over the top. Too much hair, make up, jewelry, too casual, too low cut.

Some common pitfalls of dressing etiquette are as follows:

- Wearing casual wear to the office
- Wearing beach wear in the city
- Not dressing in one's Sunday's Best at Church
- Wearing bright and color clothes at a funeral
- Wearing entirely black outfits at weddings
- Wearing flip-flops everywhere
- Ignoring the specific dress code of an event

New Words and Expressions

put your best foot forward			全力以赴
wrinkle	[ˈriŋkl]	*n.*	皱,皱褶;(皮肤表面的)皱纹
pitfall	[ˈpitfɔːl]	*n.*	陷阱;圈套;诱惑;易犯的错误
flip-flop	[ˈflipflɔp]	*n.*	[复数]平底人字拖鞋

Task Three

Building a Man's Business Wardrobe

Formal and traditional business dress

If the male employees are required to wear formal business attire, this usually means that they have to wear suits. Generally, employees can only wear dark-colored suits with white shirts, cuff links, silk ties and pocket squares. The dark tailored suits should be black or a very dark navy.

- **Suits**

When choosing a suit, look first for fabric, fit and comfort; look second for style. Your fabric should never shine or change colors in different lighting. Fabrics that are appropriate include wool, cotton, linen and various micro-fibers. Wool is the most versatile of the three coming in both summer and tropic weight and in a variety of fabric styles. Linen suits are popular especially during extreme heat and high humidity but it wrinkles immediately.

You can choose from these basic styles (and their multiple variations): American cut: These suits can have either two or three buttons and have center-vented jackets and natural shoulders and pants with a straight line. Italian cut: These suits have unvested jackets with padded shoulders and pants that are fuller than American suits. British cut: These suits have side-vented or unvested jackets with a square shoulder, tapered waist, and pants that are narrower than both American cut and Italian cut suits.

- **Shirts**

Many companies require employees to wear shirts that are specific colors. Shirts should be long-sleeved white shirts or light blue shirts. Cotton or cotton blend is preferred. It should be easy to press and wrinkle free. Conservative stripes are acceptable.

- **Ties**

Ties should be silk, understated, always be darker than the wearer's shirt, coordinated with your suit and shirt, and should end at the top of your belt.

- **Pants**

Traditional dress slacks. Always make sure they are ironed neatly and fit properly.

- **Socks**

Socks should be at least as dark as your suit or pants. Wear dark socks coordinated with the color of your suit. Patterns are permissible so long as they're not ostentatious. White socks are unacceptable in business. And wearing no socks is equally unacceptable.

- **Shoes**

Plain- and cap-toed oxfords, wingtips, and plain or tasseled loafers are the extent of men's choices for dress business shoes. Coordinate your shoe color with your suit color. Black shoes go nicely with charcoal and black or navy suits. Brown shoes match with brown and tan suits. Keep them well-shined. Running shoes, hiking boots, or sandals with a suit are unacceptable.

- **Accessories**

The little things are what matter most.

Briefcases: Traditionally are black or brown leather. If you choose a notebook computer bag instead, hold it to the same high-quality standards you would a briefcase.

Belts: Match or closely match the color and texture of your shoes.

Watches: If you go for status symbols, buy an expensive watch. Otherwise, a medium-range watch with a leather or metal band is the way to go.

Eyeglasses: Wear glasses that fit your face and personality.

Casual business wear

Casual wear for men has taken a high jump in these recent years. Most of the multinationals want their employees to be present in a simple T-shirt and jeans that makes them comfortable to do their work. A comfort and casual environment has always been a great path towards higher accomplishments. And, the major portion of changing trends of fashion and casual wear have been influenced by the sports gear which automatically makes the entire casual attire smart and trendy. Smart and yet casual wear for men usually includes dress trousers-chinos which is a long sleeve dress shirt, trendy slip-ons, dress socks, a belt and if the individual wants, then he can surely go for a tie or a blazer. Smart casual clothing is also interchangeable with business casual wear for men. Remember that business casual and Friday casual are distinct things. Business casual generally means khaki pants, a plain polo shirt or a long-sleeved button down shirt, a V-neck sweater, sometimes a sports coat or blazer and brown leather shoes.

Don't forget these general guidelines:

1. A short sleeve shirt is, by definition, always a casual shirt.
2. Khaki and flannel pants are casual for most businesses.
3. Tank tops, shorts, and sandals are weekend wear.
4. Advertising, artists, and fashion types can wear leather jackets.
5. Plain shirts are best, in general; shirts with ads on them are for fishing.
6. Button-down oxford shirts are casual; T-shirts are for musicians, computer types, and mowing the lawn.
7. Loafers and dark walking shoes are casual.
8. Blazers and sports coats are casual for some businesses, dressy for others. The fabric should never shine or change colors in a different lighting.

New Words and Expressions

cuff	[kʌf]	*n.*	袖口
cuff link			(衬衫袖口的)链扣,袖扣
fabric	[ˈfæbrɪk]	*n.*	面料;织物;布;组织;构造
linen	[ˈlinin]	*n.*	亚麻布,亚麻线;亚麻制品
versatile	[ˈvəːsətail]	*adj.*	多功能的,通用的,万能的;多才多艺的
vent	[vent]	*n.*	(上衣背部或两侧的)开衩,衩口;(裙子的)开衩
stripe	[straip]	*n.*	斑纹,条纹,线条;[常用复数]条纹织物,条纹衫
ostentatious	[ˌɔstenˈteiʃəs]	*adj.*	显眼的;炫耀的;豪华的
cap-toed	[ˈkæptəud]	*adj.*	(鞋)尖露脚趾的
oxford	[ˈɔksfəd]	*n.*	(=oxford shoe)浅口便鞋;(=oxford cloth)牛津(衬衫)布料
tasseled	[ˈtæsəld]	*adj.*	带穗的;呈流苏状的;(人)佩带流苏状饰物的

loafers	[ˈləufəz]	*n.*	懒汉鞋,平跟船鞋
sandals	[ˈsædəlz]	*n.*	(皮)凉鞋,浅帮鞋,拖鞋,女式高跟凉鞋
accessory	[əkˈsesəri]	*n.*	[常作复数](妇女的)装饰品;配件
chinos	[ˈtʃiːnəuz]	*n.*	斜纹棉布裤;丝光斜纹棉布
blazer	[ˈbleizə]	*n.*	(浅色)轻薄运动夹克衫,(颜色鲜艳的)运动上衣
flannel	[ˈflænl]	*n.*	法兰绒,棉法兰绒;绒布;[复数]法兰绒衣服(尤指男子长裤)
twill	[twil]	*n.*	斜纹织物;[亦作 twill weave]斜纹(图案)
		adj.	斜纹布的,斜纹织物的
denim	[ˈdenim]	*n.*	粗斜纹棉布,劳动布;[用作复数]粗斜纹棉布衣服
corduroy	[ˈkɔːdərɔi]	*n.*	灯芯绒,条绒;[复数]灯芯绒裤子

Task Four

Building a Woman's Business Wardrobe

Formal and traditional business dress

If your business is formal or you are attending those formal meetings and presentations, you need the right women's formal business wear. Get some women's suits and appropriate, conservative coordinates in your business wardrobe. Women have more options than men in what they can wear to work, as dresses and skirts are often appropriate business attire for women.

- **Suits**

The keys are fabric, fit and comfort. For autumn, winter and spring, wool is still the best choice. For summer cotton and linen are good choices, especially if blended with a small amount of stretchy fabric. Tropic weight wool is another good option. Navy blue, black, charcoal, taupe, white, burgundy and forest green are all acceptable colors. Although darker colors are typically worn in winter and lighter colors are worn in the spring and summer this rule is no longer hard and fast. Some women can wear red, but oranges, yellows, bright purples, and other loud colors are best used in small amounts. Have the suit professionally fitted. Choose suits with Jackets and skirts that are appropriate for your body type. Long jackets that cover the hips are flattering for most women.

- **Skirts**

The two most important things are fit and length. Make sure your skirt is not too tight or too short. Business skirts typically are hemmed just around the knees.

- **Blouses and shirts**

Blouses made of transparent material are inappropriate. However, high-quality cotton, silk, or a micro-fiber material is a good choice. Collars on lady's blouses are varied. Coordinate your blouse color with your suit color and choose opaque materials for business shirts.

- **Shoes**

In a business environment it is strongly advised to keep shoes functional, attractive, clean and shined. Low-heeled pumps are suitable for the vast majority of business situations. Heels can be as high as an inch and a half or two inches, but heels much higher than that look unprofessional. Keep the higher heels for your skirts. Two-inch heels with pantsuit are too dressy for day. Open-toed shoes and mules are inappropriate in conservative environments.

- **Stockings and pantyhose**

Pantyhose and stockings are both acceptable in the workplace, so long as they're matched to your other clothes, aren't heavily patterned, and don't suggest anything other than a commitment to work. During warm months, or if you feel comfortable doing so, going without pantyhose is fine.

- **Belts**

Belts should be leather and from one half inch to three fourths of an inch thick. Coordinate the colors with your outfits and avoid metallic belts covered with studs and jewels, and belts made with plastic or fur.

- **Jewelry**

Jewelry should be worn in moderate amounts and should not attract too much attention. Less is more. Keep it simple and understated.

- **Eyeglasses**

Glasses are among the few areas in business dress where you're allowed to assert your individuality, even in conservative environments.

- **Scarves**

Scarves are made of silk, wool, cashmere, or a blend of these fabrics.

- **Handbags**

Handbags are large enough to carry a few items of makeup and whatever technology you use to plan your week, but no larger.

- **Briefcases**

Some women carry a briefcase in lieu of a handbag, which is much neater.

Casual business wear

While some prefer only business attire, a few others may accept a business casual dress code for women. The term "business casual for women" can itself lead to quite a bit of confusion. Business casual for women should not be flashy, or over the top. The key here is to keep it simple, classy, elegant and sophisticated with the help of clothes that have a good fit and cut. It's all about classic cuts which suits your body type, and which are not too tight or too baggy. While business casuals definitely do not include your old ripped jeans and T-shirt, they definitely provide more flexibility and variety in clothes choices. Unlike men, women clothing have tons of options from skirts and pants to dresses. By following a few basic tips you can look casual yet elegant.

- **Fabrics**

While choosing fabrics for business casual for women you have to keep in mind to choose fabrics that have a rich look. They should not look drab, but rich and elegant. The following are examples of fabrics that are appropriate for business casual for women. Linen, wool, silk, cotton, gabardine, corduroy, twill and khaki can also be used to some extent.

- **Colors**

The next step is choosing the right colors. While you are not restricted to use only solid neutral colors like black, navy blue, gray, tan, etc. for business casuals, it is best to stick to them. If you love color, you can still add bright colors into your dress, the best way is in the form of scarves, accessories or belts. This will liven up your dress, but still keep you looking professional like proper working women.

- **Skirts**

For skirts, you have the option of straight and A-line skirts. The basic rule is that the length for business casual attire for women must be at least till the knee (while you are standing). Generally, the slits in the skirt should be in the center back of the skirt in order to facilitate climbing of stairs comfortably. If you have a long skirt, then you should definitely avoid slits that run above the knee.

- **Shirts and sweaters**

When it comes to choosing the right top for your skirts or pants, the best options for business casual for women are tailored shirts, tailored blouses, knit sweaters, etc. Tailored shirts are evergreen and versatile, as they can be paired with skirts or pants. Button-up shirts are the standard professional type of shirt for many businesswomen. Shirts can be accented with bracelets, necklaces, pins and other types of jewelry. The other option is wearing knitted sweaters which can add style and variety. A stylish sweater with a crew neck or V neck with three-quarter length sleeves makes you look casual yet elegant.

- **Pants**

For pants, the best choice would be to go for tailored pants in solid shades and soft fabrics, such as lightweight wool or wool crepe. Make sure that the pants have a good fit, that is, they should not be extremely tight or baggy. One classic option is with straight fit and simple silhouette.

- **Shoes**

Shoes should preferably be of leather, fabric or micro-fiber. They should cover the feet completely, and should be in colors that correspond to the dress, such as black, white, beige, tan, etc. In order to be comfortable, it is best if you do not wear women's shoes with six-inch heels. Instead, two- to three-inch heels add the feminine touch, while still being comfortable.

- **Accessories**

Do not be afraid to add bold accessories to your outfit. A printed or bright-colored scarf makes the outfit stand out, while a colorful beaded necklace on a white shirt can add color to your outfit and make you look casual while still being sophisticated.

- **KISS Principle**

Keep the KISS principle in mind even with casual clothes: Keep It Simple and Sophisticated. Dark colors convey authority; bright colors convey friendliness. Light colors such as taupe and khaki are generally more casual than black, gray or navy.

Try to avoid these fashion mistakes:

1. Avoid excessive use of bright color and wild patterns.
2. Avoid excessive jewelry and jewelry that signals your arrival with tiny clicking sounds.
3. Your shoes do not need to "match" your blouse.
4. Spiky, strappy, sandals in metallic colors or with rhinestones aren't appropriate for most businesses, nor are open-toed shoes.
5. Casual does not mean you can wear jeans. Jeans are a definite no-no in the corporate workplace unless stated otherwise in your company's dress code.

These were some basic guidelines for business casual for women. As long as you follow the basic guidelines, you can use your creativity and mix and match to come up with outfits that suit your personality and style.

Some companies insist that female employees wear a matching suit with pants or trousers and a jacket. More lenient companies allow you to pair skirts or dresses with business blazers and blouses. Companies with casual dress days may let you wear khakis or jeans to work, while other businesses prefer strictly professional dress at all times.

New Words and Expressions

taupe	[təup]	*n.*	灰褐色
burgundy	[ˈbəːɡəndi]	*n.*	深红色；（原产法国勃艮第地区的）勃艮第葡萄酒
hem	[hem]	*n.*	（布、窗帘、帷幕、衣服等的）边，缘，贴边；摆，下脚；褶边，褶缝
transparent	[trænsˈpærənt]	*adj.*	透明的；清澈的；（织物）极薄的
opaque	[əuˈpeik]	*adj.*	不透明的，不透光的；不反光的；暗的；单调的
heel	[hiːl]	*n.*	（鞋、袜等的）后跟；踵，脚跟
mule	[mjuːl]	*n.*	女式平底拖鞋；骡；倔强之人，顽固的人
pantyhose	[ˈpæntihəuz]	*n.*	连裤袜
commitment	[kəˈmitmənt]	*n.*	承诺，保证；委托；承担义务；献身
scarf	[skɑːf]	*n.*	头巾，披肩；面纱；领带；领巾；[复数]领带
tank top			[美语]背心式上衣，紧身背心装；马夹
synthetic	[sinˈθetik]	*adj.*	合成的，人造的
		n.	合成物；合成纤维
cotton blend			棉混纺
drab	[dræb]	*adj.*	单调的；土褐色的
gabardine	[ˈɡæbədiːn]	*n.*	宽松长袍；[纺]华达呢；斜纹呢
slit	[slit]	*n.*	狭缝；狭长切口；裂缝
silhouette	[ˌsiluˈet]	*n.*	侧面影像；轮廓
beige	[beiʒ]	*adj.*	浅褐色的；米黄色的
tan	[tæn]	*adj.*	棕黄色的；棕褐色的
bead	[biːd]	*vt.*	用小珠装饰；用珠连成一串；把……连成一串
rhinestone	[ˈrainstəun]	*n.*	人造钻石，莱茵石（一种假钻石）
lenient	[ˈliːniənt]	*adj.*	宽大的；宽容的；宽厚的；仁慈的

Task Five

The Power of Posture

How you stand can be as important as what you say. Here are ten categories of behavior you should monitor to improve your "presence" and effectiveness.

The way you stand could change your life. For businesspeople, stance is an important indicator of how deeply you are engaged with your job, how much you believe in the products you are selling, how confident you are that your company will survive.

And that's just for starters. Did you know that you are likely to make or break a sale by what you do in the first fifteen seconds after entering the customer's office—before you say anything? Or that you can increase your attractiveness to others—and your success in your career—by how you move your head? Or that the seat you take at a table will determine, in part, the direction a negotiation will take?

These insights and many more are at the heart of modern communications research, and *Teach Yourself Body Language*, by Gordon Wainwright (McGraw-Hill, 2003), summarizes much of it in very practical terms that readers can put to work immediately to change their lives.

Take stance. Wainwright suggests an experiment in which you stand straight, tuck your tummy in, hold your head high, and smile at those you meet. Do this for a week, concentrating especially on those who normally don't seem to be very friendly in your workplace. Wainwright predicts, based on many such experiments, that you'll find people treat you differently immediately. You'll garner more respect, you'll be taken more seriously, and you'll find that even the grumpy ones warm up to you.

Your stance, broadly speaking, signals to the world how energetic, confident, and powerful you are. Slumped shoulders, a downcast gaze, a slow pace, and a sagging belly are taken by the world to mean that you lack confidence, that you don't have much energy, and that you are probably less important, successful, and powerful as a result. These impressions may be neither accurate nor fair, but they are the inevitable results of the fleeting impressions we tend to get of one another during the course of a busy day.

Those are just the fleeting impressions. Stance, and what used to be called your bearing, can play much more important roles when you're negotiating an important contract or trying to close a sale. We like to deal with winners, and we are more inclined to yield negotiating points to people who appear to be operating from a position of strength.

And what about those first fifteen seconds after entering a room? Wainwright reports research that measured the status of people who enter an office. Low-status people tend to linger at the door. Medium-status people go in halfway. And high-status people go in all the way to the desk and sit down next to the occupant.

To increase your attractiveness, Wainwright suggests ten categories of behavior to monitor and improve. Studies show that attractive people tend to be more successful, everything else being equal, so more than mere likability is at stake here. The ten categories are:

- Eye contact: The more the better, up to visual intrusiveness.
- Facial expression: Be lively, smile a lot, and look interested.
- Head movements: Nod to show interest, keep your chin up.
- Gestures: Be expressive and open, without overdoing it.
- Posture: Stand erect, lean forward to show interest, lean back to be informal.
- Proximity and orientation: Get as close as you can to people without crowding.
- Bodily contact: Touch as often as you can without causing offense.
- Appearance and physique: Go for color in dress, fitness in physique.
- Timing and synchronization: Speed up your activities to just before the point of inefficiency.
- Nonverbal aspects of speech: Try to balance your need to talk with the need to listen.

If taking on all of these desiderata sounds like a tall order, take heart in the knowledge that doing even a few of them will begin to increase your attractiveness to others. You don't have to manage them all at once. In fact, you don't have to manage them at all, if you can find enthusiasm for your job, your colleagues, and your activities in general. If you are enthusiastic, you'll discover that you'll naturally increase your attractiveness by unconsciously doing many of the behaviors on the list.

New Words and Expressions

stance	[stɑːns; stæns]	*n.*	站立姿势;态度,立场
indicator	[ˈindikeitə]	*n.*	指示者,指示物;标志;指针;指示器;记录器
tuck	[tʌk]	*vt.*	卷起;挤进;使有褶裥;收拢;大口吃
tummy	[ˈtʌmi]	*n.*	肚子,胃
garner	[ˈgɑːnə]	*vt.*	得到,获得;收集,使聚集;积蓄
grumpy	[ˈgrʌmpi]	*adj.*	脾气坏的,常发牢骚的,性情暴躁的
		n.	脾气坏的人
slump	[slʌmp]	*vi.*	下降;衰落;倒下
		n.	衰退;暴跌;消沉
downcast	[ˈdaunkɑːst; ˈdaunkæst]	*adj.*	沮丧的;低垂的;(眼)向下看的
		n.	倒台;俯视的目光
sag	[sæg]	*vi.*	(尤指中间部分)下垂,下沉,下陷;(眼神、肩头等)垂下
fleet	[fliːt; flit]	*adj.*	快速的,敏捷的
bearing	[ˈbɛəriŋ]	*n.*	举止;风度;姿态;态度
intrusive	[inˈtruːsiv]	*adj.*	侵入的;闯入的;侵扰的;妨碍的
physique	[fiˈziːk]	*n.*	(男子的)体格,体形
synchronization	[ˌsinkrənaiˈzeiʃən]	*n.*	[物]同步;同时性
desiderata	[diˌzidəˈreitə]	*n.*	(拉丁)需要的东西

Exercises

I. Read the statements below and decide whether the behavior is True or False. Write T for true and F for false.

1. Speaking loudly in public areas
2. No legs wide apart while seated
3. Putting hands in pockets
4. Not picking ears/nose
5. Yawning without covering with hands
6. Smile when talking
7. Greeting colleagues
8. Sneezing without covering with hands
9. Speak slowly enough to be understood
10. No arms crossed

IV. Put the following sentences into Chinese or vice versa.

1. All clothing, uniform or non-uniform, must be non-faded, clean and well-ironed.
2. Acceptable jewellery is wedding/engagement rings. Small stud/sleeper earrings and a watch for timekeeping purpose, but should always match with professional attire.
3. Visible tattoos of any description are not permitted.
4. Fanciful shoes with buckles, clips or added ornament, sling shoes, sports shoes, flat shoes, moccasins, sandals and slippers are not recommended.
5. Only clear or light nail varnish is permitted.
6. 名牌需要端正地佩戴在左胸部。
7. 男员工应穿戴黑色或深色的、与制服相配的袜子。
8. 香水,须后水,古龙水用量要适度。
9. 所有有颜色的隐形眼镜都不允许佩戴。
10. 只能佩戴穿耳式的耳钉,并且每一边有且仅有一个。

▶ Speaking

1. Read the text loudly, and try to recite the following paragraph.

Most of us have heard the expression, "A picture is worth a thousand words." Our appearance speaks louder than our words. First impressions really matter; first impressions really are crucial. Giving a bad first impression can make you lose the confidence of prospective employers, customers and clients, and even cost your business. The first impressions you give a customer or client will set the tone for your future business relationship and shows that you are professional and prepared. Your appearance is important and impacts how others perceive you. Remember this when preparing to meet with a prospective employers, customers and clients. Some basic guidelines to follow are:

- Be clean and neat, including your fingernails, teeth, shoes, hair and face
- Conservative two-piece business suit in a basic color
- Empty pockets—no bulges or tinkling coins, keys, etc.
- No gum, candy or cigarettes
- Light briefcase or portfolio case if needed
- No visible body piercing (noise, eyebrow, tongue, etc.)—wear minimum jewelry and cologne
- When going for a job interview, arrive ten minutes early and arrive alone, take resumés and/or other pertinent information
- Smile and be friendly
- Demonstrate a positive attitude
- Use good eye contact
- Shake hands firmly
- Use good manners
- Don't chew gum

▶ Acting

Watch the videos and practise tying a tie.

http://v.youku.com/v_show/id_XMzM1MzY5Ng==.html

http://v.youku.com/v_show/id_XMjU3ODUyNzY=.html

http://v.ku6.com/show/ltvyzKi5kejVheP7.html

▶ Supplementary Listening

* Business Etiquette (Personal Hygiene, Dress Code, etc.)

http://www.51voa.com/Business_Etiquette_1.html

Listen to the dialogues and dictate down the important points.

* Men's Business Wardrobe and Women's Business Wardrobe

http://video.about.com/mensfashion/Men-s-Business-Wardrobe.htm

http://video.about.com/fashion/Women-s-Business-Wardrobe.htm

Watch the videos and dictate down the important points.

▶ Supplementary Reading

Wedding Dresses Around the World

We may be used to the white wedding dress in North America and women in many other parts of the world have adopted the virginal look for their ceremonies, but traditional wedding attire ranges in style, colour, fabric and decoration from country to country.

Korean

During the Korean wedding ceremony called Pae Baek, customary Korean clothes are worn with additional robes and headdresses. Bright colours are important in Korean wedding attire to inspire the brightness of spirit that is required at such a special event. The bride's outfit or hanbok is based around a long, high-waisted skirt that wraps around the body. She also wears a long-sleeved short jacket with two ribbons tied in a bow.

Hispanic

The Hispanic bride wears a slim dress and may choose to wear a bolero jacket over it. Alternatively, she may wear a flamenco style dress. A mantilla veil is a remnant of Spanish influence that has become standard for Mexican and Latin American brides. A Hispanic bride often pays homage to her ancestors by wearing a dress passed down from her mother and grandmother, representing the pride she has in her family. She sews ribbons of yellow, blue and red into the lingerie she wears under her wedding dress, which symbolize the food, money and passion that she hopes to attract to her marriage. Pearls are never part of a Hispanic bride's outfit since they are thought to bring future tears and grief to the marriage.

Chinese

The most essential element for Chinese wedding attire and decorations is the colour red. The colour means good luck in Chinese culture so everything from the dress to the lanterns is red. Traditionally, a one-piece dress called Qi Pao featuring intricate designs in gold and silver is worn in northern China. In southern China, the bride usually wears either a Qun Gua, Kwa or Cheongsam, which are two-piece outfits decorated with a golden phoenix or dragon. When arranged marriages were still the norm in China, the bride would wear a red veil during the ceremony and her face wouldn't be revealed until the wedding night.

American Indian

For a traditional American Indian wedding ceremony, the bride wears a long dress covered in beading and finished with fringes. Colours representing north, south, east and west are included in the garment.

Japanese

In Japan, a bride will wear a colourful kimono with a hood to her ceremony. The hood, called a tsuno kakushi, shows that she is obedient to her new husband. She will change into another kimono once the ceremony is finished. Both garments will be made into bedding after the wedding, which will be passed down to future generations.

African

A traditional African bridal outfit consists of items made from matching fabric in bright, cheerful colours including a headpiece called a gele, a wrap skirt called an iro, a shawl called an iborum and a blouse called a buba.

Scottish

A traditional Scottish wedding dress prominently features tartan, in ribbons trimming a white dress, in a shawl around the shoulders or in a sash around the waist. The dress may also have embroidered Celtic knot work symbolizing eternal love. The groom may pin a piece of his tartan to the bride's outfit representing her joining his clan.

Irish

In Ireland, blue is a lucky colour so the bride often wears a dress in this colour. She avoids wearing green, however, as this colour is thought to attract the attention of the meddlesome fairy folk. While many a bride would have a fit if her dress were torn on her wedding day, the Irish bride would consider it a sign of good luck.

Indian

The traditional wedding attire of Hindu brides usually consists of saris in red and white, colours symbolizing fertility, wealth and purity. In the days leading up to the ceremony, the bride's hands and feet are painted with henna in elaborate patterns by female family members. This decoration is called mehendi.

(http://suite101.com/article/wedding-dresses-around-the-world-a53708)

Answer the following question:

What are the colors of traditional wedding attire of the countries mentioned above?

Project Three

Office Etiquette

Learning Objectives

After completing this project, you will be able to:

* be aware of and follow proper office etiquette.

Warming-Up

Please answer the following questions.

❑ Can you name some inappropriate behaviours at the workplace?

❑ What do you think are good manners?

Listening

http://www.unsv.com/voanews/business-etiquette/lessons/037/

Listen to the recording and fill in the blanks.

Polite Behavior at the Office Party

陈豪在北京的 ABC 美国公司工作。他接到公司晚宴派对的邀请,但是不想去。

(*Office ambience*)

CH:Hi Amy, 我刚刚收到邀请,老板请我们去吃饭。

A:I received one, too.

C:你去吗?

A:Of course. Aren't you?

C:我不太想去。

A:Why not? It's going to be a nice party at an upscale restaurant.

C:我不想跟同事出去玩儿;他们跟我关系虽说都不错,但大家毕竟不是朋友。

A:I'm afraid that doesn't matter. Part of the reason for inviting everyone is to build rapport among all of us who work together.

C:Rapport 是什么意思啊?

A:______________________________

______________________________。

C:跟同事搞好关系也不一定非得出去玩儿啊。

A:______________________________。

To go or not to go is not a choice. The boss expects you to be there.

C:这么说是不能不去了。我要是有其他事呢?

A:______________________________

______________________________。

C:我可不想得罪老板,让我再想想吧。

* * * * * *

(到了第二天……)

A:Well, CH, did you decide to go to the party?

C:去,不过我要带个朋友。

A:I hate to tell you this, but that would not be acceptable.

C:星期六晚上出去应酬,带个朋友还不行吗?

A:Unless your invitation says "and guest", it would be poor etiquette to take someone with you.

C:那好,我打个照面,待一会儿就走。

A:That's not going to work either. This is a seated dinner party so you have stay the entire time.

C:晚餐完了我总可以走了吧?

A: ______________________________。

Then good manners dictate you don't leave before you thank him for the evening and tell him good-bye.

C：Amy，我真没想到，公司派对还会这么郑重其事。还有什么要注意的吗？

A：____
____。

Some people forget that rule and overdo it. Not only is it embarrassing, you could jeopardize your job.

C：这我知道，一定注意不会多喝。你能不能再总结一下，看看都有哪些注意事项。

A：____
____。

C：我知道，还有就是晚宴结束前不能告退。

A：That's right. Don't forget to say your good-byes. And go easy on the alcohol.

C：谢谢你，Amy，我一定照办。

▶ Reading

Task One

General Office Etiquette

Office etiquette or office manners are about conducting yourself respectfully and courteously in the office or workplace. You face office etiquette issues every day in the workplace, from how to collaborate with co-workers to saving company resources. The way you do your job, and the way you work with people is critical to your success. It is important for you to become confident with the rules of office etiquette and protocol and learn the right ways to interact with fellow employees and clients, and facilitate good working relationships and enhance efficiency. A congenial, harmonious atmosphere can make the workplace a more enjoyable place to be.

Clearly office environments and working conditions have changed radically over the last few years. Office etiquette has become more important with tighter space, more offices being shared and the lines between paid employees and contractors blurring. More employees are working from an office cubicle. With smaller spaces, more electronic communication and blurring lines between employees and contractors, many people simply don't know how to behave in an office environment. In the middle of a conversation, they will whip out their smart phones to check their email. They'll pinch people's food from the fridge. Or they'll take up your space by barging into your cubicle unannounced. According to a recent news story, the top five etiquette mistakes made by the British and American were not saying "good morning" to colleagues in the morning, not offering office guests a drink, speaking too loudly across a room, swearing and using the speakerphone function on the telephone.

Though some people have worked in office environments that have office cubicles, for some employees it is a new experience. Knowing office cubicle etiquette can make it easier to adjust to the new environment. While different offices have different codes of etiquette, there are a few universal truths about etiquette that you need to be aware of at all times whether you work as a videogame tester or a corporate lawyer.

Observe. The first thing to do when new to office cubicles is to be observant. See what acceptable etiquette is where you work. Keep in mind that supervisors and co-workers will have a different set of cubicle etiquette rules. Keep this in mind while learning more about cubicle etiquette.

Be punctual. Being punctual is very important, especially if you have an appointment. It shows that you respect the time of your colleagues and in turn it will compel them to respect your time too. Being on time day in and day out shows that you are in control of your environment and can adjust easily to the difficulties that life throws at you. Most of all, your superiors will see this and think that you are ready for that big promotion. Showing up to work late, taking a lot of days off, or simply not accomplishing your work is a sign of disrespect and will sooner or later get you fired. At the entry stage of a job, sending a clear message that you're eager and already working is vital.

Grooming. The way you groom and dress will affect how people view you. Be sure to bathe every day. To avoid bad breath, brush your teeth every morning after breakfast. All odors seem stronger in the office, so stay away from strong perfume or cologne, keep it light. Try to keep your personal odors unobtrusive. No exposed midriff to display tattoos and body piercing. Chewing gum and popping bubble gum in the presence of co-workers is neither cool nor dignified. Never do it whilst attending customers. Stand up straight and sit with legs together to avoid displays.

Dress professionally. Most offices will stick to a certain dress code. Most of the time, the dress code will be formal to semi-formal. If this is the case in your office, do not show up for work in a shirt and a pair of shorts, wearing sandals. This is definitely in bad taste. Keep your clothing within company standards and be sure it's clean and in good taste. Employees should wear their properly pressed office uniforms during office hours because it is the most visible representation that you work for the company. Some companies do not have strict uniform policy, but instead observe a casual business dress code to give enough freedom and comfort to their employees while in the workplace. Even then, employees are still expected to present a respectable and professional image. However, do keep in mind that not all casual attire fits in the office setting.

Maintain all shared items in " like new" condition and return borrowed supplies. Ask before you borrow anything. There's nothing worse than being branded the office thief because your stash of "borrowed" rulers is discovered by the cleaning lady. Leave the photocopier in working condition and be sure to take back that borrowed stapler with at least a few staples left inside. When you use up paper in the printer, load it for the next person. If a machine stalls or jams, take time to undo the jam or to alert the proper person to attend to it. We all expect and want to be able to use items and equipment when needed.

Do not abuse company time and resources. Most employees are used to the fact that what management does not know won't hurt them. For instance, taking an hour off your work time to surf the Internet and online shopping is considered stealing. Using company email and phones for personal use is considered corruption. All these are company resources and should only be used for official purposes. Obviously, you are allowed some room on this policy once in a while; however, if you want to maintain your clean and straight image, do not abuse it. Apart from being bad manners, it can get you into trouble if inappropriate material is sent or received.

Keep your personal workspace clean, neat and tidy at all times. Try not to be messy. A messy cubicle or desk shows how confused and careless you are, and that you're not clear about yourself. Also, it can reflect your personality or personal life at home. So don't let people think that you're always an unorganized person. Keep your cubicle tidy and decorative. Generally, less is better when it comes to office and cubicle decor. If you like adding a personal touch, such as photos or trinkets, choose only a few decent ones. Don't overload the space as if it's a collector's corner. Not only does having too many personal effects make it appear that you're rather territorial and sentimental but it can make it hard for others to take you as seriously in the work context. Keep personal items to a minimum, to avoid obstructing your work area.

Clean up after yourself in restrooms, and report any blockages or breakages to the correct attendant. Restrooms run a close second to kitchens as annoyance spots. After use, wipe the counter top and sink of any spilled water or soap. Be sure the toilet is clean for the next user. Notify the proper person if supplies are low or out, and of any plumbing problems.

Finally to sum up, let's quote from Forbes *The New Rules Of Business Etiquette*: knock before entering a cubicle, call or email before you arrive, don't leave voice mail messages when you know the person isn't there, if you're the boss, don't send emails over the weekend and if you get an email from your boss during the weekend, it's okay if you take a day to reply, don't wear your headphones in the elevator or hallway, don't check your email when you are out in the lobby or in the lift, don't touch your colleagues' food in the fridge, dress one notch up from office casual and use humor to recover from the inevitable faux pas.

New Words and Expressions

congenial	[kən'dʒiːniəl]	*adj.*	意气相投的；性格相似的；适意的；一致的
harmonious	[hɑː'məuniəs]	*adj.*	和谐的；和睦的；协调的；悦耳的
radically	['rædikəli]	*adv.*	根本上；彻底地；以激进的方式

electronic	[iˌlekˈtrɔnik]	*adj.*	电子的
cubicle	[ˈkjuːbikl]	*n.*	小隔间;小卧室
blur	[bləː]	*vi.*	变模糊;沾上污迹
		vt.	涂污;使……模糊不清;使暗淡;玷污
whip	[wip]	*vi.*	突然迅速地移动、离开等;痛打,拍击,拍动
whip out			突然拿出,突然取出,突然抽出
pinch	[pintʃ]	*vt.*	撮取……放入;少量加入;捏,拧,挤
barge	[bɑːdʒ]	*vi.*	闯(入),冲(入);冲击(常与 in 或 into 连用)
swear	[swɛə]	*vt.*	发誓;咒骂
		vi.	发誓,宣誓;诅咒
adjust	[əˈdʒʌst]	*vi.*	适应(环境等)(to);(在生活方式等方面)相互熟悉而适应
compel	[kəmˈpel]	*vt.*	强迫,迫使;强使发生
unobtrusive	[ˌʌnəbˈtruːsiv]	*adj.*	不唐突的;谦虚的;不引人注目的
midriff	[ˈmidrif]	*n.*	膈;上腹部
stash	[stæʃ]	*n.*	藏匿处;藏匿物
photocopier	[ˌfəutəuˈkɔpiə]	*n.*	影印机;复印机
stapler	[ˈstæplə]	*n.*	订书机;主要商品批发商
stall	[stɔːl]	*vi.*	停止,停转;拖延
abuse	[əˈbjuːz]	*vt.*	滥用;虐待;辱骂
	[əˈbjuːs]	*n.*	滥用;弊端;恶习,陋习
trinket	[ˈtriŋkit]	*n.*	小装饰品;不值钱的小玩意儿
blockage	[ˈblɔkidʒ]	*n.*	堵塞;封锁;妨碍
breakage	[ˈbreikidʒ]	*n.*	破坏;破损;裂口;破损量
attendant	[əˈtendənt]	*n.*	服务员,侍者;随员,陪从
plumb	[plʌm]	*vt.*	使垂直;探测,探索
		vi.	当管子工
		adj.	垂直的

notch	[nɔtʃ]	*n.*	[口语]等,级;(V字形)槽口,凹;(做记录、记数的)刻痕
inevitable	[in'evitəbl]	*adj.*	必然的,不可避免的
faux pas	['fəu'pɑː]		[法]失礼,失态

Task Two

How to Get Along with Your Colleagues

Your relationships with your colleagues are important. Good workplace relationships can help you do your job better. They can make going to work every day enjoyable. Bad relationships with colleagues can distract you and can turn a so-so job into a nightmare. You never know when you may rely on their help to get you out of a tricky jam. Here are a few things you should be aware of:

Respect your colleagues. Respect is the foundation of all good relationships, including those you have with your colleagues. Do your best to avoid offending those with whom you work. Be helpful, co-operative, friendly, and polite and show appreciation and respect toward others. Make new employees feel welcome and comfortable around you. Show consideration for other people's feelings. Always be particularly respectful to those older than yourself even if they are junior to you in position. Your elders are generally more mature in judgment and life's experiences and this deserves your respect even in the workplace. It pays off in the end. Treat your co-workers like teammates and support them whenever you can. If you help make them look good, they'll probably do the same for you. While you may want to stand out in the crowd, it's important to be liked, and it's a lot more fun to work in an office full of friends than one that's full of frenemies.

Watch your language. Say "good morning", "hello", "excuse me", "please", "thank you" and "I'm sorry", "you're welcome", as part of your everyday courtesy. Say "hello" to people in your vicinity when you come in every morning. When you pass co-workers in the hallway and this person isn't particularly your friend, smile or nod. Acknowledge that they are there. You don't have to run over and hug them but just say "hello". Think about what kind of message you send when you look the other way to purposely avoid contact. Always say "excuse me" when you cough, when you sneeze, and when you call someone's attention in between their work or conversation. Do not cough or sneeze in anyone's direction. Use a tissue, if possible, to contain the germs. Always say "please" when asking someone a favor. Without this, you will sound like you are demanding or giving command. When people do things for you, whether it is a superior or a subordinate, you should always say "thank You". This will show your co-workers that you appreciate them and what they do for you and for the company. Say "I'm sorry" whenever we do something wrong or make a mistake and follow with what you should do to make it up.

Most businesses and companies do not tolerate foul language in the workplace. Curse words, "swear" words, whatever you call them, the use of foul language in the workplace can be deemed appalling or even disrespectful to those around us. Foul language is a common example of profanity. Profanity is language or behavior that is considered to be vulgar, rude or offensive. The use of profanity can result in co-workers being insulted whether it was intended or not; it even can cause employees to be fired or even sued. Some employees exposed to inappropriate language, gestures or behaviors may notify their supervisor of this behavior or even file a complaint with the human resources department. Other employees may file sexual harassment or discrimination lawsuits depending on the type of profanity they are being exposed to. Therefore, profanity should be prohibited from the workplace and it is best to conduct yourself in a professional manner at work.

Respect people's privacy. Though cubicles are rarely private and they are often shared, when a person is working in their cubicle, it is there private office space for the time they are there working. To respect co-workers' space, treat cubicles and open desk areas as though you were entering someone's private office that has four walls, a door and a ceiling. Be sensitive to others' need for privacy. Don't read someone else's faxes, emails, mail or computer screens. Only share personal things at work that you wouldn't mind reading in next week's newspaper. If you need to discuss anything sensitive or private with another colleague, find a room where you can shut the door and nobody else can overhear you. Personal issues and work performance reviews are not for the ears of anyone other than the recipient. Confidential business conversations should also be kept to a minimum if you're in a cubicle for similar reasons. You don't want to prematurely spill the beans on some important deal.

Because you're most likely in a cubicle or other open office area, you inevitably will overhear snippets of conversations other people are having. Maybe you'll hear something about a project you're involved with or a problem you've encountered before, and you believe you have something to contribute. Yes, if you go over and join the conversation, you could save the day or provide valuable insight. However, you might also be viewed as a busybody.

Think carefully before joining that conversation. One consideration might be the amount of desperation you sense in their voices. The more desperate, the more willing they might be to hear from others. If you do choose to join them, I suggest you go to their office or cubicle, let them see you as you're listening to them. Then, at a break, casually mention that it sounds like there is a problem, and that if you can help, you'd be happy to. This approach is better than rushing over and telling them you overheard their conversation.

Refrain from gossiping about colleagues. If some news is heard that has the potential to damage business relationships, such as malicious rumors, speak to your manager. Gossiping will serve only to give you a poor reputation and reduce trust. So you should not talk harshly, backstab, gossip and badmouth the company.

Watch the volume of your voice. Some people have a voice that travels even at normal conversation levels. If you are one of those people, tone it down a little. Minimize laughter that can disturb your cubicle neighbors. When repeating private and protected customer information, keep your voice low enough that the customer can verify the information is correct but not so loud that others in the office can hear you. Be sensitive to how loudly you may be speaking. Do you notice that people down the hall comment on your conversations? That might indicate your voice is too loud. Consider closing your office door and lowering your voice whenever speaking in person or on the telephone. This awareness is even more critical when working in a cubicle-type workspace. If you listen to a radio or stream music, keep it low or wear a headset.

Be sensitive about what you bring for lunch. We're supposed to be inclusive and accepting of people from different backgrounds and cultures. And those other people are supposed to behave likewise. Nonetheless, be aware of how others may react to the lunch you bring. If you think about it, any reaction it causes can't be good for you. They'll either hate the smell or complain about you, or they'll love the smell, assassinate you, and eat your lunch. Either way, you lose out. If you have food with a distinctive aroma, consider either eating it outside or in the lunchroom, rather than at your desk. And some foods probably shouldn't be brought in at all, even to the lunchroom, such as stinky tofu or durian that's going to stink up the office and annoy people. If you're going to take lunch at your desk, keep it simple. A sandwich is best. When finishing, you should dispose of empty food containers and other items where they won't contribute negatively to the office atmosphere.

Fix, or attempt to fix, what you break. How many times have you gone to the photocopier to find that it was either out of toner, out of paper, or experiencing a paper jam? The problem was still around when you arrived because the previous person did nothing about it and simply left the copier in its problem condition. Don't be that person. If you can clear the paper jam safely and according to procedure, try to do so. Most photocopiers have diagrams to show you how. If you can't fix the jam or the other problem, leave a signed dated note describing the issue and what you are doing to fix it or have it fixed. Those actions could be a call to the maintenance vendor or to an administrative department. Your co-workers will appreciate your efforts, and signing your name to the note demonstrates your willingness to take ownership.

Keep the lunchroom clean. As a shared space, misuse of the kitchen or employee lounge often causes workplace tension. Label all the food in the refrigerator and cupboards with your name and date. Keep smelly foods out of the office. Clean out old food, and throw it away. Wash and return all kitchen items to their proper place, clean spills, and wipe counter tops and tables as needed. Help maintain supplies as needed. If you empty the coffee pot, always start a new one. Always know the microwave rules: stay away from popcorn or other foods with lasting smells such as fish; clean up any food spills; watch your food and don't stop someone else's from cooking. Remove all items at the end of your work week and toss or recycle empty containers.

Be punctual for meetings. If you're an attendee, be on time. If you can't make a meeting or you're going to be late, let someone know. Don't arrive late and ask for a recap. Doing so wastes everyone else's time. If you're the one who's running the meeting, start it on time and resume it on time after a break. To do otherwise (for example, to start late to accommodate latecomers) is unfair to those who showed up on time and only encourages more lateness in the future.

Be careful about solicitations. Even if your company has no strict prohibition against solicitations (for example, selling candy for a child's sports team fundraiser), be careful about doing so. Your co-workers may not appreciate being put on the spot. If you do anything at all, the best approach is to display the merchandise in a central location, with a notice about the reason, and an envelope to receive checks or cash.

Avoid borrowing or lending. Any borrowing that occurs can jeopardize a relationship if the repayment is slow, late, less than expected, or nonexistent. No matter how small the amount, the lender may feel resentment. In fact, a small amount might cause resentment precisely because the lender feels embarrassed about asking about repayment. Avoid borrowing or lending if you can. If you absolutely must borrow, write the lender an IOU with the amount and sign it. Then, pay it back as soon as you can.

Control your emotions. Always remain calm and collected. Keep cool when the office atmosphere gets "hot". Working in an office will sometimes expose you to experiences that can get you heated and angry. When these instances happen, it is always a wise move to keep your calm and to never get personal. Try to clear up any issues before they escalate. Business is business and like life, it is not fair. When faced with a heated argument or something that is not right for you, remain reserved and if you have to complain, do it in a calm and respectful manner. Never ever let your vocal chords loose. This can ruin your reputation and can even get you fired.

Don't consistently interrupt people. If your co-worker is on the phone but you need to ask a question, don't linger. Tap them on the shoulder and whisper that you need them for a minute (or leave a quick note in front of them) and ask them to call or see you when they are done. If your co-worker is having a work-related conversation, don't interrupt—just wait for them to finish or ask them to see you when they are through. Otherwise, it will suggest that your time or opinion is more important than theirs. When your colleagues are speaking, listen and don't interrupt.

Take responsibility for your mistakes. Apologize and go about correcting the mistakes. Apologize if you are clearly in the wrong. If in doubt, apologize anyway. It's no big deal. Never blame someone else if it is your mistake. If your boss criticizes your work, enquire about what precisely is wrong with it. Consider the comments, discuss them amiably if you disagree with the comments but defer to the bosses opinion if he/she is adamant. Be discreet and compassionate in your criticism of a co-worker.

Besides, avoid behaviors that may offend your co-workers. The top ten ways to annoy your coworkers are:

❶ Talk loudly on your cell phone

Your co-workers don't want to listen to your cell phone conversations. They are not as entertaining to anyone as they are to you.

❷ Take credit for your co-workers' contributions to a project

When your boss congratulates you on a job well done, don't mention that you had a lot of help. And, when you need some help on the next project, where do you think your co-workers will be? Not on your team.

❸ Come to work sick

If you have a cold or a stomach virus, spread it around. Your co-workers will thank you. On second thought, no they won't. Well, hopefully they'll have the decency to call in sick and stop spreading the illness further.

❹ Share everything with your co-workers

Your co-workers are a curious bunch so it is in their best interests if you tell them everything about your personal life—even if, not make that especially if, it makes them uncomfortable.

❺ Talk to your co-workers about religion and politics

Your co-workers may be very sensitive about these topics so if you want to offend them in a hurry, make sure they know why your beliefs are the only right ones.

❻ Tell your co-workers dirty jokes

It's not your problem so keep telling those jokes, but don't be surprised if you find yourself accused of sexual harassment one day.

❼ Spam your co-workers

Forward tons of email to all your co-workers. The content doesn't matter. Send it all—chain letters, jokes, and petitions. They'll be thinking of you as they keep hitting that delete button.

❽ Chew your gum loudly

Nothing sounds as yummy as the noise made by someone cracking their chewing gum and smacking their lips. It may drive your co-workers crazy.

❾ Don't carry your own weight

If you don't do your fair share of the work required by your department, your co-workers will have to pick up the slack. They'll be so exhausted from doing all the work, they won't be able to thank you.

❿ Talk down to your co-workers

You may think talking down to your co-workers will build you up, but a condescending attitude will not make you appear stronger. It will, however, make your co-workers resent you.

New Words and Expressions

nightmare	[ˈnaitmɛə]	*n.*	噩梦;梦魇般的经历
frenemy	[ˈfrenəmi]	*n.*	亦敌亦友

vicinity	[vi'siniti]	*n.*	邻近,附近;近处
hallway	['hɔːlwei]	*n.*	走廊,门厅,玄关
acknowledge	[ək'nɔlidʒ]	*vt.*	承认;答谢;报偿;告知已收到
germ	[dʒəːm]	*n.*	微生物;原始生物;细菌
confidential	[ˌkɔnfi'denʃəl]	*adj.*	机密的;表示信任的;获信任的
prematurely	[ˌpriːmə'tjuəli]	*adv.*	过早地;早熟地
spill the beans			泄密;说漏嘴
overhear	[ˌəuvə'hiə]	*vt.*	无意中听到;偷听
snippet	['snipit]	*n.*	小片;片断
busybody	['bizibɔdi]	*n.*	好事的人,爱管闲事的人
desperation	[ˌdespə'reiʃən]	*n.*	绝望的境地;不顾一切拼命
refrain	[ri'frein]	*vi.*	忍住;克制(常与 from doing something 连用)
gossip	['gɔsip]	*vi.*	闲聊;传播流言蜚语
malicious	[mə'liʃəs]	*adj.*	恶意的,恶毒的;蓄意的
rumor	['ruːmə]	*n.*	谣言,传闻
harshly	['hɑːʃli]	*adv.*	刺耳地;严厉地;粗糙地
backstab	['bækstæb]	*vt.*	[比喻、口语]暗箭伤(人),背后中伤
		vi.	背后中伤,背后攻击(某人)
headset	['hedset]	*n.*	耳机,头戴式受话器
assassinate	[ə'sæsineit]	*vt.*	毁谤,糟蹋或破坏(某人的名誉等);暗杀
aroma	[ə'rəumə]	*n.*	(酒、菜肴等的)香味,香气,芳香
stinky tofu	['stiŋki] ['təufuː]		臭豆腐
durian	['djuəriən]	*n.*	榴莲果(马来群岛产的);榴莲树
dispose	[dis'pəuz]	*vt.*	处理,处置,安排
		vi.	处理;安排;(能够)决定
diagram	['daiəgræm]	*n.*	图表;图解
maintenance	['meintənəns]	*n.*	维护,维修;保持;生活费用

vendor	[ˈvendɔː]	*n.*	卖主;小贩;[贸易]自动售货机
administrative	[ədˈministrətiv]	*adj.*	管理的,行政的
lounge	[laundʒ]	*n.*	休息室;闲逛;躺椅;(英)酒吧间
		vi.	闲逛;闲混
popcorn	[ˈpɔpkɔːn]	*n.*	爆米花,爆玉米花
toss	[tɔs]	*vi.*	辗转;被乱扔;颠簸
solicitation	[səˌlisiˈteiʃən]	*n.*	恳求;教唆;诱惑
fundraiser	[ˈfʌndreizə]	*n.*	资金筹集人;资金筹集活动
jeopardize	[ˈdʒepədaiz]	*vt.*	危害;使陷危地;使受危困
resentment	[riˈzentmənt]	*n.*	愤恨,怨恨
IOU	[ˌaiəuˈjuː]	*n.*	借据(等于 I owe you)
collected	[kəˈlektid]	*adj.*	镇定的,泰然自若的
escalate	[ˈeskəleit]	*vi.*	逐步增强;逐步升高
		vt.	使逐步上升;使逐步升级
reserved	[riˈzəːvd]	*adj.*	克制的,节制的
vocal chord			声带
amiably	[ˈeimiəbli]	*adv.*	亲切地,和蔼可亲地
defer	[diˈfəː]	*vi.*	推迟,延期;服从
		vt.	使推迟,使延期
adamant	[ˈædəmənt]	*adj.*	固执的,坚强的;坚定不移的;坚硬无比的
discreet	[disˈkriːt]	*adj.*	谨慎的;小心的
virus	[ˈvaiərəs]	*n.*	[病毒]病毒;恶毒;毒害
decency	[ˈdiːsənsi]	*n.*	合乎礼仪;礼貌
bunch	[ˈbʌntʃ]	*n.*	群;串;伙
sexual harassment			性骚扰
spam	[spæm]	*vt.*	群发垃圾邮件
forward	[ˈfɔːwəd]	*vt.*	(迅速地)发送(信件、电报等);寄发(货物等)

petition	[piˈtiʃən]	*n.*	请愿；请愿书；祈求；[法]诉状
yummy	[ˈjʌmi]	*adj.*	好吃的；美味的；愉快的
		n.	美味的东西；令人喜爱的东西
slack	[slæk]	*n.*	松弛；懈怠；懒散
condescend	[ˌkɔndiˈsend]	*vi.*	屈尊；谦逊
talk down			以居高临下的口吻说话

Task Three

Rules for Using Cell Phones at Work

Having your cell phone at work can be useful but it can also be very disruptive. Your friends and family can reach you anytime, anywhere, which can be annoying. When you're on your own time, the choice to turn off your cell phone is entirely yours. When it comes to using your cell phone at work, however, you have to be mindful of your co-workers and your boss, not to mention your own ability to get your job done. Here are some rules you should follow if you have your cell phone at work.

❶ Turn your cell phone ringer off

If you have your cell phone at work, it shouldn't ring. If you don't want to turn off your cell phone completely, at least you set it to vibrate. The sounds of different ring tones going off all the time can be very annoying to others. There's nothing more annoying that a ringing phone that goes unanswered. If you don't want to answer your phone, put it on silent or divert calls to your answer phone. Also, keep your cell phone on vibrate. In addition, you don't want your boss to know how often you get calls.

❷ Use your cell phone only for important calls

If you have your cell phone at work, you should only use it for important calls. What should you classify as an important call? The school nurse calling to say your child is ill, your child calling to say he's arrived home from school safely, and family emergencies that you must deal with immediately are important. Your friend calling to chat, your child calling to say the dog had an accident, or your mom calling to tell you your cousin Tally is engaged should not be considered important.

❸ Let your cell phone calls go to voice mail

While you are at work if you are in doubt about whether an incoming call is important, let voice mail pick it up. It will take much less time to check your messages than it will to answer the call and then tell the caller you can't talk. If you're on hold and waiting for someone to pick up, then yes, a speakerphone can save you time. Just keep the volume as low as possible.

❹ Find a private place to make cell phone calls

While it's okay to use your cell phone at work for private calls during breaks, don't stay at your desk. Find somewhere else to talk, where your conversation can't be overheard, even if what you're discussing isn't personal. You may be on a break but your co-workers have a job to do. Your co-workers in the area will not appreciate your disturbing them with a conference call.

❺ Don't bring your cell phone into the restroom

This rule should apply to using your cell phone at work or anywhere. Why? Well, if you must ask—you never know who's in there; the person on the other end of the line will hear bathroom sounds, e.g., toilets flushing; it is an invasion of your co-workers' privacy.

❻ Don't bring your cell phone to meetings

Even if you have your cell phone set to vibrate, if you receive a call you will be tempted to see who it's from. This is not only rude; it is a clear signal to your boss that your mind isn't 100 percent on your job. All calls can wait until your meeting is over or until there is a break. Remember, there was a time before we had cell phones.

New Words and Expressions

vibrate	[vaiˈbreit]	*vi.*	振动;颤动;摇摆;踌躇
engaged	[inˈgeidʒd]	*v.*	同……订婚(engage 的过去分词);保证;约定
voicemail	[ˈvɔismeil]	*n.*	语音信箱
speakerphone	[ˈspikəfəun]	*n.*	非手持电话听筒;喇叭扩音器

Task Four

Office Etiquette Beyond the Walls of Workplace

Office etiquette extends beyond the walls of your workplace and into any venue that involves work. This is where it gets tricky because, as they say, you should never mix business with pleasure.

If you've got a business lunch, then get there on time. Leave early if you need to but do not be late. It's a meeting in an informal location.

Turn your phone off during any business lunch you go to. Nobody wants to look inconsiderate while taking a call during an important meeting.

Keep your greeting short and sweet with the aforementioned handshake. Proper business meeting etiquette allows for a few minutes of small talk but keep it simple. The weather, the latest football results and so on.

If you invited your guest to the lunch, you're the one who should be paying for the meal. You can of course discuss splitting the bill when arranging the meeting but don't leave it till the bill arrives as some people see this as a sign of professional weakness. Don't forget to tip the restaurant staff.

When networking at business conferences you should make the first move to approach people wherever possible. Remember that first impressions count so dress to impress and keep the conversation formal.

You can build your business contacts by networking with the speakers at conferences. Do your research and find out who is speaking and what they are about. This will give you some good topics to discuss with them if you get the chance.

Set yourself a target to meet during a conference. Say, five new contacts through networking. Using the amazing etiquette tips you've learnt so far, it should be easy.

Don't get too drunk at the office party! How many people have lost respect, pay rises and even their job from drunken antics over the years? Keep your alcohol consumption in moderation and avoid fornicating with the boss's wife wherever possible.

Don't moan and complain about the lack of direction in the business while enjoying a cocktail with the girl from Accounts. It will inevitably get back to someone senior and you'll be the guy who cleans the toilets for the next 30 years.

On top of these tips, you'll need to be aware of the following as well: There is always a "mother" figure in the office who will sort out birthdays, collections and the office milk fund. When she asks for a donation to Jeff in Marketing who is leaving for pastures new, don't make the mistake of thinking the donation is voluntary. If you don't put a bit of money in there you can forget about ever getting a collection yourself and you will be branded as the office scrooge for the rest of your professional career.

New Words and Expressions

aforementioned	[əˈfɔːmenʃənd]	*adj.*	上述的，前面提及的
count	[kaunt]	*vt.*	有价值；起作用；值得考虑
antic	[ˈæntik]	*n.*	［常作复数］夸张的噱头；怪诞举动
fornicate	[ˈfɔːnikeit]	*vi.*	与……通奸
		vt.	私通
moan	[məun]	*vi.*	抱怨，悲叹；呻吟
pasture	[pɑːstʃə; ˈpæs-]	*n.*	退休；草地；牧场；牧草
scrooge	[ˈskruːdʒ]	*n.*	吝啬鬼

Exercises

I. Read the statements below and decide whether the statements are true or false. Write T for true and F for false.

1. When you are attending an office party, try wearing something that reflects your professional personality as well.
2. In an office party, ladies can wear short skirts or even bikini to display your slender figure, thus to leave good impression on your co-workers and boss.

3. Relationships that involve people at different levels of power in the workplace can be especially detrimental（不利的，有害的）.
4. You can put whatever you bring for lunch into the office fridge to keep your food fresh.
5. Discussing a confidential matter in a cubicle setting is appropriate.
6. Don't drink too much at an office party. It should not be more than one mixed drink or a glass of wine.
7. If the company has a policy against co-workers dating, it's best to avoid dating a co-worker.
8. Your cubicle is your own private space. As a result, you can listen to music as loud as you like.
9. You should not read others' faxes, email, computer screen, or mail in the workplace.
10. Dial and text messaging while driving is a dangerous distraction.

II. Choose the most appropriate one according to the situation given below.

1. When you meet clients in the office, which is the most appropriate greeting?

   A. Nodding and smiling.　　B. Shaking hands.

   C. Bowing.　　D. Kissing on the cheek.

2. In a meeting, which of these is acceptable?

   A. Arriving five or ten minutes late.

   B. Talking on your mobile phone.

   C. Arriving five minutes early.

   D. Having a private conversation with the person next to you.

3. Which of these is generally considered bad office behaviour?

   A. Speaking loudly.　　B. Eating at your desk.

   C. Borrowing equipment.　　D. Chatting by the water cooler.

4. In most offices how should you address your boss?

   A. Mr/Mrs/Miss + family name.

   B. Mr/Mrs/Miss + first name and family name.

C. First name only.

D. Sir or Madam.

5. Which of these would NOT be considered rude in an office?

A. Maintaining eye contact and looking away every now and then.

B. Standing one or two feet away from the person you are talking to.

C. Disagreeing with someone's point of view in a meeting.

D. Looking very quickly or not at all at a business card.

6. What is the first or Number One rule in conversation etiquette?

A. You should never disagree.

B. You should never interrupt.

C. Never ask questions—it shows you don't know what everyone else is talking about.

D. Make sure you monopolize the conversation to keep the focus on what you need.

7. You need to ask a co-worker a question and go to their cubicle, but they're on the phone. You should：

A. grab a pen and paper from their desk and attempt to communicate with them that way.

B. come back later.

C. stand there quietly until they're finished.

D. just talk to them；they'll realize what you're asking is more important than their phone conversation.

8. Your boss wants you to give a presentation on your latest sales figures. You：

A. show up late and go over the time allocated.

B. you make sure your presentation runs for the exact time allocated.

C. you have a back up plan in case your computer freezes or something else goes wrong.

D. fill your slideshow with useless diagrams.

9. Which of the following is TRUE in regards to office fridge etiquette?

A. Anything in the fridge is fair game.

B. You and your co-workers are responsible for keeping the fridge clean.

C. If you forget about your leftovers in the fridge, don't worry—someone will eventually throw them out.

D. Don't worry about "smell-proofing" your lunch. Who doesn't love the smell of liverwurst hitting them like a train when they open the fridge door?

10. Unfortunately, you need to fire one of your employees. What is something important to remember?

A. It's best to fire via email or phone call to save face.

B. The reason for the firing should be stated clearly.

C. Don't bother announcing the departure to the remaining staff. They'll hear it through the grapevine.

D. Do announce the departure to the remaining staff, and if it was related to poor performance, threaten those that are also poorly performing that the same can happen to them.

III. Put the following sentences into Chinese or vice versa.

1. Office etiquette is formal rules of behavior that make professional encounters pleasant and productive.
2. There is an old saying: If you can't stand the heat, get out of the kitchen.
3. You shouldn't have to be looking over your shoulder all day.
4. Workplace tension often results from poor communication, which in turn increases job stress.
5. Our company doesn't have a blanket ban on interoffice relationships.
6. 我不擅长面对面的直接对抗。
7. 你的手机铃声听起来真的很烦。
8. 如果双方都先冷静下来，激烈的争论就能解决。
9. 我在想你能否教我使用新的影印机和扫描仪。
10. 员工的隔间都应当被视作一个私人办公室。

▶ Acting

Read and practice the following dialogue in pairs.

(J:Joe, boss; S:Sam, employee; L:Lucinda, employee)

J: Hi Sam, please take a seat. Good morning, Lucinda. Please sit down. How are you both this morning?

S and L: Good, thanks.

J: I asked you both to come in this morning because there's been rumors floating around that you two are involved in a personal relationship. Now I know these kinds of things can be sensitive, but I do feel we have to discuss it.

L: Yes, the rumors are true. Sam and I are in love!

S: It's true, I feel the same way about Lucinda!

J: Well, let me be the first to congratulate you! Falling in love is great and I'm very happy for both of you.

S: But?

J: Well, our company does have some guidelines for internal relationships.

L: The company frowns on co-workers dating each other, right?

J: Let's just say such relationships are not actively encouraged.

S: But why? We are in love!

J: Well, there are many reasons, but one of the main downsides to interoffice relationships is that they can be a big distraction from work. Other employees can sometimes see such relationships as unfair. The end result can be jealousy, hurt feelings and a loss of productivity for the company.

L: But in today's modern working world, I feel like there is very little opportunity to meet people. Bars are smoky and loud. Internet dating can be very scary... it seems like I spend most of my time working at the office, so isn't it natural to find a co-worker as a partner?

S: I have to agree. Lucinda and I work on the same projects so we have a lot in common. I even think our productivity has increased as a result of our relationship.

▶ Speaking

Read the following paragraph loudly and try to recite it.

If you like to listen to music at work, use earphones. Your neighbors may not like the same type of music as you. A person's cubicle is their own private office. Do not go into that area if the person is not there. Even though your cubicle is your own private area, keep it organized. Leaving your area messy will reflect poorly on your professionalism.

▶ Supplementary Listening

* Business Etiquette (Office Gossip, Sexual Harassment, Cubicle Décor, Power Struggle, Best Behaviors in the Office, etc.)

  http://www.51voa.com/Business_Etiquette_1.html

Listen to the dialogues and dictate down the key points.

* How to Practice Good Etiquette in Your Cubicle

  http://www.howcast.com/videos/114768-How-to-Practice-Good-Etiquette-in-Your-Cubicle
* How to Practice Good Phone and E-mail Etiquette at Work

  http://www.howcast.com/videos/2404-How-to-Practice-Good-Phone-and-Email-Etiquette-at-Work
* How to Follow Video Conference Etiquette

  http://www.howcast.com/videos/314255-How-to-Follow-Video-Conference-Etiquette

Watch the videos and dictate down the key points.

▶ Supplementary Reading

6 Tips for Office Romance Etiquette

It makes sense that you find the love of your life (or, at least want to hook up with someone) at work. You spend most of your day surrounded by these people and probably share the same interests and a sense of camaraderie. Relationships are bound to happen; even romantic ones. However, it is important to follow certain guidelines of office romance etiquette. Six tips for handling co-worker relationships are found below:

1) Find out your company's dating policy. Most companies realize that when people work closely together, feelings are bound to spring up. Usually, it's not dating that causes the issue, but the more serious commitment of being engaged or married that causes some concern. If you and your significant other are in completely unrelated lines of business within the company, you are probably safe, but, if you directly report to your partner, or there could be an opportunity for confidential company information to be shared between you that shouldn't be, or a chance for co-workers to complain about favoritism, one of you might have to look for another job.

2) Use discretion! Nothing shows your co-workers and bosses that you will be able to handle an office romance professionally by behaving appropriately. This means no making out in your car during lunch, slapping each other on the butt when one of you walks by or making lewd or suggestive comments to each other. Not only will doing these things make you look bad, but companies are very concerned about sexual harassment claims these days.

3) If you and your partner get into a fight, do not bring the drama into the workplace. Keeping your business and personal lives separate is integral! The same goes for if/when your office romance ends. Some sexual harassment claims companies have to deal with stem from ex-lovers where one is bitter about the break up. Behaving professionally at all times in the workplace will not only keep your company safe, but it will ease the minds of your supervisors who might be concerned about the break up fall out, all the while keeping you on their good side!

4) Do not stare down every guy/girl your partner talks to. People at work have to deal with other people at work! Just because you guys met at work does not mean your partner is sizing up every other person they talk to at work as a potential date. However, they say how you meet your partner is how you lose your partner, so still keep an eye out!

5) Do not date the office scoundrel! Yes, the bad boy image draws them in by the dozens. You may think what you two have is "different". It's not. No "but's". It's not. He will move on to the hot new temp secretary the second he's had his way with you. Then you will be seen as just another notch in the scoundrel's bed post around the office. Unfortunately, there is a double standard here. Guys in the workplace can all hit up the office slut and there doesn't seem to be any fall out.

6) Do not date people who report to you. Do I really need to explain why this is an issue? If I do, you're not smart enough to have people reporting to you.

(http://etiquette-guide.com/office-romance-etiquette/)

Answer the following question:

What are the 6 tips for office romance etiquette?

Project Four
Business Communication Etiquette

Learning Objectives

After completing this project, you will be able to:

* understand the importance of communication etiquette in business;
* identify the various types of communication (verbal, non-verbal, oral/spoken and written);
* follow proper telephone etiquette and netiquette;
* define the term "body language" and apply it in the process of communication;
* identify and describe the different types of messages body language can convey when interacting with customers in a work environment.

➡ Warming-Up

Please answer the following questions.

❑ How do you communicate with your friends?

❑ Can you say various types of communication?

▶ Listening

http://www.unsv.com/voanews/business-etiquette/lessons/012/

Listen to the recording and fill in the blanks.

Netiquette

陈豪在美国ABC公司工作。他经常要用电子邮件和公司内外的人联系。今天他见到了一个他不认识的英文词，所以就去请教美籍华人Mary。

(*Office ambience*)

C：Hey, Mary，我知道etiquette这个词的意思是"礼节，礼貌"。可是，什么是netiquette? NETIQUETTE。

M：Netiquette是人们新创造的一个词。意思是"网上礼节"，也就是good behavior on the Internet。

C：网上还有礼节！Why don't you give me an example?

M：比如说，你最好不要全用大写来写email。

____

____。

C：噢，怪不得那天销售部的Robert问我：Why did you yell at me? 可有的人给我email全用小写，那是什么意思呀？Whisper? 说悄悄话呀？

M：No。那天财务部的Kevin不是给我们俩写的email都用小写吗？全用小写一般是不正式的，like chatting with your friends。

C：Email本身就是不正式的。

M：____。

我得去开个会，午饭时再接着谈吧！

C：Fine! See you at the cafeteria at 12:00 pm.

* * * * * *

M：哟，陈豪，你怎么吃那么快呀！

C：我刚才真是饿死了，不过我很想知道还有哪些网上礼节。

M：首先，在你送出email之前，check if there are mistakes such as spelling, grammar, punctuation and word choice. If your email is sloppy, you will be perceived as sloppy and disrespectful to the recipients.

C：我有两次发email给客户时忘了附件。几个客户马上回email问我：What attachment?

M：是呀，一旦email发出去以后，你就没法收回了。发现错误后最好的办法就是纠正错误，再重新发一次。你应该在 subject line 里写：corrected version with attachment included。

C：下回我一定这样做。

M：最好是不要出这样的差错。

____

____

____

____

____

____。

▶ Reading

Task One

Communication Etiquette in Business

Communication, simply put, is the process of encoding a message and sending it to another individual or group using a specific medium. Communication in business involves a complex set of unwritten rules governing speech, written correspondence and body language that varies in different parts of the world. All businesspeople, from the entry-level manager to the seasoned venture capitalist, can benefit from paying attention to communication etiquette in business.

Communication is vital in any business setting, and the effectiveness of your communication skills can make or break your career or your business. Fundamental issues, such as personal respect, courtesy and adherence to cultural standards, can go a long way toward making lasting, positive impressions and working productively with individuals from different backgrounds.

Effective communication between individuals in a business setting can strengthen feelings of camaraderie and group cohesiveness. This can directly enhance the productivity, creativity and adaptability of work teams and departments, as well as encouraging individuals to give their best efforts in their personal job roles.

Miscommunication, on the other hand, can have the exact opposite effect. A failure to communicate effectively can lead to missed opportunities for networking, strategic partnerships and new client acquisition.

Although communication among business leaders and among employees within a company is crucial to a business's success, all employees must also pay attention to their communication with customers. A different set of rules applies to communication with customers; the employee must be courteous and respectful even when customers are not, to curb negative word-of-mouth advertising. Communication in advertising, public relations and customer service activities must be scrutinized to ensure that the intended messages are being sent clearly and received by the desired market segment.

Communication etiquette takes on additional significance in the international business arena. Cultural norms and communication standards vary between countries and geographic regions; what is expected in one country may be forbidden in another. International businesspeople must take the time to become acquainted with the unique cultures in which they do business, and must often keep several distinct communication standards in their repertoire to strengthen relationships around the world.

Communication in business settings can take three distinct forms. Verbal communication consists of any spoken messages conveyed to others in person or through a technological medium. Written communication consists of any correspondence sent between individuals or groups, including letters and email. In addition to these fundamental forms of communication, body language plays a large role in communicating subtle nuances in the meanings behind your words. Businesspeople must understand the unwritten cultural rules governing all three types of communication to maximize the effectiveness of their interpersonal skills.

New Words and Expressions

encode	[en'kəud]	*vt.*	把……译成密码或电码；[计] 编码，译码
seasoned	['siːznd]	*adj.*	成熟的，老练的；调过味的；风干的

venture	[ˈventʃə]	*n.*	企业;风险;冒险;
		vt. /vi.	冒险;投机
fundamental	[ˌfʌndəˈmentəl]	*adj.*	基本的,根本的;主要的;最初的
adherence	[ədˈhiərəns]	*n.*	遵守,坚持;墨守(to);信奉,追随,忠诚(to);黏附(to)
camaraderie	[ˌkæməˈrɑːdəri]	*n.*	友情;同志之爱
cohesive	[kəuˈhiːsiv]	*adj.*	有黏着力的,有聚和性的;紧密结合的,团结的
enhance	[inˈhɑːns;-hæns]	*vt.*	增加,增强;改善;提高
adaptability	[əˌdæptəˈbiləti]	*n.*	适应性;可变性;适合性
acquisition	[ˌækwiˈziʃ(ə)n]	*n.*	获得物;获得
curb	[kəːb]	*vt.*	控制;勒住;抑止
		n.	抑制;路边;勒马绳
scrutinize	[ˈskruːtinaiz]	*vi.*	仔细检查;细致观察
		vt.	细看,细读;详察
segment	[ˈsegmənt]	*n.*	段,节;部分
norm	[nɔːm]	*n.*	标准,规范;准则
repertoire	[ˈrepətwɑː]	*n.*	[美国英语]全部技能;所有组成部分
correspondence	[ˌkɔːrisˈpɔndəns]	*n.*	通信;信件;符合,一致
nuance	[ˈnjuːɑːns]	*n.*	细微差别;微妙之处

Task Two

Verbal Communication

When enough people have similar talents, and are competing for the same positions and opportunities, the real differentiator is your interpersonal skills. The way you present yourself, how you communicate with other people, whether it's in an interview or with management at work, can make or break your personal brand. More and more people are starting to realize that the little things matter, especially in our current competitive environment. The most important in creating their personal brands were their verbal communication skills. Therefore, let's first figure out what verbal communication is.

Verbal communication can be defined as communicating your thoughts through words or the use of sounds and language to relay a message. By definition, verbal communication includes not only oral discussions, but also written messages, in other words, it includes both oral (spoken) and written communication, as both forms include the use of words. Groans or any noises or utterances a person makes are included in verbal communication. For instance, grunts of exasperation, screams of pain or delight, cries of sorrow, whimpers or utterances of joy can all be lumped under the same umbrella. Newspaper or magazine articles, bulletin board postings, emails, books, written announcements, faxes, memos, notes, traffic signs, street signs, billboards, advertisements and any other item that contains a written message is considered verbal communication. However, in this book, the author, like most business or communication experts, tends to use verbal communication in the context of the spoken word; therefore, items contain a written message, e. g., books, emails and memos, are classified into written communication. Electronic communication has spawned news ways of perceiving verbal communication. Live chat allows your business to interact with your website visitors in real time. There are many chat software options available in the market for us to use such as MSN, QQ, Fetion, Aliwangwang, wechat, etc. 8,500 customers around the globe, including the leading players in multiple industry segments count on LivePerson live chat software to deliver secure, reliable connections with their customers.

Every day we utilize multiple forms of verbal communication in order to do everything from working to playing, learning to relating.

Verbal communication in business is the act of expressing thoughts to others in the workplace. Communicating in a business environment indicates a face-to-face conversation or a chat over the telephone. For example, calling an employee into the office to tell him that you're impressed with the report he handed in last week is a form of verbal communication. However, verbal communication does not always consist of praise; it can consist of expressing your ideas or your disappointment with someone or a group. Starting a group discussion about ideas that can improve the workplace is another example of verbal communication. The following are examples of verbal communication in the workplace.

Meetings. Verbal communication occurs in meetings when participants share their ideas. Effective meeting organizers clearly define their objective, such as whether the intent of the meeting is to make a decision, brainstorm ideas, approve a plan, communicate a change or get a status report. At the beginning of the meeting, an organizer uses verbal communication to state the priorities of the meeting, the desired outcomes and the amount of time allowed to discuss each topic. By asking for additional input from participants, he ensures the meeting remains relevant for everyone. The meeting organizer also ensures that every participant gets a chance to speak without monopolizing the agenda.

Presentations and lectures. Using effective verbal communication, business professionals give presentations and lectures to convey their expertise on a particular topic. Whether a business professional provides instruction, describes a product to make a sale or communicates a vision or strategy, he needs to keep the message clear by preparing adequately. Using vivid language, descriptive examples and supplementary visuals, he ensures a successful presentation. By using short words and sentences, speakers tend to avoid confusion. Effective presenters allow time for the audience to ask questions and provide comments.

Workshops. Workshop organizers use verbal communication to direct the activities of participants. By providing clear instructions for group, the facilitator ensures a positive development experience. Leaders guide participants in researching issues, solving problems, negotiating solutions and making decisions.

Conversations. Conversations typically involve two people discussing a topic. Effective verbal communication occurs during conversations when the speaker acknowledges the sensitivity of the subject, time constraints and types of questions the receiver might ask. If the conversation occurs face to face, successful communicators use active listening skills such as repeating back what the other person has said. They also resist the temptation to interrupt and allow the other person to speak up as well to convey their thoughts. If the conversation occurs by telephone, the participants need to pay even more attention.

Then, what are some of the top verbal communication skills that people need to master if they want to stand out from their competitors? Below are top 10 verbal communication tips we should all strive to master. Each of these is just as important in our personal lives as in our professional lives. By improving your verbal communication skills you will quickly connect and build rapport, earn respect, gain influence, and become more likable and accepted.

Be friendly. People who communicate with a friendly tone and warm smile almost always have the edge. The reason is simple: we are subconsciously drawn to people who are friendly because they make us feel good and bring more enjoyment to our lives.

Think before you speak. Organizing your thoughts before speaking can reduce the amount of awkward pauses and verbal "hiccups". Although it's not possible to make an outline for impromptu dialogue, writing down your thoughts before planned discussions can improve your speaking prowess.

Be Clear. Most of us don't have the time nor do we want to spend our emotional energy to figure out what someone else is trying to say. People who are indirect in their verbal communication and who tend to hint at things without saying what's really on their mind are seldom respected. When there is something you want to say, ask yourself, "What is the clearest way I can communicate this point?"

Don't talk too much. Very few people like to be around someone who talks too much and dominates the conversation.

Be your authentic self. Today people are turned off by those people who feel the need to put on a show to make their point. Instead, people are attracted to someone who speaks from the heart and is genuine, transparent, and real.

Practice humility. Humility is having a modest view of one's own importance. It is one of the most attractive personality traits one can possess and is one of the most significant predictors of someone who is respected. People who speak with humility and genuine respect for others are almost always held in high regard.

Speak with confidence. You don't have to sacrifice self-confidence to practice humility. Confidence is a self-assurance arising from an appreciation of one's true abilities, whereas humility is having a modest opinion of one's own importance. Speaking with confidence includes the words you choose, the tone of your voice, your eye contact and body language.

Focus on your body language. When you are engaged in face-to-face verbal communication, your body language can play as significant of a role in the message you communicate as the words you speak. Your body language communicates respect and interest. It puts real meaning behind your words. Speaking with poor nonverbal cues such as slumping your shoulders or scowling can detract from the effectiveness of your words. Stay in positive control of your body language to ensure your words are assessed correctly.

Use direct and concise language. Sometimes using complicated words and sentence structures can cause more confusion than it explains. Avoid using "big words" to sound more educated because this can quickly backfire, unless you're sure of their usage and pronunciations. Plan ahead. Constantly ask yourself, "How can I say what needs to be said using the fewest number of words possible while still being courteous and respectful?"

Learn the art of listening. Being an attentive listener is more important in verbal communication than any words that can come out of your mouth. You must show a sincere interest in what is being said, ask good questions, listen for the message within the message, and avoid interrupting.

Active listening is a very important listening skill and yet, as communicators, people tend to spend far more energy considering what they are going to say rather than listening to what the other person is trying to say. The following points are essential for effective and active listening:

- Arrange a comfortable environment conducive to the purpose of the communication, for example, a warm and light room with minimal background noise.

- Be prepared to listen. Keep an open mind and concentrate on the main direction of the speaker's message.
- Avoid distractions if at all possible.
- Delay judgment until you have heard everything.
- Be objective.
- Do not be trying to think of your next question while the other person is giving information.
- Do not dwell on one or two points at the expense of others.

The speaker should not be stereotyped. Try not to let prejudices associated with, for example, gender, ethnicity, social class, appearance or dress interfere with what is being said.

New Words and Expressions

compete	[kəm'piːt]	*vi.*	竞赛;竞争;对抗
differentiator	[ˌdifə'renʃieitə]	*n.*	区别者,区分者;鉴别者
brand	[brænd]	*n.*	品牌;商标,牌子;烙印
		vt.	铭刻于,铭记;印……商标于
groan	[grəun]	*n.*	呻吟,呻吟声;叹息声;[口语]抱怨
utterance	['ʌtərəns]	*n.*	表达;说话;说话方式
grunt	[grʌnt]	*n.*	咕哝;呼噜声
		vi.	作呼噜声;发哼声
		vt.	咕哝着说
exasperation	[igˌzæspə'reiʃən]	*n.*	激怒,恼怒;激化,恶化,加剧
whimper	['hwimpə]	*n.*	呜咽声,抽泣声;牢骚,怨声
		v.	抽泣,呜咽;低声抱怨
lump	[lʌmp]	*vt.*	混在一起;使成块状;忍耐;笨重地移动

		n.	块,块状;肿块;瘤;很多;笨人
		adj.	成团的;总共的
spawn	[spɔːn]	*vt.*	引起,造成,酿成;使大量产生;大规模发展
spontaneous	[spɔnˈteiniəs]	*adj.*	自发的;冲动的;(举止、行为等)无意识的
supervisor	[ˈsjuːpəvaizə]	*n.*	监督者,监察者,指导者,管理人,检查员
mentor	[ˈmentɔː]	*n.*	顾问;导师;指导者;教师;良师益友
thrive	[θraiv]	*vi.*	兴旺,繁荣,旺盛;成功
combative	[ˈkɔmbətiv]	*adj.*	好斗的,好战的;准备战斗的;斗志旺盛的
priority	[praiˈɔrəti]	*n.*	先;(时间上)在前;上位;重点;[复数]优先权;先取权;[复数]优先考虑的事;优先配给
expertise	[ˌekspəːˈtiːz]	*n.*	专门技能(知识),专长;专家意见(鉴定、评价)
constraint	[kənˈstreint]	*n.*	监禁,关押;限制;抑制,压制;局促不安
rapport	[ræˈpɔːt]	*n.*	密切关系,交往;和谐一致
subconsciously	[ˌsʌbˈkɔnʃəsli]	*adv.*	潜意识地
hiccup	[ˈhikʌp;-əp]	*n.*	呃逆,打嗝儿;呃逆声;暂时的中断(停顿、下降)
prowess	[ˈprauis]	*n.*	杰出的才能;卓越的技能;英勇;英勇(或无畏)的行动
authentic	[ɔːˈθentik]	*adj.*	真正的,真实的;可信的;名副其实的;逼真的
trait	[treit]	*n.*	特性,特点;品质;少许
scowl	[skaul]	*vi.*	皱眉;怒视
		vt.	皱眉表示;对……沉下脸
		n.	愁容,怒容
assess	[əˈses]	*vt.*	评定;估价;对……征税
conducive	[kənˈdjuːsiv]	*adj.*	导致……的;有益的;助长的,促成的
dwell	[dwel]	*vi.*	细想;详述居住;存在于
dwell on			(心里)老是想着,担心,细想
stereotype	[ˈsteriəutaip;ˈstiə-]	*vt.*	使成为陈规,使变得刻板;对……产生成见
		n.	陈规旧习,旧规矩;固定的形式

Task Three

Telephone Etiquette—How to Communicate by Phone

Telephone etiquette refers to a set of rules that apply when people make calls to others or when they are receiving a phone call, i. e., how to communicate by phone. There are slightly different rules for a variety of situations. Making and receiving personal calls are not the same as making/receiving business calls. Within this set of rules there can be differences, especially for business calls where companies may want callers or receivers to say certain things.

For personal telephone etiquette, calling someone means doing several things. A caller should identify him/herself when not recognized right away. In calling a friend or relative, for instance, after the initial "Hello", the caller should come up with a greeting and identification. "Hello/Hi, this is John." Sometimes a last name is needed if the person being called is an acquaintance or a business representative.

Business telephone etiquette is similar in many ways to home phone calls and reception. Yet, the business should be even more vested in remaining polite, since poor phone manners can have a negative effect on business reputation. Calling out from a business is similar to a personal call. The person should begin with a greeting, identify self, and identify employer. This should then be met with a concise statement or request to speak to someone. In receiving the business call, a businessperson also attempts to be polite, understand the caller's needs, and take messages if required.

Since customers are the ones who infuse the profits into a business, they do not appreciate being treated with rudeness in their dealings with a company. This includes any business that is conducted on the telephone.

Proper telephone technique involves some basic common sense in which everyone who works for a company should use. Here are some basic tips:

Incoming calls

Tip 1—All incoming calls should be answered in a timely manner. Try to answer the telephone by the second or third ring.

Tip 2—Business telephones should always be answered with a phrase like "Good morning, ABC Company, Carol speaking, may I help you?", "Hello/Good Morning, Accounting Department, Syndi Seid speaking." In a busy office setting that fields hundreds of calls each day, this particular phrase may be too much to say. If so, it can be shortened to a phrase that is less wordy. But the name of the company needs to be stated as soon as the phone is answered along with the person's name who answered the phone. This lets the caller know that they have indeed reached the right business, and lets them know with whom they are speaking.

Tip 3—Before placing a caller on hold, ask their permission first and thank them. Let them know that they have not been forgotten, and that you are attending to their call. It is better to return a call than to keep someone on hold too long. Do not forget to return the call as you promised.

Tip 4—Speak clearly and slowly. Have a smile on your face when talking to the customer on the telephone. The smile shows in your voice, and projects a friendly ready to help attitude. Always use a pleasant, congenial and friendly tone. Do not slur or mumble your words. Speak with confidence so the person on the other end has the feeling that you know what you are doing.

Tip 5—Never be rude to a caller, no matter how nasty they are. Never engage in an argument with a caller. Always remember to handle yourself in a professional, business-like manner. This includes handling the situation in a calm, cool manner.

Tip 6—At the end of the conversation don't just hang up. End the call with a warm "Thank you for your call." Be genuine while making this acknowledgement.

Outgoing calls

Tip 1—Preparation. Think through exactly what you plan to say and discuss before you place a call. Jot down the items you want to discuss and questions you want answered. In other words, anticipate and expect you will be placed into a voicemail system; plan your message to be as direct and specific as possible, asking the person to respond to specific alternatives or questions. Do not say, "Hello, it's Syndi, call me back." At least state the subject about which you want the person to call you back about.

Tip 2—Same as Tip 4 below—Speak clearly and slowly when you make a business call. Example: "Hello, my name is John Doe from XYZ Corporation. May I please speak with Ms. Jane Smith?"

Tip 3—Same as Tip 5 below—All customers expect to work with a professional organization. One sign of a professional organization is how they are treated by the people who work there.

Tip 4— When calling another business, it is proper etiquette to give your name and the company's name you work for to whomever answers the telephone. Do not make them guess who it is or make them pry it out of you.

Tip 5—If you get the wrong number, apologize to the person who answers the phone—do not just hang up. This is especially important nowadays when people have Caller ID on their phone lines. All they have to do is to check their device to find out who just rudely hung up on them.

Tip 6—Do not allow interruptions to occur during conversations. Do not carry on side conversations with other people around you. The person on the telephone takes precedence over someone who happens to walk in your office or passes by while you are on the phone. If you must interrupt the conversation, say to the person, "Please excuse me for a moment I'll be right back." When you return, say, "Thank you for holding."

Tip 7—When leaving a phone message, always state your name, company, phone number and reason for calling. Do not stammer or stutter and use up an unreasonable amount of time. Repeat your telephone number at the end of your message.

New Words and Expressions

acquaintance [ə'kweintəns] *n.* [总称]熟人;认识 (with someone);熟悉,知道(with)

vest [vest] *vt.* (财产、权利等)授予,赐予;赋予

n. 背心,汗衫

congenial	[kənˈdʒiːniəl]	*adj.*	性格相同的;意气相投的,情投意合的;适合的
slur	[sləː]	*vi.*	含糊地发音; 潦草地写字
		vt.	藐视,轻视; 诋毁; 含糊地念
mumble	[ˈmʌmbl]	*vt./vi.*	咕哝; 抿着嘴嚼
		n.	含糊的话; 咕哝
precedence	[ˈpresidəns]	*n.*	优先;居先
stammer	[ˈstæmə]	*vt./vi.*	结巴地说出;口吃
		n.	口吃,结巴
stutter	[ˈstʌtə]	*vt./vi.*	结巴地说话;结巴地说出
		n.	结巴,口吃

Task Four

Written Communication

Written communication involves any type of interaction that makes use of the written word. It is one of the two main types of communication, along with oral/spoken communication. Written communication is very common in business situations. Some of the various forms of written communication that are used internally for business operations include memos, reports, bulletins, job descriptions, employee manuals, and electronic mail. Examples of written communication avenues typically pursued with clients, vendors, and other members of the business community, meanwhile, include electronic mail, Internet Web sites, letters, proposals, telegrams, faxes, postcards, contracts, advertisements, brochures, and news releases. So it is important for businesspeople to develop effective written communication skills.

Effective written communication is essential for preparing worthy promotional materials for business development. Writing ability is especially important in customer communication. Business proposals, status reports, customer documentation, technical support, or even email replies all depend on clear written communication.

Effective written communication skills start with using the proper format for the type of correspondence you want to send. For instance, a cover letter should be set up like a business letter, containing the elements found therein, such as date, return address and a body of the letter offset by the salutation and closing. Effective writing involves careful choice of words, their organization in correct order in sentences formation as well as cohesive composition of sentences.

The purpose of your communication should be clear from the beginning. Keep everything as concise as possible. Time is a valuable commodity for just about everyone. Keep the piece itself short, and use concise sentences and brief paragraphs that are written in the active voice. This brevity also shows respect for your reader's time, which will give her a better overall impression of you.

There is no excuse for sending communications that contain spelling errors and poor grammar. Thoroughly proofread any written communication piece before you send it out. Check it for incorrect grammar, misspellings, use of the passive voice and other mechanical flaws. Errors can create a bad impression, so it is vitally important that your written communication be error-free.

The tone of the correspondence also goes a long way in making it effective. It's imperative to match the tone to the audience. Business writing should have a formal tone. When you are writing to a friend, use a more conversational tone and even interject some humor. Cover letters for job openings, corporate communications and even emails to your boss should be wholly professional. "Hey, Dude, would you like to hire me?" just won't cut it for such situations. Likewise, your friends will think you're nuts if you start a note with: "Dearest John P. Doe III, how art thou?"

In effective business communications, good communication should be complete, concise, clear, concrete, correct, considerate, and courteous. More specifically, this means that communication should: answer basic questions like "who", "what", "when", "where"; be relevant and not overly wordy; focus on the receiver and his or her interests; use specific facts and figures and active verbs; use a conversational tone for readability; include examples and visual aids when needed; be tactful and good natured; and be accurate and nondiscriminatory. Unclear, inaccurate, or inconsiderate business communication can waste valuable time, alienate employees or customers, and destroy goodwill toward management or the overall business.

New Words and Expressions

avenue	[ˈævənjuː]	*n.*	[比喻]途径,手段,方法;林荫道
proposal	[prəˈpəuzəl]	*n.*	建议;计划;提案;提议;推荐
brevity	[ˈbrevəti]	*n.*	(讲话、文章等的)精练,简短,简洁
proofread	[ˈpruːfriːd]	*vt. /vi.*	[美国英语]校对
nondiscriminatory	[ˈnɔndisˈkriminətəri]	*adj.*	不歧视的,一视同仁的

Task Five

Netiquette—How to Communicate by Network

Netiquette is a term derived from the words "Internet Etiquette" or "Network Etiquette" which describes the use of proper manners and behavior online. It is a set of social conventions that facilitate interaction over networks, ranging from Usenet and mailing lists to blogs and forums. It means respecting other users' views and displaying common courtesy when posting your views to online discussion groups. Netiquette primarily involves any communication you may send out or receive from the net. It should be used in all areas of electronic means including email, chatting, blogging, forums, message boards, and so on.

The following is a summary of the netiquette guidelines.

Guidelines for business email correspondence

Much like writing a formal business letter, your business emails should not include slang terms, text message abbreviations and other common insertions used in informal emails or instant messages. By following a few tips and guidelines, your emails will reflect your professionalism and let your credentials shine.

Label your emails with a professional subject line. Make it pertinent to the topic of your email. Do not use simple sayings such as "For You" or "Please Read" in your subject line. This may result in your emailing being sorted to the Junk Mail folder. A professional subject line helps ensure your email's recipient will read the email and not disregard it for miscellaneous junk or spam.

Address the recipient by name, if possible. If you don't know his or her name, look it up. Most companies have a website or a phone directory. Make every attempt to learn the name of the email's recipient.

Establish your identity and corporate affiliation. Even if you and the recipient of your email have met before, it's always wise to include a business signature or other information to remind him who you are and where you work. It's a courtesy that lets them proceed to answering your email quickly, instead of having to look up who you are and how to contact you. For example:

Ms. Lee,

This is Art from Graphic Star International who has been in contact with you for our large printing needs.

Write the purpose of your email out clearly. Propose any deals or relationships you hope to create as a result of the email. Provide any details necessary for the reader to make any decisions or take any actions. By including all information necessary, you help to expedite any deals made as a result of the email.

Avoid slang or rambling within your email. Just because text messages use abbreviations, that is not a reason to include them in your professional email. Your email should be concise. Not only is the reader a busy person, but he or she may be reading your email on a mobile device. A shorter, to-the-point email is much easier to read and respond to than a lengthy, confusing one.

Tips

Before sending your email, be sure to run a final spell check to ensure there are no misspelled words or punctuation errors. Avoid writing your message using all upper case letters. It looks like you're shouting. Don't use all lower case letters either. Some people say it will make it seem like you're mumbling. Make sure your email includes a courteous greeting and closing. Be sure you are including all relevant details or information necessary to understand your request or point of view. When replying to a group, be cautious of choosing the "Reply All" button. If you must forward an email to more than one person, put your email address in the To: field and all the others you are sending to in the Bcc: field to protect their email address from being published to those they do not know. Make one last check that the address or addresses in the To: field are those you wish to send your reply to. Be sure your name is reflected properly in the From: field. Jane A. Doe (not jane, jane doe or JANE DOE). Always end your emails with "Thank you", "Sincerely", "Take it easy", "Best regards"—something! Don't forget attachments before sending out an email. When sending large attachments, always "zip" or compress them before sending.

Guidelines for message boards

As you become involved with online discussion groups, you will find that each group has its own accepted rules of behaviour. Many of these have come about because of technical limitations.

For example, on an email discussion list—where not everyone may have seen past messages—it's considered polite to quote from a message you're replying to, so your response has context. It's also considered polite to keep those quotes short and relevant. On a web-based forum, however, where the original messages are visible to all, quoting is often unnecessary.

The basic rules

Refrain from personal abuse. You may express robust disagreement with what someone says, but don't call them names or threaten them with personal violence.

Don't spam. That is, don't repeatedly post the same advertisement for products or services. Most sites have strict and specific rules about who is allowed to post ads and what kind of ads they are.

Write clearly and succinctly. On a site that has many non-native English speakers, avoid using slang they may not understand.

Remember that your posts are public. They can be read by your partner, your children, your parents, or your employer.

Stay on-topic, especially when you're new. Don't post about football in a hair-care forum or about hair care in a gardening forum!

Research before asking. When you're about to ask a question online, you should do a little bit of research first. Chances are that someone had the exact same question, asked it online, received an answer, and the whole thing was indexed by your favorite search engine. So instead of making someone else search Google for you, just do it yourself. You may of course ask your question, if you couldn't find anything relevant or if you couldn't make sense of it. Don't expect other people to do your homework for you. If you're looking for technical help, for example, don't ask questions you could easily answer yourself by reading the manual or online help provided with the product. When you do ask for help, include details of what attempts you've made to solve the problem. It will save time and also show people that you are making an effort to help yourself.

Do not post copyrighted material to which you do not own the rights. Sites vary in how strict they are about this, but as well as facing the possibility of legal action by the rights holder, you may also get the site sued. The site's owner, perhaps assisted by one or more moderators, has the final say in enforcing the rules.

Helpful hints

Almost every site has a page for newcomers that describe its rules of good behaviour. Usually this page will appear as the terms and conditions you must agree to when you open your account. However, sites may have additional information. You should read all of it.

Check to see if the site has a FAQ (frequently asked questions) section. FAQs typically include questions that have been asked and answered hundreds of times. If you have any queries about site protocol, you will most likely discover the dos and don'ts here.

Finally, it's always wise to see what the discussion group has been talking about for a week or two before you begin to post your messages. Online, as in real life, it can take a long time to get past a bad first impression.

New Words and Expressions

credential	[kri'denʃəl]	*n.*	凭证,文凭;[通常用复数]证书
miscellaneous	[ˌmisi'leiniəs]	*adj.*	混杂的;各色各样混在一起的;各种各样的
spam	[spæm]	*n.*	电子垃圾,(网上)垃圾函件
		vt.	向……发送垃圾函件
affiliation	[əˌfili'eiʃən]	*n.*	隶属关系;隶属,从属
recipient	[ri'sipiənt]	*n.*	接受者;接收器;容器
courtesy	['kəːtisi]	*n.*	礼貌,谦恭,殷勤;殷勤周到的举止,礼貌的行为
expedite	['ekspidait]	*vt.*	加快,加速
rambling	['ræmbliŋ]	*adj.*	(语言、文字)杂乱无章的,不连贯的;闲逛的,漫步的;闲聊的
		v.	(无目的地)漫游(ramble 的现在分词)
to-the-point			切中要害,切题
refrain	[ri'frein]	*vi.*	忍住;克制(常与 from doing something 连用)
robust	[rəu'bʌst]	*adj.*	强有力的(观点、见解);强健的,健康的;粗野的
succinctly	[sək'siŋktli]	*adv.*	简洁地;简便地
copyrighted	['kɔpiraitid]	*adj.*	有版权的,受版权保护的

Task Six

Nonverbal Communication

Although verbal communication is a primary means of expression, nonverbal actions such as body language can greatly affect the way a message is perceived. Nonverbal communication includes the overall body language of the person who is speaking, which can be divided into several categories: facial expressions, head movements, hand and arm gestures, physical space, touching, eye contact and physical postures. Facial expressions say a lot about his/her mood. Also, gestures like a handshake, a smile or a hug can independently convey emotions and do not need to be accompanied by words. Nonverbal communication can also be in the form of pictorial representations, signboards, or even photographs, sketches and paintings.

Has it ever occurred to you how much you are saying to people even when you are not speaking? Unless you are a master of disguise, you are constantly sending messages about your true thoughts and feelings whether you are using words or not.

Studies show that your words account for only 7% of the messages you convey. The remaining 93% is nonverbal. 55% of communication is based on what people see and the other 38% is transmitted through tone of voice. So think about it. In the business setting, people can see what you are not saying. If your body language doesn't match your words, you are wasting your time.

Eye contact is the most obvious way you communicate. When you are looking at the other person, you show interest. When you fail to make eye contact, you give the impression that the other person is of no importance. Maintain eye contact about 60% of the time in order to look interested, but not aggressive. Whether you communicate with a colleague or meet with a client, make eye contact to show your interest.

Facial expression is another form of nonverbal communication. It's hard to hide facial expressions; emotions ranging from happy and excited to sad, angry and nervous are identified by smiles, frowns, lowered eyes or raised eyebrows. A smile is easily recognized as friendly and welcoming. Smiling is an expression of happiness in most cultures. Smile often when meeting new people or presenting information. Avoid frowning in business settings; instead, ask questions to clarify your confusion. Otherwise, you risk offending colleagues, especially in the instance when there's a guest speaker presenting information.

Your mouth gives clues, too, and not just when you are speaking. Mouth movements, such as pursing your lips or twisting them to one side, can indicate that you are thinking about what you are hearing or that you are holding something back.

The position of your head speaks to people. Keeping your head straight, which is not the same as keeping your head on straight, will make you appear self-assured and authoritative. People will take you seriously. Tilt your head to one side if you want to come across as friendly and open. Nod your head during conversations to show that you're actively listening.

How receptive you are is suggested by where you place your arms. Arms crossed or folded over your chest say that you have shut other people out and have no interest in them or what they are saying. This position can also say, "I don't agree with you." You might just be cold, but unless you shiver at the same time, the person in front of you may get the wrong message.

How you use your arms can help or hurt your image as well. Waving them about may show enthusiasm to some, but others see this gesture as one of uncertainty and immaturity. The best place for your arms is by your side. You will look confident and relaxed. If this is hard for you, do what you always do when you want to get better at something—practice. After a while, it will feel natural.

The angle of your body gives an indication to others about what's going through your head. Leaning in, says, "Tell me more." Leaning away signals you've heard enough. Adding a nod of your head is another way to affirm that you are listening.

Posture is just as important as your grandmother always said it was. Sit or stand erect if you want to be seen as alert and enthusiastic. When you slump in your chair or lean on the wall, you look tired. No one wants to do business with someone who has no energy.

Control your hands by paying attention to where they are. In the business world, particularly when you deal with people from other cultures, your hands need to be seen. That would mean you should keep them out of your pockets and you should resist the urge to put them under the table or behind your back. Having your hands anywhere above the neck, fidgeting with your hair or rubbing your face, is unprofessional. Practice etiquette by holding the door for colleagues based upon rank, as a gesture of respect. When speaking, use your hands to help you get your points across.

Legs talk, too. A lot of movement indicates nervousness. How and where you cross them tells others how you feel. The preferred positions for the polished professional are feet flat on the floor or legs crossed at the ankles. The least professional and most offensive position is resting one leg or ankle on top of your other knee. Some people call this the "Figure Four". It can make you look arrogant.

The distance you keep from others is crucial if you want to establish good rapport. Standing too close or "in someone's face" will mark you as pushy. Positioning yourself too far away will make you seem standoffish. Neither is what you want so find the happy medium. Most importantly, do what makes the other person feel comfortable. If the person with whom you are speaking keeps backing away from you, stop. Either that person needs space or you need a breath mint.

You may not be aware of what you are saying with your body, but others will get the message. Make sure it's the one you want to send.

Communicating in a business environment requires more than just effective verbal and written communication. It's likely that your nonverbal communication cues enter the room before you speak. Everything from gestures, eye contact, posture, appearance and facial expressions offer an indication of moods and thoughts. Because of this, it's important to be aware of the nonverbal signals you send while working in the office with co-workers and clients, during business meetings and interviews, at conferences and when you're giving presentations.

New Words and Expressions

pictorial	[pik'tɔːriəl]	*adj.*	图片的;用图片表示的;形象化的
sketch	[sketʃ]	*n.*	写生;素描,速写(画);简图,略图
disguise	[dis'gaiz]	*vt.*	掩饰;假装;隐瞒
		n.	伪装;假装
account for			共计达;(在数量、比例上)占;说明(原因、理由等)
transmit	[trænz'mit]	*vt.*	传导,传递,传达;输送,传输,传播
aggressive	[ə'gresiv]	*adj.*	过分自信的,(行为等)过分的;挑衅的;积极进取的
frown	[fraun]	*vi.*	皱眉;不同意
		vt.	皱眉,蹙额

		n.	皱眉,蹙额
clarify	[ˈklærifai]	*vt.*	澄清;说明,阐明;变得明晰;得到净化
authoritative	[ɔːˈθɔritətiv]	*adj.*	有(或显示)权威的;官方的,当局的
tilt	[tilt]	*vi.*	倾斜;翘起;以言词或文字抨
		vt.	使倾斜;使翘起
		n.	倾斜
immaturity	[ˌiməˈtjuəriti]	*n.*	未成熟;幼稚;粗糙;不完全
affirm	[əˈfəːm]	*vt. /vi.*	确认;肯定;断言
posture	[ˈpɔstʃə]	*n.*	姿势;态度;情形
		vi.	摆姿势
		vt.	做……的姿势
erect	[iˈrekt]	*adj.*	(位置、姿势)直立的,垂直的
alert	[əˈləːt]	*vt.*	警告;使警觉,使意识到
		adj.	警惕的,警觉的;留心的
		n.	警戒,警惕;警报
slump	[slʌmp]	*vi.*	弯下腰;下降;衰落;倒下
		vt.	使降低;使衰落;使倒下
		n.	衰退;暴跌;消沉
fidget	[ˈfidʒit]	*vi.*	烦躁;玩弄(常与 with 连用)
		vt.	使不安,使烦乱
		n.	烦躁
arrogant	[ˈærəgənt]	*adj.*	傲慢的;骄傲自大的,妄自尊大的
standoffish	[ˌstændˈɔfiʃ]	*adj.*	冷漠的,冷淡的;不友好的
cue	[kjuː]	*n.*	提示,暗示;线索
		vt.	给……暗示

Exercises

I. Read the statements below and decide whether the statements are true or false. Write T for true and F for false.

1. If you are in a peer's office and you answer the phone for them, it is inappropriate to say "who's calling please".
2. You should never take a business call at lunch even if co-workers lunching with you don't mind.
3. You should talk about personal issues on a business call until you have established a personal relationship with your business contact.
4. You should smile when you're on the phone; it "shows" through the phone.
5. Answer your telephone promptly, after no more than two rings, and smile.

II. Read the statements below and choose the right answer.

The Office Phone Etiquette Quiz will test your knowledge of a variety of business phone etiquette topics.

1. In the unlikely event that you reach a receptionist or secretary when making a business call (instead of voice mail of the person you are calling), how should you address the call taker?

   A. Ask for the person you're calling.

   B. Ask for your party's extension without offering any other information.

   C. Ask for the person you're calling for, state your name and purpose for calling.

   D. Ask for the person you're calling for, and state your name.

2. The single most important factor in leaving a voice mail message is ______.

   A. leave a message that's short and to the point

   B. humor

   C. leaving as much information as possible

   D. speaking clearly and succinctly

3. What does not need to be a consideration before you make a phone call?

A. Who you are calling. B. The purpose of your call.

C. The best time to call. D. A brief joke to break the ice.

4. If you need to discuss sensitive issues over the phone (including exchanges of personal and protected information), how should you handle it with your phone companion?

A. Tell them you'll fax the information.

B. Confirm with them it's OK to discuss before discussing it.

C. Tell them you'll email it.

D. Avoid these discussions at all costs on the telephone.

5. It is said you should make business calls during the time of day most people are freshest to receive them. When is this?

A. 8 to 10 a. m. B. 10 a. m. to noon

C. 1 to 3 p. m. D. 3 to 5 p. m.

6. If your business call to someone will be unexpected, what should you do?

A. Tell them the purpose of your call, then ask them to call you back at their convenience.

B. Leave a message on voice mail or with a receptionist and tell them to call at their convenience.

C. Email them and ask what a good time for calling would be.

D. Call them, but first ask if they have time, before proceeding with the call.

7. What is not an active listening word that will let your party know you are listening while on a business phone call?

A. "What?". B. "Yes". C. "I see". D. "Great".

8. Why should you keep a pad and pen near the phone for use during business calls?

A. To jot down things your party says so you remember them.

B. To jot down notes about other things you need to do.

C. To jot down ideas to suggest to your party.

D. To help script your call so you don't forget anything.

9. The 7 "P"s of business phone etiquette should include (among other topics) preparation, purpose, and what else?

   A. Practice. B. Privacy. C. Packaging. D. Pinpointing.

10. Why should you generally not answer your business phone on the first ring?

    A. It's rude.

    B. You don't look busy enough.

    C. You should let the phone ring through to your voice mail so you can talk at a time of your choosing.

    D. It can catch the caller off-guard.

III. Put the following sentences into Chinese or vice versa.

1. Employees act in the best interest of the Company. They communicate openly, listening for understanding and valuing diverse opinions.
2. Whether I'm dealing with my co-workers, my supervisor, or potential clients, communication is the key.
3. We sincerely wish to maintain close communication with clients, even with the most enthusiasm, the best service, welcome the new and old customers patronizing!
4. Communication is a two-way process. You must be willing to listen as well as talk.
5. You're having a face-to-face conversation with someone and your cell phone rings. You should say "Excuse me" and then answer the phone.
6. 对话可以是一种有效的交流手段。
7. 你能给我说一些新闻组的网上规矩吗?
8. 网上聊天的时候,你要遵守网络礼节。
9. 从他们的面部表情、姿势和眼神你发现了什么?
10. 肢体语言在面试中能起到非常大的作用。

▶ Speaking

1. Read the text loudly, and try to recite the following paragraph.

Verbal communication can be defined as communicating your thoughts through words or the use of sounds and language to relay a message. By definition, verbal communication includes not only oral discussions, but also written messages, in other words, it includes both oral (spoken) and written communication, as both forms include the use of words. Groans or any noises or utterances a person makes are included in verbal communication.

Although verbal communication is a primary means of expression, nonverbal actions such as body language can greatly affect the way a message is perceived. Non-verbal communication includes the overall body language of the person who is speaking, which can be divided into several categories: facial expressions, head movements, hand and arm gestures, physical space, touching, eye contact and physical postures.

2. Make dialogues by using the following expressions.

1) Telling you are busy

- I am busy with work. Can I do this later?
- Do I need to do this now?
- Can I do this tomorrow?
- Sorry, I am a little busy. Can I do this sometime later?
- I am busy now. Can we meet in the evening?
- I don't have time for any other assignment this week.
- When is the deadline? I don't think I can meet the deadline.
- I will have to work doubly hard if I am to meet the deadline.
- I won't be able to do this on time. I need to free up my schedule.
- I am sure I will be able to do this on time.

2) Asking for business cards

- Have you got a business card? You can reach me by telephone or email.

- Can I have one of your business cards? Sure.
- When is the best time to contact you? Can I contact you by telephone?
- Can I have your telephone number? Sure.
- My telephone number is on my card. Let me give you one.

▶ Acting

Students form groups by themselves and role play. The instructor comments on performance and grade the students' work.

1. Word Description. This activity requires the participants to divide into pairs. One of the participants is given a word that they need to describe to their partner. Under the word that needs to be described is a list of five words the person cannot use in his description. For example, if the word that is being described is "coffee", the five most common words can be listed under the word such as "black", "drink", "cream", "sugar", "hot". The person describing the word will have to use his verbal skills to get his partner to understand the word without using common words.

2. Role Playing. Have two people volunteer for the demonstration. Ask one student to demonstrate and the other to describe the meaning of various body languages poses such as "happy", "sad", "angry", etc.

▶ Supplementary Listening

* Business Etiquette (Good Telephone Etiquette, Proper Way of Replying to E-mail, Unspoken Messages, etc.)

http://www.51voa.com/Business_Etiquette_1.html

Listen to the dialogues and dictate down the key points.

* Good Telephone Etiquette

http://www.ehow.com/video_12221307_good-telephone-etiquette.html

Watch the video and dictate down the key points.

▶ Supplementary Reading

Nonverbal Communication in Different Cultures

Facial expressions

Although smiling is an expression of happiness in most cultures, it can also signify other emotions. Some Chinese, for example, may smile when they are discussing something sad or uncomfortable.

Winking has very different connotations in different cultures. In some Latin American cultures, winking is a romantic or sexual invitation. In Nigeria, Yorubas may wink at their children if they want them to leave the room. Many Chinese consider winking to be rude.

In China's Hong Kong, it is important not to blink one's eyes conspicuously, as this may be seen as a sign of disrespect and boredom.

Some Filipinos will point to an object by shifting their eyes toward it or pursing their lips and point with their mouth, rather than using their hands.

Some Venezuelans may use their lips to point at something, because pointing with a finger is impolite.

Expressions of pain or discomfort such as crying are also specific to various cultures; some cultures may value a stoic affect while others may encourage a more emotive state. Expressions of pain or discomfort are also learned from one's family illness experiences, expressions and idioms of distress.

Head movements

In Lebanon, the signal for "YES" may be a nod of the head. To signal "NO", a Lebanese may point his or her head sharply upward and raise the eyebrows.

Saudis may signal "YES" by swiveling their head from side to side. They may signal "NO" by tipping their head backward and clicking their tongue.

Hand and arm gestures

The "OK" sign is interpreted in Japan as the symbol for money, because the circular shape of the index finger and thumb together suggest the shape of a coin. In

Argentina, Belgium, France, Portugal, Italy, Greece, and Zimbabwe, the sign means "zero" or "nothing". In some Eastern European countries as other countries throughout the world, the gesture indicates a bodily orifice and is highly offensive.

In some parts of the US, to hold up crossed fingers is to wish good luck, but to hold crossed fingers behind your back negates whatever pledge or statement you're thinking. In Russia, this is a way of rudely rejecting or denying something. In Argentina and Spain, this sign is made to ward away bad luck. In China, it signifies the number ten.

The "thumbs-up" gesture has a vulgar connotation in Iran.

In Colombia, tapping the underside of the elbow with the fingers of the other hand suggests that someone is stingy.

Many Chinese people point with their entire hand; using the forefinger to point is viewed as rude. Similarly, in India one may use a full hand to point, but never just a single finger.

In Latin America, a shrug with the palms facing skyward may be interpreted as a vulgar gesture.

Personal space

Compared to most people in the US, Latin Americans are accustomed to standing and sitting close to people who are not well known to them. Even within the majority population in the US there are important variations in the size of the personal space comfort zone.

People from the Middle East may stand quite close when talking with each other.

In some Muslim cultures, a woman may be alarmed if a man, even a male physician, stands or sits too close to her.

Touching

In some cultures, light touching of the arm or a light kiss to the cheek is very common, even among people who have just met. People from Latin America and Eastern Europe may be very comfortable with this kind of touching, whereas people from many Asian cultures may prefer less physical contact with acquaintances.

Touching another person's head is considered offensive by some people from Asia and the Middle East. It is therefore inappropriate to pat a child on the head.

Some Chinese may be uncomfortable with physical contact early in a relationship. Although many Chinese will use a handshake to greet a Westerner, any other contact may be considered inappropriate. This is especially important to remember when dealing with older people or those in positions of authority.

Men in Egypt tend to be more touch-oriented; a handshake may be accompanied by a gentle touching of the recipient's elbow with the fingers of the left hand.

A strong, warm handshake is the traditional greeting between men in Latin America. However, because most Latin Americans show affection easily, male friends, like female friends, may embrace. Women may lightly brush their cheeks together.

Throughout most of the Middle East, it is the custom to reserve the left hand for bodily hygiene. For this reason, one should never offer the left hand to shake hands or accept a gift. This is also true of some African cultures.

A Western woman should not initiate a handshake with a man in India. Many Indian women will shake hands with a foreign woman, but not a foreign man.

To many Indians, it is considered rather offensive to (even accidentally) step on someone's foot. Apologies should be made immediately.

Eye contact

Making direct eye contact is a sign of disrespect in some cultures. In other cultures, refusing to make direct eye contact is a sign of disrespect. Many Asians may be reluctant to make eye contact with an authority figure. For example, when greeting a Chinese, it is best to avoid prolonged eye contact as a sign of respect and deference.

Many Middle Easterners have what North Americans and Europeans consider "languid eyes". It may appear that the person's eyes are half closed, but this does not express disinterest or disrespect.

In Ghana, young children are taught not to look adults in the eye because to do so would be considered an act of defiance.

In Latin America, good eye contact is important in both social and business situations.

Physical postures

In many cultures throughout the world, it is impolite to show the bottom of the shoe, which is often dirty. Therefore, one should not sit with the foot resting on the opposite knee.

In Argentina, standing with the hands on the hips suggests anger, or a challenge.

In many cultures, slouching or poor posture is considered to be disrespectful. For example, good posture is important in China's Taiwan, with Taiwanese men usually sitting with both feet firmly fixed to the floor.

(http://erc.msh.org/mainpage.cfm? file=4.6.0.htm&module=provider&language=English)

Answer the following questions:

1. What are the verbal communication skills for selling?
2. Can you tell some gestures that have different connotations in different cultures?

Project Five Business Meeting Etiquette

Learning Objectives

After completing this project, you will be able to:

* follow business etiquette guidelines for attending meetings;
* describe bad meeting behaviors;
* identify the steps in planning and conducting effective business meetings.

Warming-Up

Please answer the following questions.

❑ Do you know how to behave in business meetings?

❑ Can you describe some bad meeting manners?

Listening

http://www.unsv.com/voanews/business-etiquette/lessons/003/

Listen to the recording and fill in the blanks.

Punctuality

陈豪在美国公司已经工作了一段时间。今天老板要找他谈话。老板找谈话会有什么事呢？陈豪心里有点不安，所以急着去请教美籍华人 Mary。

(*Office ambience*)

陈：(很着急地)Hey, Mary, 快，我有事问你。

M：What's the matter?

陈：老板的秘书通知我老板过一会要找我谈话，可说的话我没听懂，说是为了什么 punc … punc … 那个词我不知道……

M：Punctual?

陈：对，有点像，不过那个词最后的音好像是什么 ty 来的。

M：Punctuality?

陈：Yes, yes. Punctuality. Punctuality 是什么意思呀？哟，不好了，时间到了，我得去了。

(*Sound of knocking on the door; opening the door*)

Mr. Jones：Mr. Chen, it has been ____________________ that you are frequently late for meetings. I want you to know that ____________________ and in our company too.

C：Sorry, Mr. Jones, I am not sure I understand. What exactly do you mean by punc … punctuality?

Mr. Jones：____________________. If a meeting is scheduled for one o'clock, everyone is expected to be in the meeting room and ready to start.

C：(自语：噢，开会要准时！) Mr. Jones, now I understand. I'll be on time for meetings from now on.

Ms. Jones：Good.

(*Sound of pushing chairs and walking*)

M：嗨，陈豪，刚才我要告诉你 punctuality 就是"准时"，你匆忙走了，大概没有听见。哎，老板找你干什么呀？

C：他批评我开会不准时。他不懂，可我又没法和老板争。你知道有的时候我专心工作忘了时间！

M：那不行，上星期开会讨论财务，可数据全在你手上。你不到，会没法开。There's no way to have the meeting without you，所以你浪费了大家的时间。

____

C：我不是有意没礼貌，有的时候是没法控制的。那天我刚要去开会，电话铃响了。

M：That's simple. Don't answer it。打电话的人要是有重要事情他会留言。你开完会可以打回电。

陈：还有一次，开会的时间到了，可是一个客户来看我。我总不能不见吧？

M：实在没有办法的时候，______________________。这样别人就会觉得你是尊重他们的。

陈：行，知道了。哎，Mary，你再给我总结一下吧，免得我忘了。

M：____。

C：谢谢，Mary！今天又学会一个词——punc-punctua-punctuality！punctuality！

▶ Reading

Task One

Business Meetings Etiquette—Attending a Meeting

We spend approximately a quarter of our working life in business meetings, according to the US Public Health Service. But while those meetings are vital to our career success, they can often be intimidating. Many people cringe when they hear that they have to attend a business meeting. They're afraid that it will be a waste of times, that starts late and accomplishes nothing or that it will be dominated by one or two people. These common problems can be avoided by using proper business meeting etiquette. Etiquette rules allow you to attend or run the meeting more efficiently and to make sure it is productive. The following are tips of business etiquette for attending formal business meetings.

Be prepared

It is bad form to show up for a meeting for which you are completely unprepared. Bring materials that were sent in advance, like agendas and handouts. Have an understanding of the meeting topic. Review your files on the subject, if you have them, to make sure you are up-to-speed on the subject of the meeting. Do any background research you need, and check with the meeting organizer to see if you have any "homework" due during the meeting. If you are asked to come to a meeting to do a presentation or briefing, make sure you are prepared. It is frustrating for those in attendance to expect information and not receive it. Make sure you have plenty of handouts. Never show up to a meeting without a pad of paper. Also bring a backup writing utensil just in case.

Attire

Appearance matters in most business meetings. Dress appropriately for the environment. Usually, business meeting require business casual or business formal attire. When invited to the meeting, make sure to read carefully what it indicates about the dress code. If unsure, it is far better to appear overdressed. It is really embarrassing to be the only one wearing khakis among attendees with suits and ties. All clothing should be neat, clean and ironed. Avoid wearing excess perfume or cologne.

Posture and body language

Sit straight in your chair with both feet on the ground, or crossed at the ankles. Avoid crossing your arms as this sends defensive signals. Keep your hands as relaxed and still as possible. Refrain from fidgeting with paper clips or rubber bands and avoid doodling on your note pad. Don't take your shoes off. It was rude and completely distracting.

Be timely

Always arrive at the meeting at least 15 minutes early. This allows you to find proper seating and familiarize yourself with other attendees. Besides, being punctual shows respect to the person who has organized the meeting. If you think the meeting is not going to start because you are running late, think again. It is not the responsibility of those who arrive on time to fill you in on what you missed if you are tardy Plan accordingly. If you are traveling a long distance, map out your route and give yourself plenty of time to get there. Do not leave early. Although scheduling conflicts are a fact of life, a schedule that is too packed too often is an indicator of poor time-management or prioritization skills, and if given the chance people will draw negative conclusions. Likewise, do not skip meetings. People all have moments when the car won't start or a child is ill, but people who make a habit of missing meetings they committed to attend will not earn the respect of co-workers or superiors.

Be social

Get to know the other participants, if any are unfamiliar to you. Shake hands, smile and trade business cards. Learn who the key members of the meeting group are, and begin building professional relationships with other attendees. This is especially valuable for entrepreneurs or small-business owners who may attend meetings with clients or networking groups—being social today may mean additional business tomorrow.

Seating

Ask where to sit if you are unsure. Don't sit at either end of the table. Avoid taking the chair next to the chairperson as this may be reserved for the person taking the minutes of the meeting. Indeed, positioning yourself at a business meeting is as important a consideration as what ideas and questions you bring to the table. The following are some rules of the road. 1) The person leading the meeting sits at the head of the table, usually opposite the entry door so he or she can see people coming in. If a key customer is attending the meeting, that power seat would be reserved for him or her. 2) Those who are highly supportive of the boss (brown-noser or sycophant) tend to sit to the right of the manager. This person may be, or may want to be, the second in command within the group. 3) Left-hand sitters like the proximity to the power base in the room, and they are apparent supporters of the boss. 4) People who prefer to sit in the middle may be type of people who listen to all sides before expressing their own views. 5) End-of-the-table folks can maintain eye contact with all members of the group, and often qualify as extroverts. Also, they generally are the most active participants. They may want to sit close to colleagues in order to help build better relationships with them. 6) Be especially cautious about sitting at either of the following two places: the outside or the opponent's seat. The outside seats are those that are not at the table; perhaps they are along the wall of the room. If they're overflow seats, and you got to the meeting late, you may have no choice but to take one of these "out of the mainstream" seats.

Turn off electronics

The arrival of cool tools, smartphones and iPads makes meetings and taking notes easier, but the flip side is that it could make you look like you're not attentive. Refrain from the use of any electronic device. Before entering a meeting, make sure your cell phone is off or on silent. Answering calls or texting during the meeting is not only disruptive; it sends the message that you are more important than everyone else. Also while using electronic devices during meeting, you will most likely miss what is being discussed. If you require your laptop or smartphone in the meeting, announce that you'll be taking notes on it so people around the table don't think you're doing something else. If you're using your phone or laptop, do not open instant message or check email. People will—and do—notice that you're not paying attention. If your phone rings or buzzes, don't take it unless it's an emergency. If you have to take it, step out of the meeting room. If you are expecting an urgent call, then set your phone to vibrate and excuse yourself from the meeting if the call comes in.

Be professional

Stick to business matters, not office gossip. You would not want someone talking about you if you were not present. A good rule of thumb is not to say something about a person you would not be willing to say to his or her face. Remain tactful at all times. If the meeting is important enough to attend physically, then it is important enough to attend mentally, too. Avoid one-off sidebar conversations with other participants, especially about unrelated subjects. It's distracting. Never put up your hand to cover your mouth while talking to your neighbor. Rudest move ever.

Take turns

For a business meeting to be effective, everyone involved needs to practice professional courtesy in the sharing and exchange of ideas. Outgoing group members can unknowingly absorb the discussion during a meeting, limiting the free exchange of thoughts and opinions. For example, a talkative attendee might state her opinions first and then monopolize the discussion. Resist the urge to hijack the meeting by dominating the conversation or trying to seize control of the agenda from the meeting organizer. Learning how to take turns in a discussion is crucial to the success of a meeting. To effectively take turns, keep in mind that the alternative viewpoints of your colleagues are valuable and take notes if you do have ideas you want to bring up later.

Participate effectively

Asking questions demonstrates active interest and participation in the meeting. Make sure to ask questions that require a brief response and solicit additional information that adds value to the meeting. Avoid generic questions that are a waste of time and possibly present your own views without really adding any value to the meeting's progress. Avoid raising issues that are unrelated to the subject at hand, stick to the agenda. Don't repeat what someone else in the meeting has already said and take credit for it.

The effectiveness of business meetings depends on the active engagement of participants. Choosing to participate, even in small ways, can help a business meeting to be more productive and effective for everyone involved. During the meeting, share your thoughts and opinions with other participants whenever an opportunity arises.

Do not interrupt others

While another attendee is presenting, make sure to hold your comments and questions until the presentation is over. Interrupting other speakers is impolite and disrespectful. Moreover, it disrupts the flow of the meeting and it confuses other attendees. Only if open discourse is encouraged you are allowed to comment before the meeting is adjourned. Avoid confrontational language such as "You are wrong about this." Instead say, "I disagree with you on this one" or "I have some different ideas about this issue."

Be accountable

Accept responsibility for any post-meeting tasks; do not just raise issues that others must solve, but take the initiative for solving problems, particularly in a team context. If you are responsible for problems, own up to them and volunteer to fix them without trying to find blame or creating an excuse. People will forgive mistakes or missed deadlines much more readily if the responsible party owns up to it and tries to make it better.

Guests

Do not bring unannounced guests to a meeting. If you have someone you would like to bring to a meeting, then contact the chairperson for permission to bring your guest. If permission is not granted, then do not bring him.

In conclusion, when attending a business meeting, make sure to participate constructively. Be concise, clear and on topic. Be open-minded and ready to accept opposing views. Keep an eye contact with other meeting attendees and maintain a professional conduct throughout the meeting. Add value to the meeting with your knowledge and make sure to be poised and polite. Showing genuine interest in the meeting, even if you have opposing views, demonstrates professionalism and proper business meeting etiquette.

New Words and Expressions

approximately	[əˈprɔksimitli]	*adv.*	大约,近似地;近于
intimidate	[inˈtimideit]	*vt.*	使畏惧;恫吓,恐吓;威胁,威逼
cringe	[krindʒ]	*vi.*	畏缩;奉承,阿谀
		n.	畏缩;奉承
dominate	[ˈdɔmineit]	*vt.*	控制;支配;占优势;在……中占主要地位
handout	[ˈhændaut]	*n.*	文字资料;散发材料;施舍物
briefing	[ˈbriːfiŋ]	*n.*	简报,简要汇报;基本情况介绍会
in attendance			出席;值班;负责
utensil	[juːˈtensəl]	*n.*	用具,器皿
overdressed	[ˌəuvəˈdrest]	*adj.*	穿着过于讲究的
khakis	[ˈkɑːkiz]	*n.*	(khaki 的复数)卡其裤;卡其服装;卡其黄
fidget	[ˈfidʒit]	*vi.*	烦躁;坐立不安;玩弄
		n.	烦躁;坐立不安;烦躁不安的人
rubber band			橡皮筋
doodle	[ˈduːdl]	*vt.*	乱涂;闲混;随意弹奏
		n.	涂鸦

tardy	[ˈtɑːdi]	*adj.*	缓慢的，迟缓的；迟到的
		n.	迟到
packed	[pækt]	*adj.*	充满……的，塞满了……的
prioritization	[praiˌɔritaiˈzeiʃən;-tiˈz-]	*n.*	优先次序；优化；优先化
sycophant	[ˈsikəfənt]	*n.*	谄媚者，奉承者
extrovert	[ˈekstrəuvəːt]	*n.*	外向；外倾者，性格外向者
flip	[flip]	*adj.*	[口语]无礼的，轻率的；冒失的，鲁莽的
disruptive	[disˈrʌptiv]	*adj.*	妨碍的，扰乱的；分裂的，破裂的；中断的
rule of thumb			经验法则
outgoing	[ˈautɡəuiŋ]	*adj.*	对人友好的；开朗的；乐于助人的；爽直的
monopolize	[məˈnɔpəlaiz]	*vt.*	垄断；独占；拥有……的专卖权
hijack	[ˈhaidʒæk]	*vt.*	胁迫；强制；抢劫；揩油
solicit	[səˈlisit]	*vt.*	征求；招揽；请求；乞求
take credit for			因……得到好评；把……归功于
adjourn	[əˈdʒəːn]	*vi.*	休会；延期；换地方
		vt.	推迟；使……中止；使……延期
confrontational	[ˌkɔnfrʌnˈteiʃənl]	*adj.*	对抗的；对抗性的
accountable	[əˈkauntəbl]	*adj.*	有责任的；有解释义务的；可解释的
initiative	[iˈniʃiətiv]	*n.*	主动权；首创精神
		adj.	主动的；自发的；起始的
grant	[ɡrɑːnt;ɡrænt]	*vt.*	授予；允许；承认
		vi.	同意
poised	[pɔizd]	*adj.*	泰然自若的，镇定的；均衡的；静止的

Task Two

Business Meetings Etiquette—Running a Meeting

Meetings are the bane of the corporate world but even small businesses can't avoid them completely. Many people believe that no skills are needed to run a business meeting. However, this is simply not the case. To run a successful and productive meeting, you must take several many steps that require organizational skills and the ability to direct a group of people through a list of chosen tasks. Planning ahead, creating an agenda, being prepared and making sure to stay on track are important elements in ensuring that each meeting only lasts as long as it needs to. Here's how to run your meetings without wasting time or money.

Set goals. All meetings should have a purpose. When composing your goal, write a concise and easily understandable statement such as "To select an advertising campaign for fourth quarter". Before you invite anyone to a meeting, some other questions you should ask yourself are:

- What is the purpose of the meeting, and what is it intended to achieve?
- What are the desired outcomes/milestones?
- Who needs to attend and why? Can the meeting go ahead if anyone is unable to attend, or can you go ahead with the other attendees?
- Is there a more effective way of communicating besides having the meeting? Would a simple group email get the desired outcome quicker?
- What is the meeting agenda and timeline?
- What preparatory work is needed?

Arrange a venue. Arrange a suitable meeting space for your meeting and make sure the room is comfortable for the number of attendees, and that it has the right layout, but avoid rooms that are excessively large. The seating arrangement sets the tone of the meeting. A round-table meeting is less formal than the long table meeting. The seating arrangement can influence the outcome of a meeting.

When you hold a group meeting, you can consider the three forms of seating arrangement. If you are involved in negotiation with the trade union, you want to arrange the trade union leaders to sit at the opposite side of the table. The chairpersons of both parties should sit in the middle of the long table. This is the confrontation seating arrangement. If you are holding a friendly discussion, you can choose a round table. The seating arrangement indicates friendliness and informality of the meeting. You indicate your respect for all the participants in this meeting when you use a round table. If you sit at the head of the table, and arrange the lowest-ranking members to sit at the far end of the table, you are using the hierarchy seating arrangement. This is the seating arrangement to convey I am the boss message. This seating arrangement works for holding Board Meeting. The Chairman of the Board of Directors always sits at the head of the table. You cannot use a round table for Board Meeting.

When you hold small meetings, an intimate round-table setting will keep conversation flowing. For larger presentations with a small number of speakers, it may be more productive to utilize a classroom setting with tables and chairs facing forward toward a single presenter. For example, the term "conference style seating" is often used by hotels or conference centers to mean either U-Shape, Hollow Square or Boardroom.

Prepare an agenda. It should include opening remarks and announcements that the entire group needs to hear, along with recent developments that will affect the project at hand. List all of the topics that you want to discuss in the meeting in the order in which you want to discuss them. Place the name of the person(s) responsible for each agenda report and how much time is allocated for presentation or discussion. Share your goal and agenda in advance of the meeting via email, allowing the attendees to mentally prepare for the meeting as well as give them the opportunity to come prepared with paperwork or other materials relevant to the planned topic. Be sure to let the attendees know how much time they will have to present ideas or their reports. Participants should call the chairperson to express any concerns about the agenda at least 48 hours prior to the meeting. The chairperson and concerned participant will then have time to determine if changes need to be made. The agenda should also mention the meeting's start and ending times as well.

Commonly an agenda of a business meeting covers:

- opening remarks and announcements;
- meeting start time, meeting end time, meeting location;
- topic headings, Including some topic detail for each heading;

- indicating the time each topic is expected to last;
- indicating which meeting participants are expected to be the main topic participants.

Below are two sample agenda:

Sample Agenda 1

Item	Responsible	Time
Internet Marketing Association Meeting Agenda Start at 10:00 a. m. in Board Room		
Opening Remarks	President	5 min
VP Membership Report -intramural report -new member program intro	VPM	20 min
VP Financial Report -status of budget -house bill status	VPF	7 min
VP Rush Report -status of current efforts -status of next term plans	VPR	7 min
VP Internal	VPI	5 min
VP External	VPE	10 min
Guest Speaker	Community Relations	15 min
End at 11:10 a. m. **Let's keep on track!**		

Sample Agenda 2

Meeting Agenda

09:45	**Reception**	
10:00	Call Meeting to Order & Pledge-Sgt-At-Arms	Roger J
10:00	Opening by President	Alvin L
10:10	**Toastmaster of the Meeting**	Josh Yang/CP
	Timer/Ah-counter	Henson Wen /Sway Teng
10:20	**Variety Session**	Ryan /PRVP
10:35	**Prepared Speech**	
	Speak 1,	TBD
	Slow and Steady wins the race! (C10, '8~10')	Kevin Lin/ President of Linkou
	TBD (A9)	Roger Jien/
11:15	Intermission	
11:25	**Table Topic**	**Tom Cheng**
11:35	**Evaluation Session**	
	General Evaluator	**Tobie Openshaw/STM**
	The 1st Timer report / Ah-Counter report	
	Evaluator for Vicky Li(2'~3')	David Yu/ STM
	Evaluator for Kevin Lin(2'~3')	Justin Wu/Div E Gov.
	Evaluator for Roger Jien(2'~3')	Jack Tsai/Former Dis E Gov.
	The 2nd Timer report / Ah-Counter report	
11:55	Comments from Guests	Alvin L
12:00	Accouchement of Trophy Winners and Closing remarks	Alvin L
12:10	**Meeting Adjourned**	

Establish roles. Most meetings have a chairperson. Select an individual to serve as the secretary and ask this person to take notes as the meeting progresses. Assign another meeting attendee to act as timekeeper. This individual will keep an eye on the clock and help ensure that you follow your planned time allotment for each agenda item. Declare yourself the meeting moderator and take on the task of moving through the items on the agenda in a timely and effective fashion.

Stay on track, keep the meeting moving forward. Retake control of the meeting if it slips out of your grasp. Make sure everyone understands the topic of the meeting. If the meeting is about how to handle your customer service, it's not the time to talk about problems in the employee break room. If people stray, get them quickly back in focus. Don't get stuck on one point, especially if you have many other items to discuss. If someone is talking over others or dominating the discussion, acknowledge that person and tell him that you'll come back to his point after the other items have been considered. Remind participants that there are other matters to discuss.

Pay attention to people who are quiet during the meeting. Not everyone needs an opinion during the meeting, but give those people a chance to speak. Ask them if they would like to talk or offer a thought but don't pressure them to participate.

Make sure everyone receives handouts if there are. Handouts don't necessarily have to be entirely reviewed during the meeting but are a good source of information for everyone after the meeting is concluded to aid them in implementing meeting outcomes.

Breaks. Meetings should have a break every two hours. Breaks should be 20 minutes long, and meal breaks should be 30 minutes long.

Keep in mind that there are "verbal" and "visual" learners. Offer information both in writing and oral formats. Use PowerPoint presentations, handouts, charts as well as verbal presentation.

Put a question and answer session on your meeting agenda. Once the purpose of the meeting has been determined and attendees know the road that needs to be traveled so to speak, some people may have questions. A good Q&A session can also help you determine if there was an area or agenda item that wasn't fully covered.

Assign tasks. As you move through your discussion and decide on things that need doing, assign these tasks on the spot. Also set a due date for the completion of each task, improving the chances that the task actually gets done. Ask the individual taking meeting minutes to write down these task assignments.

Conclude the meeting on time. If you allow the meeting to go past its scheduled end point, you will likely find that many of the attendees mentally check out of the sit down. If you reach the end of your allotted time and you have items yet to discuss, table them to a later date out of respect for those who gave their time to attend the meeting.

Share minutes post meeting. Email the meeting minutes along with a thank you to the attendees for their cooperation and dedication. If you assigned many tasks during the meeting, include a polite reminder to the attendees to follow through with the assigned items.

Business meetings are scheduled to motivate a team, review sales figures, generate ideas, provide status reports on projects or make employees aware of new products or initiatives. Regardless of the reason you're holding a meeting, aim to run productive, results-driven business meetings.

Meeting can be informative and beneficial or be a complete waste of time. Make sure your attention, and everyone else's, is laser-focused on the topic at hand and what you need to accomplish. Don't let distractions get in the way, whether you're running the meeting or attending one. Etiquette plays a large role in the productivity of a business meeting. A lack of etiquette and poor planning are two of the main reasons why many business meetings fail.

New Words and Expressions

bane	[bein]	*n.*	祸根,祸害;毒药;灭亡的原因
venue	[ˈvenjuː]	*n.*	发生地点;集合地点;审判地;犯罪地点
trade union			工会
hierarchy	[ˈhaiərɑːki]	*n.*	层级;等级制度
Chairman of the Board of Directors			董事会主席,董事长
allocate	[ˈæləukeit]	*vt.*	分配;拨出;使坐落于
		vi.	分配;指定
cover	[ˈkʌvə]	*vt.*	包括;采访,报导;涉及
moderator	[ˈmɔdəreitə]	*n.*	议长;会议主席;调解人,仲裁人;(电视或广播节目的)主持人
stray	[strei]	*vi.*	(议论)离题;(思想)迷失方向;迷路;失败
stick	[stik]	*vi.*	卡住;坚持,固守;遵守;堵塞
on the spot			立刻,当场;在危险中;处于负责地位

Exercises

I. Read the statements below and decide whether the statements are true or false. Write T for true and F for false.

1. How well a person conducts himself during a meeting can build or demolish reputations in business.
2. It is acceptable to leave on your personal cell phone during the meeting and answer it when it rings.
3. You should usually arrive 15 minutes or more early for a business meeting.
4. If you are attending a meeting, it is not necessary for you to make preparations for the meeting.
5. As professional events, business meetings are no-nonsense with straight faces and no smiling.
6. Positioning yourself at a business meeting can not affect your business career.
7. For a formal meeting,an agenda is usually circulated in advance to all participants.
8. Put up your hand to cover your mouth while talking to your neighbor during the meeting.
9. If your are runnimg a meeting, once you make the subject and goals of the meeting clear, and identify a place and time, don't change them unless there's an emergeney.
10. Minutes holp remind participants of what was decided and defines the action plan going foward.

II. Choose the most proper answer for a business meeting etiquette quiz.

1. You have a meeting with a client but are expecting a call. You should ______.

   A. set your cell phone ring volume to high to ensure you hear any calls

   B. turn your cell phone off

   C. tell your client you are expecting a phone call

2. Your client meeting is scheduled for 9:00 am. What time should you arrive for your appointment?

A. No more than thirty minutes prior to the meeting time.

B. No earlier than 8:50 a. m.

C. Don't be early, it appears overeager.

3. If a client is waiting for a one-to-one meeting with you, but you are running a little behind schedule, what should you do?

A. Take a minute to walk out and apologize in person and offer them a cup of coffee and a magazine.

B. Have your assistant tell him you are running behind schedule and you will be a few more minutes.

C. Finish what you're working on—you'll get it done faster that way and they'll only have to wait a few more minutes.

4. It's casual Friday, but you are meeting with an important client. How do you dress?

A. As you would normally on Friday, as the concept of casual Friday is well understood.

B. Appropriate for a business meeting.

C. You don't give much thought to your dress at all and get dressed quickly and simply.

5. When you have a business meeting in the UK, you should ______.

A. get down to business straight away

B. spend an hour introducing yourselves

C. avoid talking business immediately

6. You are attending a meeting in Russia. Your host offers you Vodka, but, you have a headache and don't feel like drinking. You should ______.

A. politely decline, for your host will understand

B. take the offered drink, but don't drink any of it

C. take the offered drink and sip it occasionally

7. In India, you should greet you business partner at a business meeting with ______.

A. "namaste", while bringing your palms together, facing each other

B. a firm handshake C. a light handshake

8. While attending a meeting in China, you are given a business card. You should ______.

   A. leave it on the table when the meeting is over, for you've already copied the details into your Blackberry

   B. put it in your pocket without even looking at it

   C. place it some place safe only after admiring its details.

9. You have just walked into a business meeting in South Korea. You approach the business person with the higher status and ______.

   A. extend your hand for a handshake

   B. bow and say "pleased to meet you" in Korean

   C. nod a greeting and stay silent

10. You are a woman attending a business meeting in Singapore. You notice that one of the men from the Singapore team is wearing a tie in a pattern you absolutely love. You ______.

   A. simply compliment the person on their style

   B. don't say anything

   C. discreetly snap a picture of it with your cell phone camera so you can shop later to find the same one for your husband

III. Match the words and phrases in Column A with the definitions in Column B.

Column A	Column B
1. attendee	A. a detailed plan or explanation to guide you in setting standards or determining a course of action
2. dominate	B. to ask sb. for sth. such as money or support to try to sell sth. by visiting people and persuading them to buy it.
3. proximity	C. someone who takes part in an activity
4. accountable	D. a list of matters to be taken up (as at a meeting)
5. monopolize	E. the point in time at which something must be completed
6. guideline	F. a person who participates in a meeting

7. motivate	G. have dominance or the power to defeat over; be in control
8. solicit	H. speak, plead, or argue in favour of; a person who pleads for a cause or propounds an idea
9. agenda	I. the property of being close together
10. allocate	J. the power or right to give orders or make decisions; (usually plural) persons who exercise (administrative) control over others

IV. Put the following sentences into English.

1. 我想,我们是不是可以安排一次会面来讨论新产品。
2. 我的秘书会给你讲解其中的细节。
3. UPS 短讯追踪由 UPS 免费提供,让您了解托运货件的最新动态。
4. 用别人的工作谋个人荣誉是不诚实的。
5. 他在例行记者招待会上表示:"我们愿意在这个问题上同有关各方进行对话和沟通。"
6. 我需要跟你说明客户部经理的职责与角色。

V. Read the following passage and finish the exercise.

Action 公司第三季度会议在各部门负责人一一报告以及与会者热烈讨论之后即将落幕。会议主持人 Jennifer 此时再度上台,为会议做个总结。

That wraps up the last item on the agenda. Before we close, are there any questions?

Fine. In summary, I think we agree that this quarter's domestic sales figures show a marked trend in microwave sales. Sam, I'd like you to follow up on that, please. Let's see where this is heading. Jane, thank you for the comprehensive PR status report. I understand there are still a few problems to be worked out, but we all trust in your ability. Ladies and gentlemen, the new design is satisfactory. Let's keep Action ahead of the game.

Finally, I appreciate your comments and suggestions about the Canadian sales outlook. This is our first opportunity to promote our products in North America, so we certainly want to cover every detail.

Well, then, that covers everything. I make a motion to close the third quarterly meeting of Action Appliances. Is there a second?

Task One

Try to fill in the blanks with one of the following phrases from the passage.

wrap up	marked trend	follow up
work out	status report	ahead of the game

1. The accounting department is required to submit weekly ____________ to our general manager.
2. I'd like to quickly ____________ this meeting, so we can go home.
3. She studies hard every day to stay ____________.
4. Judging from the graph, you can see a ____________ upward on the Japanese stock exchange.
5. Things will ____________ as long as you are patient.
6. We can take care of that problem when we ____________.

Task Two

Translate the following sentences into Chinese.

1. That wraps up the last item on the agenda.
2. In summary, I think we agree that this quarter's domestic sales figures show a marked trend in microwave sales.
3. I appreciate your comments and suggestions about the Canadian sales outlook.
4. This is our first opportunity to promote our products in North America, so we certainly want to cover every detail.
5. I make a motion to close the third quarterly meeting of Action Appliances.

▶ Speaking

1. Read the text loudly, and try to recite the following paragraph.

In conclusion, when attending a business meeting, make sure to participate constructively. Be concise, clear and on topic. Be open-minded and ready to accept opposing views. Keep an eye contact with other meeting attendees and maintain a professional conduct throughout the meeting. Add value to the meeting with your knowledge and make sure to be poised and polite. Showing genuine interest in the meeting, even if you have opposing views, demonstrates professionalism and proper business meeting etiquette.

2. Read the dialogue and role play it.

Discussing Ideas at a Meeting

(*C = Chairman*, *R = Robert*)

C: I'd like to open today's meeting. Robert?

R: First, I'll quickly go over the main points of the last meeting.

C: ... (*finishes*), if no one has anything to add, let's move on to today's agenda.

R: I suggest we each give a little background on the suggestions we discussed last week.

C: Could you repeat that, please?

R: Let's start by going over the research you've done on the suggestions.

C: You'll find most of the information outlined in the summary documents in front of you.

R: These figures are interesting. It's clear to me that customer communications are not working as they should.

C: Yes, our marketing efforts really haven't been effective to date.

R: I suggest we break up into groups and discuss how we can improve our message.

C: Unfortunately, we're almost out of time. I suggest you submit your ideas on marketing and we can discuss the best next week.

R: Before we close, could we quickly discuss the Armstrong situation?

The following are some expressions that are often used in meeting.

❑ **Starting a meeting**

I think we'll make a start. The first item on the agenda is ...

Since everyone's here, shall we get started?

I'd like to call the meeting to order. Today, we are going to discuss ...

❑ **Asking for opinions**

What are your views on this?

What do you think about this?

What's your opinion?

❑ **Making interruption and giving opinions**

If I could just make a point here ...

Sorry to interrupt, but I'd just like to say that ...

Could I make a suggestion?

It seems to me that ...

❑ **Agreeing/Disagreeing**

I totally agree with you.

That's exactly the way I feel.

Unfortunately, I see it differently.

Up to a point I agree with you, but ...

I'm afraid I can't agree.

❑ **Ending a meeting**

I'm afraid our time is up. Let's call it a day.

We have to close today's discussion now.

Let's stop here. We'll go on with the talk this afternoon.

Let's discuss it in more detail tomorrow.

▶ Acting

Students form groups by themselves and role play. The instructor comments on performance and grade the students' work.

A sales agent from one of the real estate company in Suzhou is meeting with a family of three, husband, wife, mother-in-law. These are first-time buyers who are shopping for this residential quarter. They are at the sales office located next to the site of the future place. Construction has not begun but a large billboard sign outside the sales office proclaims "over 80% sold-starting at MYM195,000". The four people sit down for their meeting inside the fashionably decorated office.

▶ Supplementary Listening

* Business Etiquette: Getting the Point Across, Unspoken Messages, Getting Noticed at Meetings in a Positive Way, Obscenity in the Office, etc.

  http://www.tingvoa.com/html/20120310/67211.html

Listen to the dialogues and dictate down the key points.

* How to Practice Proper Business Meeting Etiquette

  http://www.howcast.com/videos/424457-How-to-Practice-Proper-Business-Meeting-Etiquette

* How to Be Professional During a Meeting

  http://www.howcast.com/videos/265142-How-to-Be-Professional-During-a-Meeting

* Rules on How to Conduct a Business Meeting

  http://www.ehow.com/video_5112540_rules-conduct-business-meeting.html#ixzz2BADiJr54

* How to Follow Proper Business Etiquette in France

  http://www.howcast.com/videos/429915-How-to-Follow-Proper-Business-Etiquette-in-France

* How to Follow Proper Business Etiquette in Germany

  http://www.howcast.com/videos/429874-How-to-Follow-Proper-Business-Etiquette-in-Germany

Watch the videos and dictate down the key points.

▶ Supplementary Reading

How to Act in a Business Meeting in France

Traveling overseas to France can be an exhausting experience especially if you are worried about making a faux pas in an important business meeting. Before your meeting, learn some common French phrases like "bonjour" for hello, "au revoir" for goodbye, "s'il vous plait" for please and "merci" for thank-you. Arrive the day before your meeting to unwind from the long, transatlantic flight. Minimize jet-lag by getting a good night's sleep. Prepare for your meeting by researching some of the cultural differences between the United States and France. You may find that the cultural divide is not as large as you may have thought, allowing you to relax and focus on the business at hand. The following are some instructons.

1. Be on time. Punctuality is prized in France. When arriving, give a business card to the receptionist and to each person that you meet regardless of position. Business cards are exchanged more frequently than in the United States. You may wish to have a card printed in French if you are doing a great deal of business in France.

2. Shake hands quickly with everyone present at the start of the meeting. You may notice that some French business people may lightly kiss each other on both cheeks. This type of greeting in common among people very familiar with each other. Avoid cheek-kissing until you have developed a friendly relationship with your co-workers.

3. Address people in a formal manner using their last name proceeded by Monsieur, Madame or Mademoiselle. France is a conservative and formal country. First names are only used by family and friends, and not commonly used in a business setting. For women, err on the side of caution, and wait to see if the woman is addressed as a Madame or a Mademoiselle.

4. Speak softly and in a formal manner. The French tend to stick to business in meetings and do not tell jokes or exchange many personal pleasantries, such as asking

about children, spouse or sports teams.

5. Get down to business. By law, the French can only work a maximum of 35 hours per week. Meetings are organized around an agenda and stick to the planned topics. The French do not waste time by getting sidetracked from the main issues as is common in the United States. Speak in details and specifics about what you would like to accomplish in the meeting. Make sure that you are well prepared.

6. Be patient. Although the French stick to business and avoid the personal chit-chat common in the United States workplace, detailed discussions typically occur before a decision is made. Debating the issues from all angles is a cornerstone of French business. Be prepared to wait until an issue is thoroughly examined by all team members before a final decision is made. A logical argument on your part will be better received than an emotional plea or a hard-sale approach.

7. Dress conservatively and professionally in neutral colors. Men should wear a jacket and leave it on in the meeting. Women should avoid wearing bright colors and err on the side of caution when choosing an outfit.

(http://www.ehow.com/how_6612294_act-business-meeting-france.html)

Answer the following question:

What are the tips on how to act in a business meeting in France?

Read more business meeting etiquette in different countries:

- http://www.ehow.com/about_6382913_business-meeting-etiquette-united-states.html
- http://www.foreigntranslations.com/languages/korean-translation/korean-business-etiquette/
- http://www.foreigntranslations.com/languages/finnish-translation/finnish-business-etiquette/
- http://www.foreigntranslations.com/languages/german-translation/german-etiquette/

Project Six
Business Reception Etiquette

Learning Objectives

After completing this project, you will be able to:

* follow the basic guidelines when preparing to meet with people;
* summarize the tips on receiving foreign clients and meeting clients;
* summarize the top tips on visiting a client.

Warming-Up

Please answer the following questions.

❑ What should you prepare before you are going to receive a foreign guest?

❑ When making introductions, do you know whom to introduce first?

Listening

http://www.hjenglish.com/beczhongji/p400603/

Listen to the recording and fill in the blanks.

Receiving

Dialogue 1

F: How can I help you?

M: Yes, I am Jims Mirson from Edison Associate. I would like to see Mr. Smith.

F: ____?

M: Yes, he knows I am coming. ________________________________.

F: I'm wondering if Mr. Smith forgot your meeting, I am afraid he left this office this morning and he is not expected back until after 4 p. m. Let me find out if he ________ ________________ for someone else to meet with you in his place, ________ ________________?

M: Sure.

F: Yeah, Mr Mirson, I just checked with their office manager Ms Terry, she said Mr. Smith ________________________, she is just finishing up our meeting now, and she should be with you shortly. ________________________________?

M: That would be very nice, thank you!

F: Right this way, Mr Mirson, we can start with our front office, when Ms Terry is ready, you may take the elevator at the front to the 6th floor, ________.

Dialogue 2

http://www.hjenglish.com/beczhongji/p401624/

F: Good afternoon, what can I do for you today?

M: Yes, ____

____.

F: Do you have any appointment with ________________________________?

M: I was not aware I need to make an appointment.

F: Oh, it is no problem, ____.

Can you please wait just a moment? ________________________________.

M: Thank you!

F: Thanks for waiting! I just talk to our crew, it is a busy time for us right now, but if you don't mind waiting about 10 minutes,

____,

she can help to answer the question you have about investment accounts, here, take this number and I will let you know when it is the time, when your number is called, Susan would be ready to see you.

M: Where is her office?

F: ____,
and when you get off the elevator it is the first door on the right.

M: Thank you, I am sure I shouldn't have any problem of finding it!

▶ Reading

Task One

Tips on Receiving Foreign Clients

Ensure some information

When the client mail or phone you that he will come to your factory for a visit, you should make sure some basic information such as the schedule of his stay in China, the flight number and arriving time. Does he need you to reserve a room for him or pick him up in the airport? Does he need you make a reservation at the hotel he used last time. After making sure these information, you can tell him your mobile phone number, ask him to call you for anything urgent.

Preparation

Before picking up the clients in the airport, you should make some preparations.

1) Make your office, factory yard, workshop and sample room clean, make everything in order.

2) Make the necessities available: you will use in the negotiation, and show to the clients stationeries: such as laptop, projector, white board, marking pens (make sure they have enough ink), eraser, stapler and even tea and coffee are available. Materials: such as your catalogs, some paper you can write on, enough name cards, price list.

3) Get enough information: Google the clients' country and get the information about their business habits and native customs, their favorite food, especially the taboos in their nation. Then you can avoid doing that when staying with them. Find the famous things in their country, such as place of interest, celebrities, even the latest news recently. They are the good topics you can chat with your clients outside the negotiation. Make sure you can describe your products' making process fluently in

English. At first, you should know your products well. You can also print some necessary business spoken English and keep them in mind. Then you can blurt them out in the related situation. Google some good restaurants with special dishes for your choice.

In the airport

You should arrive at the airport earlier and wait in the hall. When the flight is arriving, you can raise the board with the clients' name on. When you find the clients or they's find you, shake hands and show your hospitality. After the clients get the baggage, you can lead him to your car, during the way, you can ask him if they had a good flight or if he need your help to manage the baggage. You should make sure where the clients want to go first. Go to the hotel for a rest or go to the factory for a visit and negotiation after dinning. On the way back, you can chat with the clients about the topics you prepared, or ask the client to have a rest.

In the factory

Lead your clients to your workshop, and explain the making process at the same time. After visiting the workshop, you can lead them to the meeting room and begin to talk business.

In the dinner

Ask the clients' favorite food. Then go to the restaurant for one of your choices and let the clients choose the dishes they like. Then you can enjoy the food and talk during the dinner. You can chat with them with some easy topics such as food, music, or even teach to say some Chinese langue such as "Xie Xie" or "Ni Hao".

Other things

If necessary, you can give the clients gifts as a token of your friendship. You'd better choose something with Chinese elements. If the clients need, you can see them off in the airport, and keep in touch in the email or msn later to get more and regular orders.

New Words and Expressions

ensure	[in'ʃuə]	*vt.*	保证,担保,确保;使确实,确定
schedule	['ʃədju:əl;'skedʒu:əl]	*n.*	[美语]预订日期;预定计划;计划表,进度表;一览表,明细表;表格;报表
stationery	['steiʃənəri]	*n.*	文具;信纸;信封
		adj.	文具的
stapler	['stæplə]	*n.*	订书器;纤维切断机
celebrity	[si'lebrəti]	*n.*	名声,名望,声誉;[pl] 名人,名流
blurt	[blə:t]	*vt.*	(通常与 out 连用)不假思索地说出,脱口说出;无意中漏出
token	['təukən]	*n.*	标志;象征;特征;证件,执照,凭证;纪念品

Task Two

Meeting and Greeting Clients

A day in the life of every businessperson is made up of a series of meetings and greetings. Whether you are making the initial contact with a client or a colleague, you want to get off on the right foot. Doing so will make the first encounter and subsequent ones go smoothly and easlly. Getting off on the wrong foot can make for a difficult recovery. Save your energy for later and use these simple strategies for a successful start.

Stand up when you meet someone

This allows you to engage the person on an equal level- eye to eye. By remaining seated, you send a message that you don't think the other person is important enough to warrant the effort it takes to stand. If you find yourself in a position where you can't stand up (such as being trapped behind a potted plant), offer your apology and explanation. You might say something like "Please excuse me for not getting up. I can't seem to get around the foliage."

Smile

Your facial expression says more than your words. Look as if you are pleased to meet the other person regardless of what is on your mind. Put a smile on your face for the person standing before you.

Make eye contact

Looking at the people you meet says you are focused and interested in them. If you are staring off somewhere else, you may appear to be looking for someone more to your liking to come along.

Introduce yourself immediately

As soon as you approach people you don't know or are approached by them, say who you are. Don't stand around as if someone else is in charge of introductions.

Include a statement about who you are when necessary

It is not always enough to say, "Hello, I'm Mary Jones." Give more information. "Hello, I'm Mary Jones. I work for XYZ Corporation."

Offer a firm handshake

Extend your hand as you give your greeting. The person who puts a hand out first comes across as confident and at ease. Make sure that this physical part of your greeting is professional. Don't offer bone-crushing grips or wimpy limp-wristed shakes. If you are confused about men and women shaking hands, don't be. There once was a time when women didn't shake hands with men. We are past that.

Learn how to make smooth introductions

In business you always introduce less important people to more important people. The way to do this is to say the name of the more important person first, followed by the words "I'd like to introduce ..." and then give the other person's name. Be sure to add something about each person so they will know why they are being introduced and will have some information with which to start a conversation.

Know who the more important person is

The client or the business prospect is more important than your boss. Just hope your boss agrees.

Pay attention to the names of people who you meet

It is common to be thinking about what you are going to say next without focusing on the other person. If you concentrate and repeat the name as soon as you hear it, you stand a better chance of remembering it later.

Use the first names of people who you have just met only after they give you permission

Not everyone wants to be addressed informally on the initial encounter. It is better to err on the side of formality than to offend the other person right off the bat.

Learn how to exchange business cards

Whether you are looking for a job or running a business, giving out business cards is crucial to marketing your skills or services. Hold the card in both hands when offering it or present your card with your right hand. Give business cards out to everyone. Have the information facing the recipient. Business cards are always received with two hands. When accepting a business card, have a good look at it for a few seconds, making the person feel important. Don't just take it and place it in your pocket. In your conversation, offer a compliment about the logo, design, etc. Unlike in Asia where the exchange of cards is taken very seriously, the exchange of business cards is very casual in Western countries, and the business card has little meaning other than a convenient form of capturing essential personal details.

Your goal within the first few minutes of meeting other people is to make them feel comfortable and to put them ease so they will want to do business with you. When you are confident of the rules for those critical initial encounters, you will have a solid start for long-term profitable relationships.

New Words and Expressions

initial	[iˈniʃəl]	*adj.*	开始的,最初的;原始的;初期的;第一的
subsequent	[ˈsʌbsikwənt]	*adj.*	连续的,接下去的;随后的,后来的
foliage	[ˈfəuliidʒ]	*n.*	全部叶子;一簇叶子;[总称]叶子
grip	[grip]	*n.*	紧握,抓牢;紧咬;紧夹
wimpy	[ˈwimpi]	*adj.*	衰弱的;无能的;智力欠缺的 [亦作 wimpish]
limp-wristed	[ˈlimpˈristid]	*adj.*	[美国俚语]软弱无力的;柔弱的;脆弱的

prospect	[ˈprɔspekt]	*n.*	合适的人选；期望，预期，指望；期望的事物
address	[əˈdres]	*vt.*	称呼；（直接地）对……说话；写信给
err	[əː]	*vi.*	犯错误，弄错；（陈述、仪器等）出差错，发生偏差
formality	[fɔːˈmæliti]	*n.*	礼节；拘谨；仪式；正式手续；繁文缛节

Task Three

Top Tips on Visiting a Client

Pat Walden (VP of Business Development) and I (Rich Templeton—Marketing Director) are currently traveling through the southern California area visiting current and potential clients. I thought this would be a good time to share these top customer service visit tips.

- Confirm the appointment before the visit. Make sure the date and time are accurate. You don't want to surprise the client.
- Confirm you have the correct address of the client in advance. This will save you time when searching for the visit location and avoid the unprofessional act of the client guiding you five minutes before the meeting.
- Confirm your agenda. Avoid aggravation by reviewing what you will be covering in the meeting ahead of time.
- When you meet the clients, greet them by names.
- If you have any documents for the clients, be sure to organize them in a folder or binder before handing them over.
- Clearly identify signatures that might be needed in the documents. Use post-it notes or a highlighter.
- A few days after the meeting, follow up with the client thanking them for the opportunity to visit and find out if they have any questions.
- Let the clients know when you've received the paperwork back and go through future procedures so they can be aware of upcoming events.
- Your attention to detail can make all the difference in world to the client.

New Words and Expressions

potential [pəuˈtenʃəl] *adj.* 潜在的,有潜势的;可能的,有可能性的

aggravation [ˌægrəˈveiʃən] *n.* 令人恼火的事;[口语]恼怒;烦恼;激怒

binder [ˈbaində] *n.* (书的)活页封面;活页夹;(书籍)装订工;装订机

highlighter [ˈhaiˌlaitə] *n.* (彩色)标记笔;荧光笔,亮光笔

Exercises

I. Match the country with its type of greeting.

Although handshaking is the standard form of greeting around the world today, different countries are known for different types of greeting. Surf the Internet or consult books and try to work it out properly.

---

1. Japan 2. France 3. Germany 4. Latin and Arab countries 5. America 6. Italy, Mexico, Latin America and Spain

---

A. a light handshake with one to two pumps

B. a limp, slow handshake a limp, slow handshake; shaking hands throughout the greeting

C. a firm shake with one brisk pump

D. a handshake and a bow (There are three levels of bows: 15 degree, 35 degree and 50 degree angled bow. The more senior the executive is, the lower your bow will be.)

E. a firm grip, two quick pumps

F. women may kiss on both cheeks after knowing you awhile

II. Choose the best answer.

1. When you receive someone else's business card you should ______.

A. immediately put it into your back pocket

B. immediately pass him your business card

C. look at the card but say nothing about it

D. look at the card and acknowledge it

2. What should you do if you see someone at a business event that you have met before, but you can't remember his name?

A. Ignore the person.

B. Introduce yourself, apologize for not remembering his name but say where you met him before.

C. Walk up to him or her and say, "Hi, mate!"

D. Try to find out the person's name from others at the event and then introduce yourself.

3. You are introducing two people to each other. When you suddenly forget the name of the second person, what will you do?

A. You tactfully apologize and ask for the person's name.

B. You leave them to introduce themselves to each other.

C. You introduce them with their titles, without mentioning their names. They will eventually say their names during the conversation.

4. You are a highest-ranked female in your company and you are sitting in the lobby of your office, talking to your subordinates. When the newly hired director of the department is approaching you to introduce himself, you ______.

A. stand up, extend your hand, introduce yourself and your colleagues

B. remain seated, extend your hand, introduce yourself and your colleagues

C. remain seated and extend your hand

5. The statement "A first impression is formed within the first 5 seconds." is ______.

A. correct B. incorrect

6. How low should a tie hang? It is supposed to reach ______.

A. the buckle of your belt

B. just above the belt

C. to any place

7. You are supposed to hang your name badge on ________.

A. the left lapel B. the right lapel

C. any place

8. You are talking to the president of the company at a cocktail party, when a client of yours comes to you and starts a conversation. You have to kindly greet your client and then you have to ______.

A. apologize to the president of your company for the interruption

B. introduce the president to your client

C. introduce your client to the president

9. You are at a cocktail party and do not see any familiar faces among the guests who are gathered mostly in groups. The host is not around and thereby cannot introduce you. How do you proceed?

A. You stay aside and wait for somebody to start a conversation with you.

B. You introduce yourself, start a small conversation on a hot political topic and start passing out business cards.

C. You try to lend your ears on the conversation of a group of guests and wait for the right moment to introduce yourself.

10. The statement "Business cards are always reciprocated in the USA." is ______.

A. true B. false

III. Read the passage carefully and decide whether the following statements are true or false. Write T for true and F for false.

Knowing how to introduce people in business and social settings is an important social skill that you should not overlook. Why are introductions important? They help others get to know each other and put guests at ease. Fortunately, knowing how to introduce people gets easier with practice. Below are the steps in making introductions.

1) The first step in making introductions is to determine who should be

introduced to whom. The basic rule is that the name of the older or higher ranking person should be said first.

When all other things are equal, the name of the person that you know better should be said first. In a business situation, the client is always considered higher ranking. Finally, at a party, guests should always be introduced to the guest of honor.

2) Unless you are in an informal setting, introductions should be made using first and last names, as well as titles such as "Dr." when appropriate. If the person that you are introducing has a clear relationship to you, this should be made clear.

How does this look in practice? Below are some examples:

"Edith Smith, I'd like you to meet Natalie Jones." (Edith is older than Natalie)

"Mr. President, I'd like to introduce my husband Paul Brown."

3) In a group setting such as a party, you should introduce a person to the group first. For example, "David, these are my friends Steve, John, Elizabeth and Natasha. Everyone, this is David."

Introductions like this should be made for a group of up to six people. If there are more than six people present, only make introductions to those that are nearby or those that the person will be sitting with. You should never lead someone around a room making introductions.

4) In general, when you are introduced to someone, it is polite to say "How are you?" If it is someone that you have been told about, you might make a comment along the lines of "Jeff has told me so much about you".

If someone has forgotten to introduce you, there is nothing wrong with introducing yourself and explaining how you know the host if you are at a party. The following are tips.

- If you have forgotten someone's name, it is more polite and less awkward to simply acknowledge the fact than to avoid an introduction.
- If you are being introduced to a group of people, you do not need to say something after each introduction. It is fine to just nod after the first

introduction to avoid repeating yourself.

- Formal etiquette rules dictate that men should stand when being introduced to women and women should stand when being introduced to older women. However, it is best to judge the situation and the actions of those around you when deciding whether to stand up.

The following are

1. The first step in making introductions is to determine who should be introduced to whom.
2. In a group setting such as a party, you should introduce a person to the group first.
3. If you have forgotten someone's name, it is not polite and less awkward to simply acknowledge the fact.
4. In business, the most important person is always the client.
5. When making introductions, first and last names must be stated.
6. Men should not stand when being introduced to women and women should not stand when being introduced to older women.
7. Suppose you are making introductions. You turn to Ms. (Mr. or Mrs.) Important and say something like "Ms. Important. I would like to introduce Mr. Unimportant, my associate (or whatever relationship you have with Mr. Unimportant)." Then turn to Mr. Unimportant and say something like "Mr. Unimportant. I would like you to meet Ms. Important, a director of XYZ Company."
8. Suppose you are making introductions. "Mary, I would like to introduce my grandmother, Frieda Abbott, to you." Then turning to your grandmother say, "Grandmother, this is my girlfriend, Mary Smith."

IV. Put the following sentences into Chinese or vice versa.

1. Excuse me, are you Mr. Wilson from the International Trading Corporation?
2. How was your flight? Was it comfortable?

3. I'm Maria. How do I address you?
4. We've made a reservation at the hotel you used last time.
5. Our new product line has been very successful. We've expanded the factory twice this year already.
6. 车正在那边等着,咱们现在就赴宾馆吧。我来帮您拿行李可以吗?
7. 祝您一路顺风,旅途愉快!
8. 您用餐时需要喝点酒吗?
9. 我带你出去吃饭好吗?这次我请客。
10. 昨天晚上你睡得好吗?

▶ Speaking

1. Read the following paragraph loudly and try to recite the eight etiquette errors.

Etiquette Mistakes at Business Events

Business etiquette doesn't have to be complicated. But there are certainly some bad manners that can be easily avoided at business meetings and events, such as seminars, conferences, business meals or cocktail receptions.

Avoid these meeting etiquette errors and you should be fine.

- **Failing to respond to the RSVP**

Etiquette tip: Respond within five days of receiving any invitation.

- **Failing to follow the dress code**

Etiquette tip: Read the invitation prior to the event and recognize the dress code information. When in doubt, always overdress for circumstances.

- **Failing to arrive on time**

Etiquette tip: Corporate managers and staff are always expected to be the first to arrive at an event.

- **Failing to extend the correct handshake**

Etiquette tip: Nobody is interested in shaking your wet, clammy hand. Shake hands after you've properly eaten and washed. At this point, greet verbally and your client will understand.

- **Failing to introduce new people to those around you**

Etiquette tip: Remember to introduce everyone in the group, and make every effort to introduce lower ranking individuals to the higher rank in the group (in that order). Also, remember to include titles and formal names. ("Mr. John Smith, let me introduce you to Dr. Jane Jones, our vice president of product development. Dr. Jones, Mr. Smith is director of client relations at Acme Corporation.")

- **Failing to speak to appropriate topics**

Etiquette tip: Several topics should be avoided in group event situations, and personal health topics are among them. Other topics that should be avoided include matters of personal finance, divisive topics and anything in the realm of gossip.

- **Failing to yield respectful courtesies to others at the event**

Etiquette tip: Show deference to others in a variety of social and business settings.

- **Failing to follow other business etiquette rules**

A few of the additional topics include:

* Excessive drinking at company events
* Inappropriate table manners
* Lack of thank you messages/acknowledgements, etc.

▶ Acting

Students form groups by themselves and role play. The instructor comments on performance and grade the students' work.

1. Meeting Clients at the Airport
2. Receiving Clients in the Company
3. Showing Clients Around the Company

▶ Supplementary Listening

* Business Etiquette (Handshake, Big City Comaparison 1, 2, etc.)

http://www.51voa.com/Business_Etiquette_1.html

Listen to the dialogues and dictate down the key points.

► Supplementary Reading

Top Tips to Become the Worst Sales Person in Your Company

Sean McPheat

Have you ever had sales people who just never seem to make it no matter how hard they try? These sales people are one of the main factors for decline in business. Your sales people are the heart of your company and without good ones you will find it difficult to succeed in selling your products. To train good sales people you sometimes need to take a different approach.

Here are 10 tips that will save you from becoming the worst sales person in the company:

1. Not being punctual: Being on time is very important to a customer. Take into consideration that many of your seasonal Christmas customers will be new. Your sales people will represent the first contact these customers have with your company. First impressions are lasting ones and your sales person need to make a good impression. Being on time will give a good impression to the client and increase their confidence in your company.

2. Poor presentation: Some sales people just do not have all their ducks in a row and simply do not present the product well. A presentation is the first thing a customer will know about your product. If your product is not shown correctly to the customer he is very unlikely to buy.

3. Bad attitude: Rudeness and unprofessional behavior is not acceptable under any circumstances. It is quite surprising that you will meet some sales people who are just plain rude and short with you. This gives the potential buyer the wrong impression about your company. They do not get a proper picture of the product, as they will probably not even wait for the presentation to end. You will lose many sales like this.

4. Not being articulate: A sales person must know how to express himself with confidence and fluency. He needs to be able to greet the prospect and introduce himself with assurance. This will start the whole presentation off to a good start. When he actually presents the product, he must be sure to do this in a confident manner. He should also be prepared to answer all questions concisely and well. If your sales person cannot do this, your sale will not go through.

5. Not listening to a customer: A sales person should not only be able to present your product but listen to the prospective buyer. There is nothing more irritating to the consumer than having a sales person go on about a product and not letting you ask a few simple questions. After all whose money is on the line here? Worse still is when you do finally get to ask your question and instead of giving you a straight answer they go off on a tangent and have clearly not been listening to you. This will make a customer angry and they will probably never do business with you.

6. Basing a sale on cost: It is extremely risky for a sales person to depend on cost to close the sales. The prospective buyer will be quick to take advantage when he sees that the deal depends on the cost factor. He will drive the price as low as he can and you will take a heavy cut in profits for the sake of a sale. The buyer may hold off and then not even buy.

7. Not knowing when to close a sale: This is a common fault but a lethal one. Many sales have been lost because the sales person did not know when to close the sale. A good sales person is in tune with the prospective buyer and knows instinctively when to move to close the sale.

8. Hard sell: Hard sell is when sales people try to push the sale on the prospective customer. This will make the buyer aggressive and he will try to get rid of your sales person as soon as possible. It is a proven fact that nobody likes to be sold to.

9. Inflexibility: A sales person should be aware of different personalities and various situations. They must be flexible and able to adapt to different circumstances. The presentation may be the same but the buyers are rarely the same. Each buyer wants to feel special and expects the sales person to understand his circumstances. Inflexibility will cost you many sales.

10. Not following up a hot prospect: Following up is very important. It is actually plain good manners. You have spoken to a person who has expressed interest in your company's product but may not have been able to make a decision yet. It is courteous and good for business to follow up with him. You may even make a sale this way. If your sales person does not know how to do this, you will end up losing valuable customers and sales.

Being the best sales person in your company is a tough task whereas being the worst is a synch! Read on to learn how to guarantee that you are the worst sales person in your company and whether you already hold the crown!

Sean McPheat provides sales training across the UK, Europe, US and the Middle East. Visit his sales blog for free information about how to increase your sales and close more deals.

(http://www.positivearticles.com. PositiveArticles.Com does not vouch for or necessarily endorse the contents of this article.)

Top 10 Tips for Visiting Egypt

Stuart Cheese

In my capacity as the UK Director of Operations for One World Tours Limited, one of my jobs is to ensure every client has the best tour possible, so here's my top 10 tips if you are considering holidays in Egypt.

1. Consider your dress. Egypt is a largely Muslim country and with this in mind, men and women should consider what they wear. You certainly do not have to be over the top, lets face it, it's a hot climate. But you should avoid shorts and short sleeved shirts. Women may also want to consider taking a head scarf too, not for general use, but just in case they visit particularly important temples, etc.

2. Pens. Offer a child an Egyptian pound or a pen and they will take the pen every time. Pens for children are like gold-dust. So if you want to give the kids a treat, pack a box of cheap pens and give them out whenever you get the chance. Do note though, that you need to do this not too openly as if you don't. You may have a very good natured riot on your hands as kids will appear out of nowhere when you start handing them out.

3. Toilet Paper. Toilet paper is often at a premium at historical sites and so it's a really good idea to take a roll out of your hotel and take it in your back whenever you are out for the day. It should also be noted here that toilets at many historical sites are not of a "Western standard" so arranging toilet visits in hotels, restaurant stops, etc. is not a bad idea.

4. Water. Like with any other hot climates, you should look to take plenty of water with you on your days out and make sure it's sealed of course.

5. Avoid ice/salads, etc. This related partly to Number 4. People generally know not to drink non-bottled water (to avoid possible upset stomachs), but often they over look that ice is frozen water and that salads have often been washed in water. Keep these things in mind when ordering food and drinks.

6. Take small notes. If you are going to tip, it's a good idea and it avoids embarrassment to change up some bigger notes for a number of 1 LE (Egyptian Pound) notes.

7. Be strong. This applies to people begging. Egypt is a relatively financially poor country and with that comes the fact that people (children and adults) will beg. This is obviously a very personal issue, but obviously it's possible to personally sort out all of Egypts financial problems. So feel free to help out where you can and when you feel comfortable, but realise, it's just not possible to give to everyone who asks.

8. When in Rome. This again partly relates to Tip 1. You are ultimately holidaying in a more reserved country and therefore you need to just think about things like public shows of affection. Obviously we want you to have a good time, just be respectful to a different culture and you'll be just fine.

9. Haggle. As a tourist, when you buy almost anything, anywhere, the price will be marked up. You therefore have to bargain your socks off. We generally suggest offering a maximum of 1/3 to 1/2 of the asking price and work up. If you can do it, you are even better not to offer a price at all, but just keep saying no and let them lower the price. The best tip is to just keep saying no until the person selling stops and lets you walk. At that point, you just won't get a better price and then you have the option to go back and say—OK, I'll take it at that price!

10. Baksheesh. If you do not know what this is, by the end of your holidays you will! Baksheesh is a tip in Egypt for just about anything, from carrying your bags at the airport to offering to have a picture with you or showing around a tomb. So just be aware. If you chose to pay (it's completely optional), pay with the smallest bills/nots possible (1 LE will be just fine).

(http://www.approvedarticles.com)

Answer the following questions:

1. What are the 10 top tips to become the worst sales person in the company?
2. What are the top 10 tips for visiting Egypt?

Project Seven
Business Negotiation Etiquette

Learning Objectives

After completing this project, you will be able to:

* demonstrate proper etiquette in business negotiation;
* follow the principles of negotiating international business.

Warming-Up

Answer the following questions.

❑ Can you tell us when we will negotiate?

❑ What do you learn from the quotation "In all negotiations of difficulty, a man may not look to sow and reap at once; but must prepare business, and so ripen it by degrees"? (Francis Bacon, "Of Negotiating")

Listening

http://www.unsv.com/voanews/business-etiquette/lessons/001/

Listen to the recording and fill in the blanks.

The Eyes Have It

(*Office ambience*)

A:陈豪,Do you have a few minutes to talk?

C:Sure, 有什么事吗?

A:I noticed something in our meeting just now. 作为朋友,我觉得应该告诉你。

____。

C: 我有什么地方做得不对吗？西方礼节对我来说还有些陌生，你可得随时提醒我。

A: ____。

C:肢体语言？Amy，你能说得具体点儿吗？

A:____

____。

C:你是说从我眼睛里能看出我的想法吗？

A:没错。比方说，今天开会时，______________________

____。

Todd 介绍提案时，我能看出你不同意他的意见。

C:噢，你从我眼睛就能看出来？我真的是有异议。可你看出来的？我可是一字都没说呀。

A: ____。

C: 我翻眼睛了吗？我怎么一点儿都没觉得。

A:你是下意识的。______________________________。

C:那就是说虽然我嘴上没表示反对，其他人还是能够看出来。

____。

A: ____。

C:这有什么不好吗？他说的我都听过好几遍了。

A:没错。______________________________________

____。

C:这我可没想到。我一直在努力管住自己的嘴巴，不要乱讲话。

A: ____。

C:Amy，你还从我的眼神儿里看出什么了？

A:____

____。

C:“车前灯里的鹿”是什么意思啊？

A:____

____。

C：你是说我的眼睛虽然看着 Todd，但是别人能看出来，我其实并没有听进去？

A：____。

C：Amy，你能不能再提醒我一下，以后要怎么做，省得我的眼睛把我的想法都泄漏出去了。

A：记住，眼睛是心灵的窗口。____。

▶ Reading

Task One

Etiquette in Business Negotiation

Etiquette in business negotiation is essentially about building relationship between/among negotiating parties to create strong deals and building good relationships. To achieve the goals, it's very important for negotiators to know the etiquette associated with negotiating, such as how to speak to a potential client and how to behave when the negotiation process is prolonged. These courtesies will help you to avoid awkward situations and make a positive first impression.

Greetings

Before the negotiations officially begin, it is essential that you present yourself as friendly and polite to give the impression of trustworthiness. The most common form of greeting in the corporate world is the handshake. However, if you are in countries such as France or Brazil, kisses on the cheek are the norm. If you are in the Middle East, a nod of acknowledgment may be best when greeting someone of the opposite sex. Learn the culture of the people you will be negotiating with. This is a sign of respect and an indication of how you will behave during the business process.

Small talk

It is also common for some professionals to engage in small talk before the negotiations begin and to have short conversations after negotiations have ended for the day. This gives everyone time to become more comfortable with one another and is the gateway to building a lasting business relationship. However, in some countries such as Finland and Germany, small talk is not part of business culture, and meetings start precisely on time. After negotiations, a German or Finnish professional may host a dinner or a trip to the sauna for casual conversation. In places such as Mexico and Saudi Arabia, small talk is expected, but it's best to know which subjects are off-limits. For instance, it is not proper etiquette to discuss the poverty in the country with Mexican professionals, and one should not inquire about the well-being of a female family member in Saudi Arabia.

Presentation

If you will be presenting information that is meant to sway a client in a certain direction in a business deal, be sure that your presentation is concise, fact-based and easy to follow. While some companies depend more on a favorable relationship when making a final decision in a negotiation, it is always proper etiquette for you to have facts and figures ready to present to each meeting participant. Being thoroughly prepared for the presentation and ready to answer any questions is likely to make new clients more at ease when it comes to doing business with you.

Deciding on strategy

When you are deciding which negotiation strategy to use, considering the negotiation etiquette of the professionals you are working with is imperative. For example, in the US, it is appropriate to use "hard selling" or persuasion to get a businessperson to side with you in the negotiation process. However, in countries like Australia this is inappropriate and could result in the end of a potentially positive business relationship. In the Middle East and parts of Africa, bargaining is common and expected—both sides make offers on an item or service until a satisfactory price is reached. In some cases, it is best to simply state the facts regarding your stance in the negotiation, to be honest about your intentions and to respectfully listen to all the opinions presented at the meeting.

Waiting for a decision

Once all the information has been presented and it's time to come to a decision, using proper etiquette to respect this part of the process will help to secure the business deal. In many companies, the final negotiation decision is made from the top down, meaning that executives will likely have additional meetings to determine the negotiation outcome. Being patient and accommodating during this time shows that you respect the process and are not simply focused on getting "your way". Following up with the negotiation proceedings in the appropriate way, such as sending a short email, will show that you are genuinely interested but don't want to seem too pushy.

New Words and Expressions

prolong	[prəˈlɔŋ]	*vt.*	延长;拖延
trustworthiness	[ˈtrʌstwəːθinis]	*n.*	可信赖;确实性
sauna	[ˈsɔːnə]	*n.*	桑拿浴
		vi.	洗桑拿浴
sway	[swei]	*v.*	影响;统治;使摇动
		n.	影响;摇摆;统治
secure	[siˈkjuə]	*vt.*	保护;弄到;招致;缚住
pushy	[ˈpuʃi]	*adj.*	有进取心的;爱出风头的;有冲劲的;固执己见的

Task Two

Principles of Negotiating International Business

Negotiation is an activity that all managers and professionals engage in. It's necessary to negotiate at every stage of a project or business transaction in order to reach an agreement. International business negotiation takes place between the interest groups from different countries or regions. It includes consultation, bargaining, mediation, arbitration and sometimes, even litigation. In international business negotiation, negotiators should take into account the following issues such as language barrier, cultural differences, international laws and domestic laws in force, international political factors. The difficulty and the cost are greater than that of domestic business negotiations.

World globalization is making it easier to deal with cultural differences in business. Still, unfamiliarity with a country's culture can cause issues to arise in any business negotiation. Learning basic cultural business etiquette can help make a business transaction or negotiation successful. To get basic etiquette practices, international business negotiators should follow the following principles:

Before negotiation

First, know our goals and their goals. We must always make certain we understand our goals or objectives clearly, before we board the plane. Similarly, if our negotiations are through a third party acting on our behalf, we want to ensure that they fully understand our objectives. By knowing and understanding each sides goals and objectives, affords both parties a better opportunity to explore creative solutions. One of the best ways to determine the other side's interests is to interact with the agent or parties who will already be involved with the preliminary arrangements.

Second, organize a competent delegation. Most international arrangements are generally performed by a team of players. Some will be at the table, while others may either be in the background in the country where the deal is being negotiated, or they will be stationed at home base. Carefully consider the structure of the team, so that only the relevant players are involved. It is better if we have a single spokesperson who can integrate all the components into a single vision. Team members should understand their responsibilities fully, and any tasks assigned to them. Whether it be logistics for the team, communication, research, travel, etc. They can identify a couple of dependable contacts in the host country and work with them on logistics prior to our visit. We may also need to arrange for the use of a qualified and competent interpreter or translator. Interpreters need to be considered as an equal and functioning member of the team. They have to be briefed on the nature of the negotiations, and how they are to provide their translation such as whether it will be a summary or verbatim translation. They may be asked to provide assistance in understanding the cultural nuances that might be encountered.

***Third*, research the other side and their perspective on the pending partnership.** Do homework on the host country's time consciousness, communication styles, protocol and etiquette, etc. Learn the basics about the behavioral norms in your partner's culture, especially concerning appointments, punctuality, planning and the best time to hold an important business meeting. It is crucial we gain as much understanding about the business background and personalities of the other side. We will need to know and understand the country's political climate, economy, culture and laws. The department that represents international trade for our own country, plus our own embassy in the country where we are conducting business, can provide us with a wealth of information. The more information we have on hand, the more we are able to consider and overcome any obstacles.

***Fourth*, consider all your options and estimate the other side's options.** If our deal collapses, then what do we do? It is unwise to assume that the agreement will automatically succeed. We have to consider our BATNA (Best Alternative to a Negotiated Agreement). Of the available options, we then have to compare our best alternative to a proposed agreement, to see how it measures up. Similarly, we need to estimate what alternatives may be available to our counterpart.

***Fifth*, clearly identify the issues.** Technical and logistical problems are often the most common issues we might face. Anything that is an issue to our counterpart is also an issue that will influence our business arrangement.

***Sixth*, consider multiple proposals that are of mutual benefit.** With everything else in place, we can now consider the proposals that will best address the goals and objectives of both sides. We might choose to either present these proposals in person, or submit them in writing prior to the talks. A draft agreement proposal that is presented beforehand is a common practice used by many negotiators. It permits us the opportunity to talk about the draft later. It may also provide us with a tactical advantage.

***Finally*, don't forget to bring proper gifts because gifts are appreciated in every culture.** Learn how to pronounce names of host contacts correctly and clarify their positions and job titles.

During negotiation

Upon entering the board room or any other negotiation with due preparation, start each negotiation with a friendly handshake and decent eye contact. Be sure as always that you have dressed in a manner that the other party will not find offensive. Remember to maintain your composure, your posture throughout with good eye contact. This reflects well on you that you are willing to listen. Chances are the other person will offer less than they would actually deliver. Though you would be tempted to pepper the person with the presentation with question after question, hold onto them by taking notes. Unless there is a serious misunderstanding, do not try to ask questions until after the presentation. This could break the flow of their presentation. While in negotiations, avoid negative body movements such as sloped shoulders. This means disinterest. Make sure not to tap or shuffle. Maintain a studious composure. Don't doodle! Listen to the presentation and take notes. It means that you're interested and that they do have points of interest. It also helps you to stay on task. When it is a natural break or the presentation is over, ask questions. Praise the good points in the presentation. Put down some points on paper that you both can mutually consider and make a copy. Try not to get hung up in the details. These can be tied up later.

Don't say the word "between", it tends to be tantamount to a concession, and any shrewd negotiator with whom you deal will swiftly zero-in on the cheaper price or the deadline. In other words, you will find that by saying the word "between" you will automatically have conceded ground without extracting anything in return. Don't say "I think we're close." It indicates that you value simply reaching an agreement over getting what you actually want. And a skilled negotiator on the other side may well use this moment as an opportunity to stall, and thus to negotiate further concessions. Unless you actually face extreme time pressure, you shouldn't be the party to point out that the clock is loudly ticking in the background. Create a situation in which your counterpart is more eager to finalize the negotiation than you are. Don't say "Why don't you throw out a number?" Many people believe you should never be the first person in a negotiation to quote a price. Let the other side start the bidding. Study shows that the final outcome of a negotiation is affected by whether the buyer or the seller makes the first offer. Specifically, when a seller makes the first offer, the final settlement price tends to be higher than when the buyer makes the first offer.

Never tell the other side when you are leaving because this gives them control over your time.

Respect the sensitivities (hot buttons) of your partner in the area of personal status and national pride.

Allow yourself plenty of time, and even more. Patience is an asset for negotiation and it is destroyed by time pressure.

Do not get fooled by the other party seemingly sharing your time pattern: try to set realistic dates and deadlines and plan modestly and realistically. Tight deadlines may result in jumbo delays that ruin the credibility of the whole planning process.

Try to balance relationship—orientation and deal-orientation: wait for the negotiation process to extend beyond the signature of the deal.

Adopt different negotiation approaches. The most frequently employed ones are: distributive and integrative. Distributive negotiation is competitive in nature (also called competitive or win-lose approach), whereas integrative negotiation is characterized by cooperation (also called a cooperative or win-win approach). Distributive negotiation largely entails that one party essentially attempts to maximize its set of winnings and reduce the gains of the opposite party to the lowest amount possible. Integrative negotiation is an attempt to identify joint gains for the benefit of all involved parties. It has often proven to work better in negotiation, especially for parties interested in maintaining long-term relations. Distributive negotiation may still be appropriate in simple market contexts; however, integrative negotiation will be an important approach in developing long-term relationships.

Be ready for different communication styles (verbal) and be cautious in interpreting (non-verbal) silence, emotionality, threats and any kind of manipulative/instrumental communication. Body language and communication will also differ in other countries.

Although the entire conversation may be conducted in English there may still be communication differences. For instance, in some countries the physical communication is done at a much closer proximity than you may be used to and pulling back from a person may be seen as an insult. In some countries a "yes" answer may only be an acknowledgement of a conversation, but not an authorization of a transaction. In other areas a shaking of the head from side to side (as Americans do to indicate "no"), may indicate agreement or acknowledgment. In these cases it is best to simply address the cultural difference and explain your conclusion of the conversation. Always apologize for your misunderstanding, and make it clear that it is a misunderstanding. The foreigner is more likely to help you understand when you have expressed your lack of cultural knowledge.

When speaking, recognize the foreign associates business and cultural practices. Asian cultures encourage lengthy decision making, concentrating on everything detail, and avoids confrontation and debate. Whereas the American culture emphasize quick, efficient decisions on major points while leaving the details to be worked out later and encourage open disagreement. Avoid talking negatively about the business partner's country, principles, religion, or business practices. Instead, talk of the advantages of the country and their positive cultural customs and beliefs. Your appreciation of a country will make up for any etiquette mistakes you make during a meeting or conversation.

After negotiation

When both parties have acknowledged mutual agreement, there is no need to continue negotiating. Closure should be sought in as concrete a form as the participating cultures are ready to accept at that point. In cultures where reflection and relationships is the key, an agreement in principle, such as a memorandum of understanding that recapitulates the agreed conditions, can be a perfectly acceptable sign of trust, to be followed by a formal agreement. Finally, should an agreement not be possible, a future relationship may be possible, so it makes sense to remain positive and respectful.

Signing the agreement is a useful common practice. As a symbol of the success of negotiation, signing ceremony is of great importance and a good preparation is necessary. The signer will be determined by the contracting parties. Based on the importance and nature of the agreement, the signer can be the leader of local government or the person in charge of local business or companies. The signer of the party should have the same or similar rank or status. People attending the signing ceremony should be those who participated in the negotiation. Many nations assign more officials or officials of higher ranks to attend the ceremony to show the importance of the agreement. The procedures of signing ceremony are as follows: Participants from both parties enter the signing hall at the same time. The signers take their seats and others stand behind their signer. The signers sign their own copy first. The signer's assistant of each side stands by the signer, turning the pages of the document for him and pointing at the space for him to sign. The assistants of both sides pass on the signed copy to the signer of the other party for signature. After signing it, the signers exchange the signed copy and shake hands. Champagne is served to celebrate the signing of the agreement.

New Words and Expressions

mediation	[ˌmi:diˈeiʃən]	*n.*	调解;仲裁;调停
arbitration	[ˌɑ:biˈtreiʃən]	*n.*	公断,仲裁
litigation	[ˌlitiˈgeiʃən]	*n.*	诉讼;起诉
preliminary	[priˈliminəri]	*adj.*	初步的;开始的;预备的
		n.	准备;预赛
logistics	[ləuˈdʒistiks]	*n.*	[军]后勤;现代物流
verbatim	[və:ˈbeitim]	*adj.*	逐字逐句的,一字不差的
		adv.	逐字逐句地,一字不差地
nuance	[ˈnju:ɑ:ns]	*n.*	(颜色、音调、表情、措词、等的)细微差别
pending	[ˈpendiŋ]	*adj.*	未决定的;行将发生的

		prep.	在……期间;直到……时为止
		v.	待定;悬而不决(pend 的 ing 形式)
embassy	[ˈembəsi]	*n.*	大使馆;大使馆全体人员
collapse	[kəˈlæps]	*vi.*	倒塌;瓦解;暴跌
		vt.	使倒塌,使崩溃;使萎陷
counterpart	[ˈkauntəpɑːt]	*n.*	对应者,对手;地位相同者;极相似者
composure	[kəmˈpəuʒə]	*n.*	镇静,沉着,泰然自若
pepper	[ˈpepə]	*vt.*	使布满,使活跃;使(文章等)辛辣(或有煽动性);加胡椒粉于
		n.	胡椒,辣椒;胡椒粉
shuffle	[ˈʃʌfl]	*vi.*	坐立不安;拖着脚走;支吾;推诿,搪塞
studious	[ˈstjuːdiəs]	*adj.*	用功的;热心的;专心的;故意的;适于学习的
tantamount	[ˈtæntəmaunt]	*adj.*	同等的;相当于……的
shrewd	[ʃruːd]	*adj.*	精明的;狡猾的;机灵的
		n.	精明(的人),机灵(的人)
stall	[stɔːl]	*v.*	停止,停转;拖延,使陷于泥中
		n.	货摊
bidding	[ˈbidiŋ]	*n.*	投标;出价;命令
jumbo	[ˈdʒʌmbəu]	*adj.*	巨大的,巨型的,特大的
		n.	庞然大物;体大而笨拙的人或物
credibility	[ˌirediˈbiləti]	*n.*	可信性,可靠性;确实性
distributive	[disˈtribjutiv]	*adj.*	分配的;分发的;分送的
entail	[inˈteil]	*vt.*	必需,使承担;引起;使需要;必须包括
manipulative	[məˈnipjulətiv]	*adj.*	操作的;控制的;操纵的;巧妙处理的
instrumental	[ˌinstruˈmentəl]	*adj.*	作为手段(或工具)的;有帮助的;起作用的
memorandum	[ˌmeməˈrændəm]	*n.*	备忘录;便笺
recapitulate	[ˌriːkəˈpitʃulcit]	*v.*	概括;重述要点;摘要

Exercises

I. Read the statements below and decide whether the statements are true or false. Write T for true and F for false.

1. Since negotiation is fundamentally confrontational, it is most important to know how to defend one's position without budging.
2. The process of negotiating brings out many of the key value orientations linked to culture, including the degree of formality, the approach to time and the way action is taken.
3. Relationships necessarily interfere with efficient, focused negotiation.
4. The best negotiators speak in terms of objectives, not positions.
5. Foreign counterparts are likely to be most impressed by determination, not cooperation.
6. When both parties have acknowledged mutual agreement, it is important to try to obtain at least one additional concession in order to save face.
7. The signers turn the pages by themselves to find the space for signature.
8. A Westerner is preparing for a round of negotiations with a Chinese delegation: The choice of meeting room and seating arrangement make little or no difference.
9. Negotiations are usually all or nothing: Either the deal is signed, or the experience is a failure.
10. Spending more time on relationships can reduce time negotiating.

II. Choose the best answer.

1. When seeing the other party off at the train station, as courtesy, you should ______.

   A. have the station before the train departs

   B. walk away when the train begins to move

   C. wave at them and stay there until the train disappears from your sight

2. At the final stage of negotiation, an agreement needs to be signed. A signing

ceremony is ______.

A. a useful common practice
B. a ritual
C. both of the above
D. unnecessary

3. The signer of the agreement will be determined by ______.

A. the leader of the nation
B. the minister of the government
C. the head of the local firm
D. the contracting parties

4. The host signer will take ______.

A. the chair on the left side
B. the chair on the right side
C. the chair on either side
D. the chair at the end

5. Which of the following is ideally NOT a component of the negotiation process?

A. Defending positions.
B. Comparing objectives.
C. Sharing information.
D. Listening.

6. Pre-negotiation research ______.

A. is rarely helpful, because the other side inevitably hides its true intentions
B. should focus exclusively on data and other "hard evidence"
C. helps participants to con their underlying interest in reaching an agreement
D. is superfluous, because either side has presumably already decided that they want to do project/programme purpose together

7. Good relationships are relevant to negotiation because ______.

A. they improve communication
B. provide an additional positive consequence to reaching agreement
C. potentially bring to the surface additional options that are mutually beneficial
D. all of the above

8. Which of the following items is a negotiation team from a direct "doing" culture likely to arrive to the meeting with?

A. Thoughtfully chosen gifts.
B. Data, charts and contract forms.
C. An extensive presentation of the organization background and its founders.
D. A large number of team members, each a specialist in a different area of

project/programme purpose.

III. Contrast cultural differences in negotiation and mediation and fill in the blanks with "ASIAN" and "WESTERN".

<table>
<tr><td></td><td colspan="2"></td></tr>
<tr><td>Low Context (Direct) Communication</td><td colspan="2">High Context (Indirect) Communication</td></tr>
<tr><td>Low Power Distance</td><td colspan="2">High Power Distance</td></tr>
<tr><td>Individualism</td><td colspan="2">Collectivism</td></tr>
<tr><td>Low Uncertainty Avoidance</td><td colspan="2">High Uncertainty Avoidance</td></tr>
<tr><td>Masculinity (Assertive)</td><td colspan="2">Femininity (Cooperative)</td></tr>
<tr><td>Short-Term Orientation</td><td colspan="2">Long-Term Orientation</td></tr>
<tr><td>Monochronic Time</td><td colspan="2">Polychronic Time</td></tr>
<tr><td>Space—Far Apart</td><td colspan="2">Space—Close</td></tr>
<tr><td>Risk Takers</td><td colspan="2">Risk Avoiders</td></tr>
<tr><td>Brief Rapport Building Time (Short)</td><td colspan="2">Extensive Rapport Building Time (Long)</td></tr>
<tr><td>Aggressive</td><td colspan="2">Passive</td></tr>
<tr><td>Contract Focus</td><td colspan="2">Relationship focus</td></tr>
<tr><td>Win-Lose Approach</td><td colspan="2">Win-Win Approach</td></tr>
<tr><td>Informal Approach</td><td colspan="2">Formal Approach</td></tr>
<tr><td>Show Emotions</td><td colspan="2">Hide Emotions</td></tr>
<tr><td>Preference for Specific Agreement</td><td colspan="2">Preference for General Agreement</td></tr>
<tr><td>Contract Is Fixed</td><td colspan="2">Re-Negotiation Is Possible</td></tr>
<tr><td>Individual Decision-Making</td><td colspan="2">Group Decision-Making</td></tr>
<tr><td>Logical Decision-Making</td><td colspan="2">Emotional Decision-Making</td></tr>
<tr><td>All Equals</td><td colspan="2">One Leader</td></tr>
<tr><td>Face Saving</td><td colspan="2">Face Giving</td></tr>
<tr><td>Inductive Logic</td><td colspan="2">Deductive logic</td></tr>
<tr><td>Low Government Involvement</td><td colspan="2">High Government involvement</td></tr>
<tr><td>Linear-Active</td><td>Multi-Active</td><td>Reactive</td></tr>
</table>

IV. Put the following sentences into Chinese.

1. Many Asians, Africans and Orientals will look down and avoid direct eye

contact as a sign of respect, while for Europeans and North Americans lack of eye contact is often an indication of lack of attention, and could be regarded as impolite.

2. In the Middle East, people of the same sex stand much closer to each other than North Americans and Europeans, while people of the opposite sex stand much further apart.
3. In many regions of the world, to ask someone to approach you by beckoning with the upright forefinger is distinctly rude.
4. It is obvious that touch is a sensitive issue and, to be on the safe side, avoid touching during negotiation as far as possible.
5. If you also keep your arms crossed over your chest and lean back in your chair besides just keeping your legs crossed, you could be demonstrating distaste or defensiveness.
6. Other gestures to avoid during negotiation are "thumbs up" and "okay" signs. These have positive connotations in the UK and America, but in Iran and Spain the "thumbs up" sign is considered obscene, while the "okay" sign has a similar meaning in Greece, parts of Eastern Europe and Latin America. It could also mean "worthless" or "zero" in France.
7. The inability of customers to keep to time is probably one of the most significant irritations in cross-cultural negotiation.
8. Some officials, such as traffic police or those at immigration or customs posts, appear rude in their demands: "Give passport now" and "I want documents" without the adoption of "please" and "thank you". To many Westerners this is inexcusably rude English and quick offence is taken.
9. Most Westerners find silence embarrassing and will seek to fill a gap in conversation.
10. Plan to negotiate on the least-important issues first. Negotiating on the less-significant issues first can give you more time to focus on concessions that are more of value.

▶ Speaking

1. Read the text loudly, and try to recite the following paragraph.

Ask questions, rather than simply interpreting a statement in the way you believe to have understood it. When asking, use certain key words that the other party mentioned in their last statement. "The one who asks, leads" as the old German saying goes. Skillfully formed questions show that you are listening attentively and that you are trying to figure out the motives and the background behind the other's argument. They also give you the opportunity to think things through and to elegantly change the direction of the discussion. Depending on the reply that you want to elicit out of the other party, you can work with different types of questions.

2. Read the dialogue and role play it.

A: So, thank you for coming, everyone. It's really a pleasure to see you all here. First of all, may I suggest you take a look at the agenda I sent you? Would you like to make any comment on that?

B: Yes, I wonder if we can begin with shipment question first. We really need to come to an agreement on that before anything else.

A: That's true, but it's also a very difficult issue. That's the reason why I put it last. I thought it might be a good idea for us to start with the points we have in common. We'll move on to the shipment issue after that.

B: All right. That sounds reasonable.

A: Well, before we go any future, I would like to say strongly how I feel that it's in both our interest to reach an agreement today. The market is becoming even more competitive and our combined strength will give us some big advantages, not least in terms of the dealer network. Now, I think Richard would like to say a few words about that.

▶ Acting

Students form groups by themselves and role play. The instructor comments on performance and grade the students' work.

Work in pairs for possible solutions to the following problem: Suppose that you are the seller and your partner is the purchaser. The seller's position is stated as selling a certain number of cell phones at X dollars per unit whereas the purchaser's position is expressed as receiving a certain number of cell phones within a month's time at X minus US $30 per unit. Please jointly work out a solution and report to the class.

▶ Supplementary Listening

* Business Etiquette (Asking for a Raise (1,2), Raising Prices (1,2), etc.)

http://www.voanews.cn/voaet/17705.htm

Listen to the dialogues and dictate down the important points.

▶ Supplementary Reading

International Trade Negotiation Tips

Negotiating successfully in international trade requires a delicate balance of finely tuned people skills and technical expertise. The starting point for a winning strategy in global trade is a sensitive understanding of foreign cultures.

- **Rule #1: Culture Drives Negotiations**

Prudent negotiators first research a foreign culture to find out whether negotiations require a formal or informal approach.

On his website, Professor Geert Hofstede explains that an American or Canadian negotiator strives to achieve a target of mutual understanding. When the opposing sides from these Western cultures reach an agreement, the negotiating parties shake hands to show that negotiations are over and that the working together phase has begun.

In contrast, negotiators from Middle Eastern cultures shake hands to signal that serious negotiations are about to proceed. After a handshake at the end of a hard day of bargaining, an American or Canadian representative might be under the false impression that a multi-million dollar deal has been struck. One negotiating side will be shocked when they learn that the Middle Eastern business persons are expecting more detailed presentations and compromises in the next round of negotiation.

- **Rule #2: Manage Time Wisely**

Rule number two is that negotiators must use their time wisely. This is much trickier than simply showing up on time. Prudent time usage means being sensitive to how the opposing side wants to spend their hours, minutes and seconds.

American, British and German cultures demand that the other side be punctual. A German executive frowns both on opposing negotiators that show up either too early or too late, as this shows a lack of planning—a deadly sin for any party to German negotiations.

Mexicans and Brazilians are generally more relaxed in their approach to time. It's not unusual for people from these more emotional cultures to spend the first hour of their working days discussing family or social matters before getting down to business. While being late isn't as serious in these cultures, failure to spend enough time chatting about personal matters before starting business proceedings is.

- **Rule #3: Respect Negotiation Opponents**

Rule number three is universal: To be respected in international trade negotiations, one has to first respect his or her opponents.

Regardless of culture, negotiators must avoid confrontations and never show any belligerence. This applies whether checking in with a junior administrative assistant at an international trade show or greeting a senior executive from a foreign country.

To achieve skills in showing genuine respect for one's opponent, negotiators often practice self-control assignments at home, school or at the office. Personal development courses are available that enable participants to grade themselves on how well they think they show respect. Others are then surveyed on how each participant comes across. Role-playing exercises are video-taped, providing more valuable feedback on self-perception versus how other people actually perceive the negotiator.

Some cultures, like the Japanese, have historically shown more respect to older male figures. Sending a bold younger leader like Sarah Palin to negotiate with an old school Japanese board of directors can present some cultural issues of respect, depending partly on how smoothly verbal and non-verbal communications flow. One approach would be to team a younger female executive with a cohort of local Japanese representatives with many years of negotiating experience.

- **Rule #4: Listen Before Making a Point**

Rule number four is to be a good listener. The most successful negotiator isn't necessarily the person who talks the loudest or the longest. By listening well, the negotiator shows that he or she is seeking to understand and will accept a reasonable compromise.

The flipside to being a good listener is that one never reveals essential information in the first meeting. That's because the initial meeting is about learning what each side wants and the best way to proceed. The most effective negotiators also know that good timing is key to clearly communicating one's position.

- **Rule #5: Lead Discussions Humbly**

Rule number five is to be humble but assertive. That way, the negotiator shows the other side a willingness to enter into meaningful discussions that often lead negotiations to win-win solutions.

- **Rule #6: Trust Opponents but Do Homework**

The foundation for all relationships is trust. Negotiators must be as accommodating as possible, particularly in face-to-face meetings. After all, the only way that negotiations can move forward is if all parties trust each other.

Still, all major findings presented at negotiations must be thoroughly vetted and fact-checked with authoritative sources.

If the other side has valid points, the negotiator is respectfully verifying another perspective. This should reassure everyone that the negotiators want an optimal solution based on essential facts.

(http://suite101.com/article/international-trade-negotiation-tips-a85876)

Answer the following question:

What are the tips that Dana Persia gives in international business etiquette?

Read more negotiation cases and business negotiation etiquette in different countries:

* Negotiation Case Studies
  http://www.negotiations.com/case/
* Negotiation and Etiquette Guides in 70 Countries
  http://www.globalnegotiator.com/country-guides-how-to-negotiate-in-70-countries.html

Project Eight
Business Dining Etiquette

Learning Objectives

After completing this project, you will be able to:

* follow the proper Chinese dinner etiquette;
* demonstrate the internationally accepted Western dining etiquette and table manners and increase confidence when eating in Western dining settings;
* behave properly at the buffet;
* follow the proper Japanese table manners.

Warming-Up

Discuss the following questions with your classmates.

- ❑ Have you ever been to a Japanese restaurant? Share your experience with your classmates.
- ❑ Is it considered rude to take a sip of your drink while still chewing?
- ❑ Is it wrong to stand when a lady excuses herself from the table? What is the proper etiquette when the woman excuses herself and returns?
- ❑ What should you do if you spill a beverage on yourself while dining?

Listening

http://www.unsv.com/voanews/business-etiquette/lessons/058/

Listen to the recording and fill in the blanks.

Coats and Ties at the Business Meal

(*Office ambience*)

C: Hi, Amy! How are you?

A: I'm fine, thank you, and you?

C: 我感觉很疲惫。昨天晚上我跟老板 Mr. Brown 一起请客户吃饭,很晚才到家。

A: ______________________________

C: 我觉得有个客户的举止很不得体。

A: What did he do?

C: 我们一入座。他就把西装外衣脱下来,搭在椅子背儿上。当时饭店里确实有点热,可 Mr. Brown 没脱西装,所以我也就没脱。

A: ______________________________

____

C: 那个客户显然没有想到这一点。不过 Amy, 我记得你告诉过我,应该尽量让客户觉得自在。

A: ______________________________

C: 因为过了一会儿,那个客户也发现,只有他一个人没穿上衣,所以觉得很尴尬。如果我是主人,我肯定会主动跟着他把西装脱下来。

A: ______________________________

____

C: 如果我是 Mr. Brown, 看到客户脱西装,我肯定会说,"是挺热的,我也穿不住了。"

A: ______________________________

____

* * * * *

(中午陈豪和 Amy 一起吃饭)

A: ______________________________

C: 还有,汤上来的时候,刚才脱西装的那个客户一下子把领带甩到了肩膀上,可能是不想把领带弄脏。

A: ____

____

C:原来男人戴领带是为了保护衬衣不被弄脏。那我们能不能把餐巾掖在脖子下面呢?

A: ____

____

C:哦,餐巾一定要搭在腿上。我以前见过不少人把餐巾掖在脖子下面,我昨天差点那么做。

A: ____

C:Amy,你能不能总结一下刚才说的,跟客户吃饭的注意事项呢?

A: ____

____

____

▶ Reading

Task One

Chinese Dinner Etiquette

To Chinese business people, the banquet dinner is a common way of entertaining and giving thanks to foreign guests. Banquets can be held to celebrate a variety of occasions from closing a business deal to saying farewell to a departing foreign business associate to reciprocating for the hospitality the Chinese may have received. Like many other aspects of Chinese business culture, there are rules of etiquette that both Westerners and Chinese business people should follow when invited to banquets.

Reception formalities

Be punctual—it is rude in Chinese society to arrive late. Guests should present themselves to the host upon arrival. This is important since it is the host who determines the seating arrangement, and in order to do this properly, the host needs to know who among the invited guests actually arrived. If one is more or less a stranger to the other guests and needs introducing, the host will generally take care of this, either personally, or by delegating this function to an appointed person.

One may bring a small gift if one is a low-ranking guest (a stranger or a near-stranger, a distant relative, etc.) while one brings a finer gift such as a bottle of quality wine if one is a higher-ranking guest.

Seating arrangement

The seating arrangement follows some strict rules. Usually, the first place and importance is given to the oldest member of the family. The first seat that is given to the most respected person of the family gives the best view of the room. If in case there is no seat at the entrance of the room, then the "seat of honor" will be the one facing the eastward position of the room. The second general rule is that the seating order proceeds in accordance with one's "social ranking". The person with the highest rank gets a closer seat to the "guest of honor". However, there is no fixed ranking between the seats on the left side and right side. This provides a huge flexibility to the guests. At Chinese meal time, Chinese people use a round or square table. Person of the most importance would usually take the seat the farthest away from the door whilst the youngest or the person of the least importance would take the seat closest to the door. Generally, seats on the left or east or facing the door are seats of the honor. For a round table, the seat facing the door will be for the guest of honor. The importance of the seats to the right and left hand are in descending order with their proximity to the seat of honor, and the ones on the left are better than those on the right if their distance to the honored seat is just the same. For a square or a rectangular table, if there are seats facing the door squarely, then among them the one on the right end is for the guest of honor. And if there is no seat facing the door, then the seat on the right end of the east sides of the table would do. For a grand banquet, the order of the desk shall be arranged as follows: the top table shall always be in the front or the center, the 2nd, 4th and 6th table shall be on the left, and the 3rd, 5th and 7th table shall be on the right. And the host and guest shall be seated according to their status and the closeness to the host. The host should arrive in advance and wait to usher in the guests, while the guest should be seated where the host arranged him to. Each seat will have a name card for each guest. Do not try to rearrange the cards as they are almost always carefully chosen in regards to seniority and importance. Trying to change the seating arrangement without a very good reason can confuse the Chinese hosts and possibly cause them to lose face.

Table setting

The table setting itself will usually look like this: a small bowl, a medium size plate, three glasses, a large porcelain spoon and chopsticks. The bowl is to be used for rice, soup or noodles. The plate holds regular food and can be used for bones, shells and other scraps. The largest of the three glasses is for beer, soda, yogurt and juice. The second glass, a small wine glass, is for wine. The third glass is for strong alcohol, particularly Baijiu, the national drink of China. The large porcelain spoon is a typical Chinese spoon and is used like a regular spoon.

Lazy Susan

A Lazy Susan is a rotating tray at the center of the table. It is put there so that everyone has equal access to the food; so that there is no bias. The basic purpose of the Lazy Susan is to make everybody realize that each one is honored. This is one of the signs of hospitality and equality. It is customary to start with the dishes at the guest of honor first, and then rotate clockwise after, but not starting with the host. If there is only one table and there is no obvious guest of honor, then start with the person to the left of the host and continue clockwise. This shows that the host is taking care of all of his guests, by waiting and being willing to be last in line for the food; it's a sort of show-face action. When there are multiple tables at a banquet and the guest of honor is not obvious per table, starting with the eldest person at the table is usually acceptable. It is rude to turn the Lazy Susan when someone is transferring food from the communal dishes to their own bowl, even if the movement is only slight and will not prevent the other person from still being able to get their food. It is impolite to hoard a dish. It is appropriate to take a small amount, then let that same dish go at least one circle before you take seconds.

Chopstick usage

The use of chopsticks is a must in the Chinese cuisine. There are many no-no's such as waving chopsticks around, licking chopsticks, or using them to stir up the food, gesture with them or point them at others. Don't dig in the food on a plate but just get the piece which you want to get. Don't pick one piece then drop it back in the plate and change to another piece. Do not impale food with chopsticks. Unless they are disposable, chopsticks will be washed and reused. Consequently, don't use them to pick at your teeth or for other unseemly endeavors. Do not chew on the ends of chopsticks. When not in use, chopsticks must always be placed neatly on the table with the two sticks lying tidily next to each other at both ends, and place the front end of the chopsticks on the chopstick rests if the restaurant provides them. These are usually small ceramic rests placed near your napkin on the right hand side of your bowl. If there are no rests, place your chopsticks on the rim of a dish; they should never touch the table. If you happen to drop some food or your chopsticks on the floor, you do not need to pick them up. Service staff will do this and provide you with new chopsticks. Don't put chopsticks vertically in rice in a bowl since it resembles the incense sticks for the dead. This is disturbing to adults. Also, never direct a chopstick towards one of your table companions as it is considered as being a serious insult. If there are *gongkuai* available, do not use your personal chopsticks in shared dishes. Using your personal chopsticks when there are *gongkuai* available is the equivalent of spitting in the food and considered unhygienic. If you accidentally start using the shared chopsticks as your own, as soon as you notice it, you must quickly apologize for it and ask if it would be possible to obtain another pair of shared chopsticks, and place the new pair of shared chopsticks where they need to be.

Dining

At the beginning of Chinese dinner, the first wet towel served by the waiter is for the hands, not the face. Along with lobster, chicken and fruits would come a small basin Where some lemon slices or rose petals are floating on the water, which is for hand-washing not for drinking. When washing your hands, you should wet your fingers in turn and wash them quietly, then dry your hands with wet towel.

When the food comes, the host will usually begin the meal by eating first or by allowing the guest of honor to eat first. The guest of honor "breaks the ice" by taking the first drink or by proposing the first toast, just as it is the guest of honor who is the first to begin eating. Generally, the chief guest will say "shall we eat" first to invite everyone to the dinner. This politeness gesture will impress the rest of the guests and they will take it as a signal and will start eating. It's a rude thing to start the dinner before the "guest of honor". Hence, everyone start taking dinner after the chief guest.

When helping yourself to food placed on the table (on platters, etc.), always take from the side nearest to you. It is considered ill-mannered to take food from the side of the platter facing others, and it is considered outright uncouth to "dig for treasures" as the Chinese put it, or to "cherry pick" for choice morsels as one would say in English.

Banquet meals may have as many as a dozen or more courses, so remember not to overindulge at the beginning of the meal. It is considered good manners to at least sample all that is offered to you during a meal. Conventionally, all the dishes should not be eaten up completely, or you will give the host the impression that he has not provided a good banquet and the food was insufficient.

Dining manner should be gentle. For example, avoid touching the neighbor, be careful not to make the dishes out of the plate or spill the soup. Please do not make slurping sound when drinking the soup or chewing the dishes. Do not spit the bones or the fishbone directly to the desk. You had better cover your mouth and pick it out on the plate with your chopsticks. Do not take the dishes again after it falls to the desk. Do not play with the tableware. Do not use your hand to pick teeth. When you use the toothpick to pick teeth, please cover your mouth with the towel. Do not let the tableware make noise. After the dinner, you can use the napkin or the towel served by the waiter to wipe your mouth, but do not wipe your face or chest with it. Avoid burping or belching.

Business is not generally discussed during a meal. Good topics of conversation include Chinese art, food, and sights, inquiries about the health and well-being of family members. As in all cultures, conversations are to be kept light and general, without heavy politics or religion.

Toasting/Drinking

Drinking and toasting are an important part of the Chinese banquet. Guests will usually have their choice of various wines, beers, and spirits as well as non-alcoholic offerings. It is okay to decline alcohol. It is considered rude to pour your own drink without offering to pour someone else's drink first. It is common etiquette to never pour your own drink. Instead, you let the host or someone else pour your drink for you, and then you return the favor to him or her.

At the beginning of a formal dinner, the host will begin the dinner with a toast of welcome or make an introductory toast for the guest of honor, and then after the second or third course, the chief guest might say a few words and propose a toast, thereafter, toasts are free for all to propose. You can toast anyone from superior to inferior at their convenience. When someone toasts you, you should immediately stop eating and drinking to accept and toast in response. If you cannot keep up with the toasting, don't drain your glass because it will quickly be filled up again. Toasts are performed with the utmost respect using both hands around the cup or glass, raised to shoulder height, make eye contact with the host and all, smile, and take a sip or "bottoms up", similar as in Western culture. If one hand is used, it must only be the right hand and the Chinese do not typically clink glasses. After all the courses have been served, the guest of honor should thank the host on behalf of the guests.

Leaving the table

The serving of fruit signifies the end of the meal. Generally, guests do not linger much past the end of the meal. If you want to leave the banquet midway, you have to tell the host the reason and apologize for the early leaving, because it is not polite to leave without any words. Leave immediately after saying goodbye to the host and do not make the host too much time chatting with you at the gate. The host needs to entertain other guests and do a lot of thing; taking too much of his time will be inappropriate.

New Words and Expressions

banquet	[ˈbæŋkwit]	*n.*	宴会,盛宴;宴请
		vt.	宴请,设宴款待
		vi.	参加宴会
depart	[diˈpɑ:t]	*vi.*	离开;出发,起程;违反;去世
		adj.	逝世的
associate	[əˈsəuʃieit]	*n.*	同事,伙伴;关联的事物
		vi.	交往;结交
		vt.	联想;使联合;使发生联系
		adj.	副的;联合的
reciprocate	[riˈsiprəkeit]	*vt./vi.*	报答;互换;互给
hospitality	[ˌhɔspiˈtæləti]	*n.*	好客;殷勤
delegate	[ˈdeligeit]	*vt.*	委派……为代表
		n.	代表
flexibility	[ˌfleksiˈbiliti]	*n.*	灵活性;弹性;适应性
descend	[diˈsend]	*vi.*	下降;下去,下来;遗传;屈尊
		vt.	下去;沿……向下
proximity	[prɔkˈsimiti]	*n.*	最近;接近;亲近;(地方、时间等)最接近
rectangular	[ˈrekˈtæŋgjulə]	*adj.*	矩形的,长方形的
squarely	[ˈskwɛəli]	*adv.*	直角地;诚实地;正好;干脆地;正当地
status	[ˈsteitəs]	*n.*	地位;状态;情形;重要身份
seniority	[ˌsi:niˈɔ:rəti]	*n.*	长辈;老资格;前辈;上级;年长,年高
porcelain	[ˈpɔ:səlin]	*n.*	瓷;瓷器
		adj.	瓷制的;精美的
scrap	[skræp]	*n.*	碎片;残余物;打架;少量
yogurt	[ˈjɔgət; ˈjəu-]	*n.*	酸奶酪,[食品] 酸乳(等于 yoghurt)

rotate	[rəuˈteit]	*vt. /vi.*	使旋转;使循环;(使)轮流
tray	[trei]	*n.*	托盘;(浅)盘;碟
bias	[ˈbaiəs]	*n.*	偏见;偏爱
clockwise	[ˈklɔkwaiz]	*adj. /adv.*	顺时针方向的(地)
communal	[ˈkɔmjunəl]	*adj.*	公有的,公共的;集体公用的;公社的
hoard	[hɔ:d]	*vt.*	聚藏,贮藏;囤积
		vi.	积聚钱财;贮藏货物
impale	[imˈpeil]	*vt.*	刺穿,戳穿;钉住
disposable	[disˈpəuzəbl]	*adj.*	可任意处理的;可自由使用的;用完即可丢弃的
endeavor	[inˈdevə]	*n.*	努力;尽力
ceramic	[siˈræmik]	*adj.*	陶瓷的;陶器的;制陶艺术的
		n.	陶瓷;陶瓷制品
napkin	[ˈnæpkin]	*n.*	餐巾;餐巾纸;尿布
rim	[rim]	*n.*	(圆形物的)边,边缘
vertically	[ˈvə:tikəli]	*adv.*	垂直地
incense	[ˈinsens]	*vt.*	向……焚香;使……发怒
		n.	香;奉承
		vi.	焚香
companion	[kəmˈpæniən]	*n.*	同伴;朋友
equivalent	[iˈkwivələnt]	*adj.*	等价的,相等的;同意义的
			等价物,相等物
unhygienic	[ˌʌnhaiˈdʒi:nik]	*adj.*	不卫生的;不健康的
lobster	[ˈlɔbstə]	*n.*	[复数]龙虾
petal	[ˈpetəl]	*n.*	花瓣
		vi.	绽出花瓣
		vt.	用花瓣覆盖
platter	[ˈplætə]	*n.*	(通常为椭圆形的)大浅盘;肉盘,鱼盘;主菜盘

outright	[ˈautrait]	*adv.*	全部地
		adj.	完全的,彻底的;直率的;总共的
uncouth	[ˌʌnˈku:θ]	*adj.*	笨拙的;粗野的;不舒适的;陌生的
morsel	[ˈmɔ:sl]	*n.*	一口;(食物)少量
overindulge	[ˌəuvəinˈdʌldʒ]	*vt.*	过分放任,过分沉溺;过分纵情(于)(与 in 连用)
slurp	[slə:p]	*vt.*	出声地吃或喝
		vi.	出声地吃或喝
		n.	吃的声音;啜食声
toothpick	[ˈtu:θpik]	*n.*	牙签
burp	[bə:p]	*n.*	打嗝,饱嗝儿
		vt. /vi.	(使)打嗝;(使)打饱嗝
belch	[beltʃ]	*vt. /vi.*	打嗝;喷出
		n.	打嗝;喷出物
drain	[drein]	*vt.*	喝光,耗尽;使流出;排掉水
utmost	[ˈʌtməust]	*adj.*	最大的;最高的;极度的,极端的

Task Two

Western Dinner Etiquette

Invitation

A dinner party invitation will inform guests of the upcoming event. The invitation should go out early enough to give the guests time to respond and make plans. Two weeks in advance is usually enough time for a casual invitation to be sent. For a formal dinner party, the invitation should be sent 4 to 6 weeks in advance. Casual invitations can be an informal note or extended by telephone or email. For very formal dinners, invitations may be engraved or written by hand in the third-person style. The invitation include, at minimum, the full name of the host and hostess, the date and time the party will take place and where and why the party will take place. A celebratory dinner party includes the reason for the celebration. The host may inquire of his guests if there are any food allergies and food preferences, i. e. , likes and dislikes, and request an RSVP (short for "respondez, s'il vous plait", a French term meaning "respond, if you please") with a specific reply date.

Guests must acknowledge invitations promptly. Hosts need to know how many they must plan the dinner for. For less formal invitations, a telephone response is all right, but for formal invitations, a letter is expected.

Dress code

Formal wear: cocktail dresses or long gowns; dinner jackets and dark suits; tuxedos. Informal wear: a nice dress or pants outfit for women; jacket, shirt and tie (optional) for men. Casual wear: sporty outfit for women or casual dresses; sport shirts, sweaters, slacks.

Table setting

Table setting or place setting refers to the way to set a table with tableware—such as eating utensils and dishes for serving and eating. The arrangement for a single diner is called a place setting.

Setting a table is not as difficult as it seems. The basic rule is: Utensils are placed in the order of use, that is, from the outside in. A second rule with only a few exceptions is: forks go to the left of the plate, and knives and spoons go to the right.

Top row from left to right: bread plate with butter knife (top left of dinner plate), coffee cup (top right of dinner plate), water glass, wine glass, liqueur glass.

Bottom row from left to right: salad fork, dinner fork, dessert fork, dinner plate with salad or soup bowl on it, knife, small spoon, soup spoon.

The napkin is placed at the left of the forks or on the service plate. Some restaurants might place the napkin in the water goblet. If the napkins are placed in the glasses for the table setting, the napkins will be on the right, as the cups or goblets should be situated to the right of the main plate. In some formal situations, the napkin can be folded into an elegant pyramid or envelope shape. The napkin may be used occasionally to wipe the lips before or after taking a drink. Women should avoid soiling the napkins with lipstick, which is often difficult to remove.

Seating plan

For formal dinners of more than eight, place cards help guests to know where to sit, thus avoiding awkward seating. Use first names for a party of close friends, and first and last names, or correct designation protocol for distinguished guests. At very large formal banquets, the seating plan may be displayed at the entrance to the dining room or guests who confirm, and may receive a seating plan with their place marked on it. Sometimes male guests are informed in advance that they are to escort a lady to the table. If they do not know her, they are expected to get acquainted with her before the dinner, and say something like: It would be my honor to escort you to the table. Then, they must make sure to be by her side just before dinner is announced.

A man is expected to draw out the chair for the woman on his right. He sits down only after she is seated. At a small table, all the men wait for all the ladies to be seated before sitting down. At a larger table, where it takes longer for all to sit, when a woman is being seated or has to get up for any purpose later during the meal, the men in close proximity rise briefly. The host and the hostess are the last to take their seats.

Seating at a formal dinner

At a formal dinner, the host enters the dining room first with the woman guest of honor on his right arm. The other guests follow in couples; the hostess enters last with the most important man. The host sits at one end of the table and the hostess at the other, unless by so doing women would sit together, as is true when there are eight, twelve, or sixteen in the dinner party.

Then, the hostess moves one place to the left, and the most important man sits at the end of the table in her place. The woman guest of honor is seated at the right of the host. The most important man or the man guest of honor is seated at the right of the hostess.

Seating at an informal dinner

At an informal dinner, the hostess leads the women guests into the dining room followed by the host and the men guests. The hostess then tells her guests where to sit. She must always have the seating planned in advance in order to avoid confusion and delay. The host and hostess sit at opposite ends of the table. While customarily the oldest woman sits at the right of the host and the oldest man at the right of the hostess, guests may be placed wherever they will be happiest.

Each person stands casually behind his chair until the hostess starts to take her seat. Each person moves to the left of the chair to be seated and also rises from the left.

Do not lean back in the chair; yet do not sit too close to the table. Keep your feet on the floor. Your feet may be crossed if you wish, but not your knees.

Order of dinner courses

A formal dinner usually starts with soup and ends with the nut course. FIRST COURSE: appetizer (or "starters" as the British call it, or hors d'oeuvres as the French call it), soup, fresh fruit cup, sliced melon, or shellfish (such as clams, oysters, or shrimp). There is a choice of a clear soup or a cream soup. In hot weather a cold soup such as Vichyssoise or Gazpacho is a welcome change. The gentlemen will generally select a heavy, cream soup and the ladies will opt for the lighter clear soup. SECOND COURSE: fish course unless shellfish is served first. THIRD COURSE: the entrée or main course which typically includes pork, beef or poultry along with a green or yellow steamed or roasted vegetable and a starch such as pasta, rice, risotto or potatoes. FOURTH COURSE: salad. It should be a light, crisp refreshing salad with a light dressing. FIFTH COURSE: dessert. There are two methods of serving dessert. One is to put the dessert fork and spoon on the dessert plate. If the dessert is served in a glass bowl, the bowl is placed on the plate before it is served. If finger bowls are used, they are brought on another plate after dessert has been served. Another formal way to serve dessert is to bring the finger bowl, as well as the fork and spoon, on a small doily on the dessert plate. The diner puts the finger bowl, with the doily, to the left above his plate and places the fork and spoon each to its proper side. After dessert, the diner dips his fingers, one hand at a time, into the water and then dries his fingers on his napkin. SIXTH COURSE: fresh fruit crackers and cheese with after dinner coffee (demitasse) and decorative sweets, such as mints, are passed last. SEVENTH COURSE: nuts and raisins. A simple but complete formal menu could include: appetizer, soup, roast or fish with vegetables and a starch, garden salad, dessert and coffee. To add a European touch you could offer fresh fruit and cheese for dessert served with cookies, chocolate truffles, sponge cake or pound cake. The main course is usually served by the host himself, especially if it is a fowl or a roast which need to be carved. He will often ask each guest what piece he prefers, and it is quite proper to state your preference as to lean or fat, dark or light.

Announcing dinner

Guests must wait for the hostess to announce the dinner. At an informal dinner, guests may carry their unfinished drinks to the table. Very courtly men sometimes offer to carry a lady's glass to the table. But at formal dinners, carrying unfinished drinks to the table would upset the dinner arrangement. Leave the glass and proceed to the dinner table.

As soon as the hostess picks up her napkin, pick yours up and lay it on your lap. Sometimes a roll of bread is wrapped in it; if so, take it out and put it on your side plate. Remember the golden rule: always work from the outside in. Use the outside knife and fork for the first course (entrée), and then simply work inwards for each subsequent course.

Late arrivals

The formal dinner never begins before seven o'clock; the time usually is eight or eight-thirty. It is very discourteous for a guest to be late. Arrive at least five minutes before the hour set for the dinner. If for some unavoidable reason you cannot arrive on time, telephone the hostess and explain the reason to her. If it has been impossible for you to notify her and she has started the meal after having waited the required fifteen minutes after the hour set, go to her, offer apologies, and take your place at the table as quickly as possible. The host gets up and welcomes the tardy guest and introduces him very briefly to the two sitting next to him or if it is a small table, announce the names of the others. The tardy guest begins with the course that is then being served. There is no need to break away from the rest at the table to offer tardy guests a drink, or bring on courses that are over.

Dinner fork

When using the knife and fork together, as in cutting meat, the fork is held in the left hand so that the end of the handle touches the center of the palm of the hand, and the handle is grasped with the thumb and the first and second fingers, the first finger pointing toward the prongs. To get the correct idea, grasp the fork handle (prongs down) as if it were a hammer; then slide the first finger down the back of the handle; do not let the finger extend along the prongs. Never hold the fork at right angles with the plate. Don't use the broomstick grip.

After the portion of meat has been cut, the knife is laid down and the fork is transferred to the right hand. The meat is then carried to the mouth with the fork, prongs up. This is the American method. According to the English or continental method, after the portion of meat is cut, the knife is still held in the right hand and the meat is carried to the mouth with the fork in the left hand, prongs down.

The fork is held with the thumb and the first and second fingers. Vegetables should be eaten with the fork. Do not pierce vegetables or bread with the fork, slip the fork under the vegetables. Bread should be taken from the plate with the fingers. Put only one kind of food on the fork at a time. Use the fork to put butter on vegetables and jelly on meat.

Eat juicy uncooked fruits, soft or sticky cake, pie, and brick ice cream with a fork. When eating pie, hold the fork the same as you do for vegetables. Watermelon is eaten with a fork, cantaloupe with a spoon.

Dinner knife

Use the knife for cutting firm meat and other foods that can not be cut with a fork. The knife is held in the right hand in exactly the same manner as the fork. Grasp the knife handle with the thumb and the first and second fingers; slide the first finger out on the handle, but do not let it extend along the blade.

Cut chicken from the bone with the knife and fork just as you would any other kind of meat. Never take chicken in the fingers unless you are at a picnic where silver is not provided. After cutting meat, do not clean the knife by rubbing it against the fork or a piece of bread; however, keep the knife as clean as possible.

The dinner knife may be used to spread butter on bread if a butter knife has not been provided. Break off a small piece of bread and hold it on the edge of the bread-and-butter plate or the dinner plate to spread it. When this is eaten, break off another small piece and spread it. A whole, small biscuit may be buttered at one time without removing it from the plate as it is considered more delicious if it is buttered while hot. Jelly—except jelly eaten with meat-jam, and butter should be put on the bread-and-butter plate and is spread with a knife.

Corn on the cob is buttered with the knife. Spread a small area—not too wide—and eat this, holding the ear with both hands if you wish. Then butter more, and continue to eat as quietly and daintily as possible.

When the knife is not in use, place it with the cutting edge in, on the upper right arc of the plate; keep both the blade and handle on the plate. Always place the silver quietly on the china; don't drop it. Never let the knife and fork hang from the plate like a pair of oars.

When passing the plate for a second helping or at the end of a course, place the knife and fork in the center of the plate with the handles at the lower right edge; then there will be little danger that the silver will fall when the plate is lifted from the table.

Spoon

When eating soup, put only the side of the spoon to the mouth. Put the spoon in the soup, tip it away from you until it fills sufficiently, and then lift it to the mouth. Do not fill the spoon more than three-fourths full. Dip away from you with soup, but toward you with everything else.

If soup is served in a bouillon cup, you may leave the spoon on the saucer and drink from the cup. Vegetable soup, rice soup, clam chowder, or other thick soups are usually served in soup plates. Leave the spoon in the soup plate, not on the service plate.

Stir a beverage gently, not vigorously round and round. Never leave a spoon standing in a cup or glass. Ice cream served in a sherbet glass or an ice served with the meal is eaten with a spoon. Do not leave the spoon standing in the sherbet glass; when the spoon is not in use, put it on the plate under the glass.

In eating cherries or other cooked fruit containing pits or seeds, it is easier to extract the pits or seeds with the spoon before the fruit is put in the mouth. However, seeds, pits or bones may be removed from the mouth with the finger and thumb. Do not put potato peelings or fish bones on the bread-and-butter plate, on the table cloth, or in a saucer; leave them on the dinner plate.

Spoon and fork

When serving yourself with a serving spoon and fork, hold the spoon in the right hand and the fork in the left, using the spoon to lift the food from the dish or platter and the fork to hold the food in place while serving it.

Glass

Do not look around the room while you are drinking; look into the glass. Use the napkin for the fingers or mouth whenever necessary, so that you will not soil the glass. Do not drink while you have food in your mouth.

Finger foods

Use the fingers for bread, rolls, cookies, potato chips, small pickles, olives, radishes, celery, nuts, or candy. Bread, rolls, olives, radishes, and celery are put on the bread-and-butter plate.

All sandwiches, unless they are of unusual thickness, are held with the fingers. Thick sandwiches may be cut into small pieces and the pieces picked up with the fingers. Cake too may be eaten with the fingers unless the icing is sticky.

Finger bowl

Dip the tips of your fingers, one hand at a time, into the water in the finger bowl; then wipe them on the napkin, wrinkling it as little as possible.

Helping yourself and refusing

If a servant passes food around, he will pass the dish in at your left hand so that you can conveniently serve yourself with your right hand. Never serve yourself while the dish is on your right; it is then the turn of your neighbor on the right. It is polite to take some of everything that is passed to you. But if there is something you may not like, you may quietly say, "No, thank you."

Second helpings

The hostess may or may not ask if you would like a second helping, according to the formality of the meal. If she does and you accept it, you should pass your plate to her or to the servant with the knife and fork still lying on it.

Miscellaneous hints

At a small dinner party, do not start to eat until all guests are served. At a large dinner party, you may start to eat as soon as those near you have been served. Do not eat too fast.

Do not talk while you have food in your mouth, and keep the mouth closed while you chew your food. Elbows should not be put on the table when you are eating; however, between courses at a restaurant, if you cannot hear your companion, it is permissible to lean forward on your elbows.

If silver is dropped on the floor, leave it there. If an accident happens at the table, apologize briefly to your hostess.

If you must use your handkerchief at the table, turn your head slightly and use the handkerchief as inconspicuously as possible. If you cough or sneeze, use your napkin to cover your mouth.

Sit up straight on your chair. Do not put much food in your mouth at a time. Drink only when there is no food in your mouth. Try not to get into your mouth anything that will have to be taken out. Do not make any noise when you eat. Do not clean your teeth at the table or anywhere in public, either with your finger or a toothpick, not even with you tongue. Never tuck a napkin to your shirt, belt, and waistband or between buttons. Never wipe your mouth with your napkin. Never dip your napkin or fingers in your water glass. Never spit anything into your napkin. If a guest needs to leave the table but will return, the napkin should be placed to the left or the right of the plate. This indicates to the waiter or hostess that the guest has not yet finished eating. It is not necessary to refold the napkin completely, but the napkin should be semi-folded, not wadded or crumpled. It is not proper etiquette to place the napkin on the seat or the back of the chair.

One should avoid sprinkling salt and pepper onto the food. It is seen as an insult to the hostess and the chef. A good idea is to watch the hostess. If she shakes some salt on her food, go right ahead and do the same. If you do not like the taste of something you have just put in your mouth, be adult and eat it anyway. Typically, if you discover something inedible in your mouth (e. g., a fish bone, a fruit pit, a piece of gristle) you should remove it (as "dry" as possible) with the same utensil that delivered it (which may be your hand). Place it on the edge of your dinner plate (not your bread plate). When there are things on the middle of the table, such as bread, butter, jelly, pickles, nits, candies, you should not take any until the hostess has suggested that they be passed.

Conversation rules

To prevent talking across the table, which can get noisy, conversation rules say that for the first course, the hostess talks only with the man on her right, who is the most important male guest. The woman seated on the right of this male guest of honor, engages in conversation only with the man on her right, and so on. For the second course, the hostess talks only to the guest on her left, and so on. If the table seats less than ten, side conversations are avoided. When one person talks, the others listen. Diners do not cross talk across the table. Conversation during a meal is to be light, pleasant, and about non-controversial topics. Keep your voice low. Loud laughter is considered gauche.

A tip for women diners

Do not place your purse on the table. Put it on your lap, or on your chair, if that is possible. Today, even in the best of restaurants, it is not safe to hang it on the back of your chair, though you may do so at a home. Reserve personal grooming for the ladies room. Do not comb your hair, or apply lipstick on the table.

Leaving the table

At a dinner party, once the host places his napkin on the table, this symbolizes that the meal is over. She will start to rise from her seat and all the guests will rise from theirs at the same time. It is impolite for a guest to leave the table during a meal or before the hostess gives the signal at the end. Guests are expected to place their napkins on the table at this time as well, in a semi-folded fashion to the left of the dinner plate. Napkins should also be folded to the left of the plate at restaurants; this gives the waiter the indication that the plate can be taken away from the table.

It is not necessary to remain longer than thirty minutes after a dinner if the invitation does not include the entire evening.

New Words and Expressions

celebratory	[ˌseləˈbreitəri]	*adj.*	庆祝的，庆贺的
allergy	[ˈælədʒi]	*n.*	过敏症;反感;厌恶
promptly	[prɔmptli]	*adv.*	迅速地;立即地;敏捷地
gown	[gaun]	*n.*	宽大的长外衣;女裙服;女式礼服,晚礼服
tuxedo	[tʌkˈsi:dəu]	*n.*	男士无尾半正式晚礼服,无尾礼服
slack	[slæk]	*n.*	[常用复数](男女)宽松长裤,便裤
tableware	[ˈteiblwɛə]	*n.*	餐具
utensil	[ju:ˈtensəl]	*n.*	器皿,用具;厨房用具,炊具
liqueur	[liˈkjuə]	*n.*	利口酒,白酒,烧酒,香酒
goblet	[ˈgɔblit]	*n.*	高脚杯
pyramid	[ˈpirəmid]	*n.*	角锥形;角锥体,棱锥体;棱锥,角锥;金字塔
soil	[sɔil]	*vt.*	弄脏,弄污
		vi.	变脏
distinguished	[disˈtiŋgwiʃt]	*adj.*	著名的;卓著的;高贵的;地位高的
escort	[iˈskɔ:t]	*vt.*	护送;陪同
	[ˈeskɔ:t]	*n.*	陪同;护航舰;护卫队;护送者
hors-d'oeuvre	[ˌɔ:ˈdə:v]	*n.*	(正餐前的)开胃菜,前菜;冷盆

vichyssoise	[ˌviʃi:ˈswɑ:z]	*n.*	奶油浓汤;有马铃薯的奶油汤
gazpacho	[gɑ:zˈpɑ:tʃəu]	*n.*	西班牙凉菜汤
entrée	[ˈɔntrei]	*n.*	主菜,正菜;(正餐前的)开胃菜;入场权;进入许可/资格
roast	[rəust]	*n.*	烤肉
poultry	[ˈpəultri]	*n.*	家禽
doily	[ˈdɔili]	*n.*	小型装饰桌巾;垫杯盘的小饰巾
light	[ˈlait]	*adj.*	(果酒等)清淡的,淡味的;酒精含量低的;(面包等)蓬松的,松软的
crisp	[krisp]	*adj.*	脆的,酥的;易碎的;鲜嫩的
refreshing	[riˈfreʃiŋ]	*adj.*	提神的;使清爽的;使人重新振作的
dressing	[ˈdresiŋ]	*n.*	调料,调味品;装饰;梳理;穿衣;加工
demitasse	[ˈdemitæs]	*n.*	小型咖啡杯;小杯清咖啡
raisin	[ˈreizən]	*n.*	葡萄干
starch	[stɑ:tʃ]	*n.*	淀粉;(浆衣服等用的)淀粉浆;[复数]淀粉质食品
pasta	[ˈpɑ:stə; ˈpæs-]	*n.*	意大利面食;面团
risotto	[riˈzɔtəu]	*n.*	意大利调味饭(用米、洋葱、鸡肉等制作的米饭)
truffle	[ˈtrʌfl]	*n.*	[植] 松露;块菌;松露巧克力糖
sponge	[spʌndʒ]	*n.*	海绵;海绵状物
carve	[kɑ:v]	*vt.*	雕刻;切开;开创
		vi.	切开;做雕刻工作
fowl	[faul]	*n.*	家禽;鸟;飞禽
discourteous	[disˈkə:tiəs]	*adj.*	失礼的,无礼貌的;粗鲁的
prong	[prɔŋ]	*n.*	耙子;叉状物
broomstick	[ˈbru:mstik]	*n.*	扫帚柄,帚柄
grip	[grip]	*n.*	紧握;柄;支配;握拍方式
		vt.	紧握;夹紧

		vi.	抓住
cantaloupe	[ˈkæntəlu:p]	*n.*	哈密瓜,香瓜;[园艺]罗马甜瓜
blade	[bleid]	*n.*	叶片;刀片,刀锋;剑
cob	[kɔb]	*n.*	玉米穗轴;结实的矮脚马;雄天鹅;圆块
ear	[iə]	*n.*	穗,谷穗
daintily	[ˈdeintili]	*adv.*	讲究地;优美地;难以取悦地;可口地
arc	[ɑ:k]	*n.*	弧(度);弧光;弧形物;天穹
oar	[ɔ:]	*n.*	桨;橹;桨手
bouillon	[ˈbu:jɔn]	*n.*	[法]牛肉等的清汤
saucer	[ˈsɔ:sə]	*n.*	茶托,浅碟;浅碟形物;眼睛
chowder	[ˈtʃaudə]	*n.*	[美]杂烩;海鲜杂烩浓汤
clam chowder			蛤蜊浓汤
sherbet	[ˈʃə:bit]	*n.*	冰冻果子露
pit	[pit]	*n.*	[美国英语](桃、杏、梅子等的)果核,核
peeling	[ˈpi:liŋ]	*n.*	[木]剥皮,去皮;剥下的皮
icing	[ˈaisiŋ]	*n.*	结冰;糖衣;酥皮
miscellaneous	[ˌmisiˈleiniəs]	*adj.*	混杂的;各种各样的;多方面的
inconspicuously	[ˌinkənsˈpikjuəsli]	*adv.*	难以觉察地;不显著地
tuck	[tʌk]	*vt.*	把(被单、餐巾、衬衫等)的边塞进,折进;把……塞进,把……挤进
waistband	[ˈweistbænd]	*n.*	腰带,裤带,裙带
wad	[wɔd]	*vt.*	把……压成一团;[美国英语]把(纸等)卷成一卷
inedible	[inˈedibl]	*adj.*	不能吃的
gristle	[ˈgrisl]	*n.*	软骨;软骨结构
gauche	[gəuʃ]	*adj.*	笨拙的;粗鲁的;不善交际的;偏转的

Task Three

Japanese Dinner Etiquette

Whether eating with new Japanese friends in a home or attending a business lunch, following a few simple rules of Japanese dining etiquette will make you shine.

Being invited to dine at a Japanese home is usually a time that calls for the purchase of an *omiyage* or gift for the host. Though this is not expected, it will certainly be appreciated and is a nice, thoughtful touch.

In Japan, some restaurants and private homes have low tables and cushions on the floor, rather than Western style chairs and tables. These are usually found on *tatami* floors. The formal way of sitting for both genders is kneeling (*seiza*). Foreigners are not usually expected to be able to sit in *seiza* style for a long time, and an increasing number of Japanese people themselves are not able to do so either. In casual situations, men usually sit cross-legged, while women with both legs to one side. The former sitting style is considered exclusively male, while the latter is considered exclusively female. The most important guest sits on the honored seat (*kamiza*) which is located farthest from the entrance. If there is a *tokonoma* in the room, the guest should be seated in front of it. The host or least important person is supposed to sit next to the entrance (*shimoza*).

To begin a Japanese meal, when the food is served, join your hands in the *namaste* gesture and say quietly "*itadakimasu*" meaning I gratefully receive. Giving compliments to the host is often a polite and appreciated thing to do in Japanese homes as much as anywhere else. Saying a sincere *oishii* or delicious will be pleasing to the host as the food they provide are essentially their gifts to their dining friends.

At a Japanese restaurant, if you are provided with a wet towel, you should use it to wipe clean your hands. It will be hot in the winter and cool in the summer. Don't wipe your face with it, as this is very bad manners.

Food that may be readily available at the table will usually be *wasabi*, a green paste made of spicy horseradish that looks similar to avocado. *Wasabi* is normally eaten stirred into the soy sauce dish and due to its strong flavour, only eaten in small doses.

Natto is also likely to be present as some Japanese take great interest in people's reactions to the fermented soybeans that is even considered unpalatable by many Japanese. Should one have the ability to stomach *natto*, it has great health benefits such as having large doses of protein and is said to provide copious amounts of energy. It is usually eaten in the morning at breakfast but may turn up elsewhere.

If the piece of food is too big to be eaten in one bite (like some kinds of dumplings, croquettes, meat dishes, or vegetable chunks), you can either separate off a bit-size piece on the plate using your chopsticks or you can pick up the whole piece, bite off a mouthful, and set the remainder back down on your plate. Don't try to stuff it all in your mouth at once; an overflowing mouth is very impolite.

Be aware of how you treat the food! For example, *sushi* is considered an art form. As such you are supposed to eat each piece in one bite; two bites usually results in a mangled, destroyed piece of "art". Aesthetics matter a lot at the Japanese table, so try to be aware and respectful of how you treat the food served to you. If you're not sure how to eat something, try to sneak a peek at others around you, and imitate their approach.

Gently serve yourself a bit of sauce by pouring a small amount into your dish. It is considered rude to pour soy sauce directly over the white rice, or to use an excessive amount. Dip your *sushi* into the soy dish, and then bring it to your mouth for one or two bites. Don't hover over your dish. When eating rice or soup, you are allowed to bring the entire bowl closer to your mouth so that you don't spill any food. Slurping noodles, especially ramen or soba, is common but not a universal practice in Japanese dining etiquette. However, it is considered rude to burp at the table unlike in some other Asian cultures like Chinese or Korean, where it can be received as a sign of satisfaction. Similarly, nose-blowing in public is a serious offense, especially at the table.

If you wish to share your food, first you must place a morsel of food onto a small plate and then pass it to another person. Do not pass the food at the table from chopsticks to chopsticks—it's a very offensive gesture because when a family is sifting through the ashes after the cremation, the Japanese handle the bones of the deceased in a similar fashion.

Never plant your chopsticks in a bowl of rice—in the Japanese tradition it resembles the burning of incense sticks at a funeral. Instead, lay your chopsticks on the chopsticks holder or at the edge of your individual plate.

At the dining table, do not pour yourself a drink but rather serve others at the table. If you're out of tea, water, beer, whatever—don't ever refill your own glass. Also, the drink is supposed to be completely empty before it's refilled. It's everyone's job to keep an eye on the glass of people sitting near them, and politely offer to refill anyone who's running dry. If you need more to drink, try offering to fill your neighbor's glass. They'll probably take the hint and offer you up in return.

Talking about toilet related and similarly unappetizing topics during or before a meal is not appreciated by most people. Blowing your nose in public, and especially at the table, is considered bad manners.

At the end of the meal, thank the chef by saying "*Gochisosama deshita*!" —Thank you for this great meal! It is also considered considerate to empty your dishes completely because the Japanese are very economical. After eating, try to move all your dishes back to the same position they were at the start of the meal. This includes replacing the lids on dishes and putting your chopsticks on the chopstick holder or back into their paper slip.

New Words and Expressions

tokonoma	[ˌtəukəˈnəumə]	*n.*	(日本房屋中的)壁龛,床之间
wasabi	[wɑːˈsɑːbi]	*n.*	芥末酱
horseradish	[ˈhɔːsrædiʃ]	*n.*	山葵
avocado	[ˌævəuˈkɑːdəu]	*n.*	鳄梨;鳄梨树
unpalatable	[ˌʌnˈpælətəbl]	*adj.*	味道差的,难吃的;讨人厌的,使人不快的
dose	[dəus]	*n.*	剂量;一剂,一服

copious	[ˈkəupiəs]	*adj.*	丰富的;很多的;多产的
dumpling	[ˈdʌmpliŋ]	*n.*	饺子,汤团;面团布丁
croquette	[krəuˈkwet]	*n.*	(法)炸肉饼;炸丸子
chunk	[tʃʌŋk]	*n.*	大块;矮胖的人或物
remainder	[riˈmeində]	*adj.*	剩余的;吃剩的
		n.	残余;剩余物;其余的人
stuff	[stʌf]	*vt.*	塞满;填塞;让吃饱
		vi.	吃得过多
		n.	东西;材料;填充物
sushi	[ˈsu:ʃi]	*n.*	寿司
mangle	[ˈmæŋgl]	*vt.*	将(皮肉)撕裂,乱砍,乱压,压碎;轧布;损坏
sneak	[sni:k]	*vi.*	溜;鬼鬼祟祟做事
		vt.	偷偷地做;偷偷取得
peek	[pi:k]	*n.*	偷看;一瞥,看一眼
		vi.	窥视,偷看
hover	[ˈhɔvə]	*vi.*	踌躇,彷徨,犹豫;波动,摇摆不定;盘旋,翱翔
		vt.	孵;徘徊在……近旁
ramen	[ˈræmən]	*n.*	拉面;面条
soba	[ˈsəubə]	*n.*	荞麦面
cremation	[kriˈmeiʃən]	*n.*	火葬;火化
deceased	[diˈsi:st]	*adj.*	已故的
		n.	死者;[法] 被继承人
		vi.	死亡(decease 的过去式)
funeral	[ˈfju:nərəl]	*n.*	葬礼;麻烦事
		adj.	丧葬的,出殡的

Task Four

Buffet Etiquette

A buffet is a system of serving meals in which food is placed in a public area where the diners generally serve themselves. Buffets are offered at various places including hotels and many social events. One form of buffet is to have a table filled with plates containing fixed portions of food; customers select plates containing whichever food items they want as they walk along. This form is most commonly seen in cafeterias. Another form, known as the all-you-can-eat buffet, is more free-form; customers pay a fixed fee and can then help themselves to as much food as they wish to eat in a single meal. This form is found often in restaurants, especially in hotels. Buffets have become a trend, whether in a corporate event, wedding, or with just a bunch of friends, as they are cost-effective and a quick way to serve meals to large numbers of people. By following a few simple rules, you can have an enjoyable buffet experience.

Approach

Before heading to the buffet line for the first time, look for eating utensils at your table. If utensils and/or plates are already there, you don't need to look for them at the buffet table. Use a plate, not a platter. Remember, if place cards are on the tables, do not shift them around to suit yourself.

Buffets usually have one or two lines. If there are two lines, both sides usually have the same item so get in the shortest line.

Take your place in line. Gender, age, and status privileges do not apply in the buffet line, so don't try to get ahead of anyone and don't break up a couple or a group going through the line together. Keep in mind there are others behind you and keep the line moving! Turn away from the food and cover your mouth if you must sneeze or cough when in line.

Dishing

Do not use your fingers to pick up food in the buffet line. Use tongs and serving utensils to transfer food from the buffet to your plate. If one item is in short supply, go easy on it. At a restaurant or hotel, it is fine to ask to have a dish replenished. At a private party, don't ask.

Use the serving spoon or fork provided for a particular dish and put the serving piece next to the platter or chafing dish when you are finished. A hot metal spoon in a chafing dish could burn the fingers of another diner.

Do not put an item back if you took it and then changed your mind once you put it on your plate. Double dipping is not allowed. If you want dip or sauce, put a dollop of it on your plate.

Don't overload your dish. Take only an appropriate portion to help ensure there is plenty for everyone to sample. Going back for seconds, thirds, and fourths is perfectly acceptable. You can go get more after all the guests have had a chance to access the buffet the first time. Never fill your plate so full that you have to hold the food as you walk to your table to keep it from falling off. When going back for seconds, do not take your plate. Leave the empty one behind and a server will pick it up, usually before you return. Get a new, clean plate at the beginning of the buffet line. When leaving your seat to go back for more, place your napkin on the seat of your chair. Clean the plate each time, please.

Serving stations

When various dishes are served at serving stations, as at a brunch buffet, remember that the attendants are limited in what they can provide. Special requests are OK as long as they are easily accomplished. For example, you can ask for scrambled eggs at the omelet station, but don't ask for "sunny side up" if no whole eggs are in sight. And only ask for ingredients in your omelet that are in sight and readily available. Similarly, don't ask for an end cut of beef if you don't see one.

Plates

In a restaurant, plenty of clean, freshly polished plates should be available, which means you should not have to reuse a plate. When you're going back to the buffet for seconds, don't hesitate to ask a server to replace a plate or silverware or retrieve what you need at the buffet table.

In a private home, use common sense to determine whether you should retain your plate or ask for a new one. In any case, never scrape and stack your plates when you're finished.

Sitting down

If people invite you to join their table as you leave the buffet line, either accept graciously or find a way to decline just as graciously. For instance, you could say, "I'm sorry, but I promised Tom and his family that I'd eat with them."

Even though people at your table will be sitting down to eat at different times, it's still a good idea to generally keep pace with others at the table and engage them in conversation. If you need to leave the table temporarily, be sure to place your napkin on the seat or arm of your chair.

Standing up

If you're eating while standing up, it's even more important to avoid overloading your plate. That way you can circulate a bit.

Indeed, one of the few—maybe the only advantages of a stand-up buffet is that you can drift around and chat with a lot of people. For example, food at cocktail parties is often consumed while standing. When you settle on a place to stand, make sure you are not blocking a path to the buffet table or anything else.

At last, remember you cannot take home a doggie bag with leftovers from buffets. Don't even think about it.

Tipping at buffets

While it is typical to tip 15% –20% at a traditional restaurant, 10% is the norm at buffets for servers who refill glasses and remove plates. But as with all tipping, if your server is attentive, tip more and if you have to throw yourself in your server's path to get service, feel free to tip less.

New Words and Expressions

buffet	[ˈbufei]	*n.*	自助餐;小卖部;打击;猛烈冲击
portion	[ˈpɔːʃən]	*n.*	(饭菜的)一份;一部分;一定数量

cafeteria	[ˌkæfiˈtiəriə]	*n.*	自助餐厅
gender	[ˈdʒendə]	*n.*	(男性、女性的总称)性别;性
status	[ˈsteitəs]	*n.*	地位;状态;情形;重要身份
privilege	[ˈprivilidʒ]	*n.*	特权;优待;基本权利
tong	[tɔŋ]	*n.*	[复数,常与 pair of 连用]钳子;夹具
replenish	[riˈpleniʃ]	*vt.*	补充,再装满;把……装满;给……添加燃料
chafing dish			暖锅;火锅
scramble	[ˈskræmbl]	*vt.*	煎炒;攀登;搅拌;搅乱;使混乱
omelet	[ˈɔmlit]	*n.*	煎蛋卷;炒鸡蛋
sunny-side up			半熟的煎蛋;单煎一面的荷包蛋
retrieve	[riˈtri:v]	*vt.*	取回; 恢复; 重新得到
scrape	[skreip]	*vt.*	擦,刮; 擦去; 擦伤,刮破
stack	[stæk]	*vt.*	使堆叠;把……堆积起来
		vi.	堆积,堆叠
graciously	[ˈgreiʃəsli]	*adv.*	和蔼地;仁慈地;雅致地
temporarily	[ˈtempərərili]	*adv.*	临时地,临时
drift	[drift]	*vi.*	无目的(或随意)地移动;闲逛;漂流
doggie bag			食物袋(餐馆供顾客剩菜打包用);狗食袋
leftover	[ˈleftˌəuvə]	*n.*	残留物;吃剩的饭菜;剩余物
norm	[nɔ:m]	*n.*	规范,基准;定额

Exercises

I. Read the statements below and decide whether the statements are true or false. Write T for true and F for false.

1. When socializing at a cocktail party, it is best to hold your glass in your left hand.
2. During a business meal, it is permissible to place your cellular telephone on the

table.

3. When you finish eating, your napkin should be folded loosely and placed on the left side of your plate.
4. When dining in India, it's appropriate to eat with your left hand.
5. During a business meeting at an up-scale restaurant, a gentleman must pull the chair out for a lady.
6. You should dismiss yourself from the table if you need to sneeze or blow your nose.
7. You're hosting a dinner at a restaurant. You should preorder for everyone and indicate where they should sit.
8. The waiter's coming toward you to serve wine. You don't want any. You should turn your glass upside down.
9. Hold your napkin and utensils in your right hand, leaving your left hand free to use the utensil provided to serve the buffet food items.
10. If you are not sure if you will like something or not, take a small sample. You can get more on your next go-round if you like the dish.

II. Choose the proper table behavior when dining out or with others.

1. How will the letters "b" and "d" (in that order) help you at dinner?
   A. Bread on the left, drink on the right.
   B. They will remind you of good manners, or to "be docile".
   C. They will remind you to always compliment your host, "best dinner".
   D. Beverage on the left, dessert on the right.
2. When you are almost done with your soup and want to get at the last little bit, how should you do this?
   A. Keep spooning up as much as you can, then stop eating.
   B. Tip the bowl slightly, then spoon up the last bit.
   C. Tip the bowl and sip from the side.
   D. Leave the last little bit; it's poor etiquette to get every last drop.
3. If you don't drink, but wine is being served at dinner, what should you do?

A. Turn your wine glass upside down to decline.

B. Hold your hand over the glass, and shake your head at the host or waiter.

C. Announce your desire not to drink and ask that your glass should be taken away.

D. Allow the wine to be poured; there's no need to draw attention to yourself. You don't have to drink it.

4. What does Miss Manners say about how you should behave while dining at home alone?

A. You should behave as well as if you were dining with other people.

B. You should behave however you want—elbows on the table, eating without utensils, etc.

C. You should behave almost as well as you would in public, including putting a napkin in your lap.

D. You can relax most etiquette standards, but she insists you should still sit at the table, use proper silverware and not gobble food.

5. When is it proper to season your food?

A. Never; it's an insult to the cook. B. After your first taste.

C. Before you taste it. D. After you've had several bites.

6. If you stop eating briefly to talk or have a drink, where should you place your utensils?

A. To the right of your plate.

B. To the left of your plate.

C. Fork and knife crossed at the top of your plate.

D. Above plate, placed horizontally.

7. What is the only fork you'll find to left of your plate in a place setting?

A. Oyster. B. Dessert. C. Salad. D. Dinner.

8. When you are finished eating, where should you place your napkin?

A. On your chair behind you. B. On top of your plate.

C. To the right of your plate. D. To the left of your plate.

9. When passing someone an item on the table, how should you pass?
   A. To the right.
   B. To the left.
   C. Directly to whoever is requesting an item.
   D. Items should never be passed, and it's in poor taste to request something.
10. Say you're eating a steak, how many bites should you eat at a time?
   A. 1 – 2.
   B. 3 – 4.
   C. 5.
   D. You will generally be excused if you cut the steak, especialy if your dining is informal.

III. Put the following sentences into English.

1. 第一次参加西式宴会的人或许会惊诧于西方文化的餐桌礼仪。
2. 有良好的餐桌礼仪意味着知晓(一些礼节),例如:如何使用刀叉,何时祝酒及该有怎样的举止。
3. 宴会开始,先上一盘小菜,这通常叫做开胃菜。
4. 吃完自己盘子里的所有东西是礼貌的,所以不要往自己的盘子里放过多的食物。
5. 在中国的一些地方,干杯表示把杯中的酒一次喝光,但西方人则通常是呷一小口。

IV. Translate the following paragraph into Chinese.

Chinese eat with chopsticks while most of the Westerners eat with knives and forks. Some Westerners may be quite good at using chopsticks, but most of them are not, therefore when setting a table at which Westerners are entertained, it is always advisable to place knives and forks alongside the chopsticks. At Chinese dinner parties, the dishes are usually placed in the middle of the table. Westerners are not used to reaching for something over the table. But in China, it is usual to help oneself to the food placed at the center of the table. So when we entertain foreign guests, we should explain such table manners to them.

▶ Speaking

1. Read the text loudly, and try to recite the following paragraph.

A formal dinner usually starts with soup and ends with the nut course. FIRST COURSE: appetizer (or "starters" as the British call it), soup, fresh fruit cup, sliced melon, or shellfish (such as clams, oysters, or shrimp). SECOND COURSE: fish course unless shellfish is served first. THIRD COURSE: the entrée or main course which typically include pork, beef or poultry along with a green or yellow steamed or roasted vegetable and a starch such as pasta, rice, risotto or potatoes. FOURTH COURSE: salad. It should be a light, crisp refreshing salad with a light dressing. FIFTH COURSE: Dessert. SIXTH COURSE: fresh fruit crackers and cheese with after dinner coffee (demitasse) and decorative sweets, such as mints, are passed last. SEVENTH COURSE: nuts and raisins. A simple but complete formal menu could include: appetizer, soup, roast or fish with vegetables and a starch, garden salad, dessert and coffee.

2. Read and practice the following dialogue in pairs.

Gordon: I sure am glad to see you.

Molly: How can I help you?

Gordon: If I want to facilitate a casual atmosphere at my company dinner, what food and beverages should I serve?

Molly: Will you be hiring a craft service caterer?

Gordon: No, I will be doing it all in house.

Molly: Then I suggest you set up a buffet with appropriate finger food and draft beer.

Gordon: What about for non-drinkers?

Molly: Non-drinkers like mineral water, a variety of juices and soft drinks.

Gordon: Is that all?

Molly: You have to decide if you want regular or paper plates.

Gordon: Planning a business dinner is a hard work.

Molly: This is only the tip of the iceberg. (The beginning)

▶ Acting

Students form groups by themselves and role play. The instructor comments on performance and grade the students' work.

1. Suppose each group is in a Western-style restaurant, please set a table with tableware.
2. Suppose each group will entertain business associates at home, one played the role of the host and one the hostess, the others business associates, please arrange the seating.

▶ Supplementary Listening

* Business Etiquette (The Continental and American Table Manners, The Details of Dining Out, Food (1, 2), RSVP—Reply, if you please, etc.)
  http://www.voanews.cn/voaet/17705.htm
  Listen to the dialogues and dictate down the important points.
* Chinese Dining Etiquette
  http://www.ehow.com/videos-on_7260_chinese-dining-etiquette.html
* Table Manners Across Cultures
  http://www.videojug.com/interview/table-manners-across-cultures-2
* Dinner Etiquette
  http://www.cctv.com/english/special/chinese/20090817/107298.shtml
  Watch the videos and dictate down the important points.

▶ Supplementary Reading

International Dining Etiquette

The country you are visiting may have very different dining etiquette rules than what you are used to. Depending on the country, be prepared to sit on the floor, eat with your hands, not eat with your hands, or try some exotic foods. To avoid too many surprises, take some time to review the dining etiquette rules common at your destination. Have a humble and respectful attitude when you make a mistake.

Asia

Everywhere in Asia you will be expected to eat with chopsticks. Try to use them if you can. A few guidelines will help you cope with chopsticks:

Ask for help if you need it. Your hosts will probably be flattered and pleased to help. Use chopsticks as a scoop if you cannot manage more intricate movements. (think about practicing at home for a week or two before you leave) Use the small end of a chopstick as your eating utensil, and the large end to serve others. Rest chopsticks on your plate or a chopstick rest when not using them. Never rest them in or across a rice bowl.

. You may use your rice bowl as a safety net, holding it close to your mouth as you eat.

Africa

Africa is so huge, so diverse, so complicated, and so rich that it is difficult to say much about a shared dining etiquette across the continent. A few general things exist that can be pointed out, however.

Africans are famous for the pleasure they take in eating and entertaining and for their generosity. If you're invited to someone's home almost anywhere in Africa, be prepared to be impressed by your host's generosity. In many countries, you will find no utensils of any kind and will be expected to eat with your hands. Remember, in Muslim countries, not to eat with your left hand. Watch your hosts in other countries for similar taboos and follow their lead.

Middle East

Arabs are known for their hospitality and their meals, which often start considerably later than ours. You may be expected to take several helpings, so pace yourself.

Alcoholic beverages are becoming more common even in Muslim countries, but Muslims do not drink, so do not ask for alcoholic beverages. Even when drinking is permitted, drunkenness is considered gauche.

If you eat with your fingers, use only your right hand to eat.

Israeli food is both mid-eastern and western. Eating customs are the same, generally, as in the West.

Central America and South America Caribbean

Business lunches are common throughout Latin America, and usually long, from 1:00 or 2:00 p. m. until 3:00 or 4:00 p. m. Dinner is a purely social event, and can occur very late; it's not unusual to sit down to dinner at 10:00 or 11:00 p. m. throughout Latin America. In general, you should keep your hands above the table at all times when eating, and pass food and drink with your right hand.

Western Europe, Mediterranean Europe and Eastern Europe

Throughout Europe, table manners are much like those in the United States, and you will feel comfortable despite a few minor differences.

The minor differences:

Europeans eat using the Continental style. When using this style, hold your fork in your left hand and your knife in your right. You then eat with your fork still in your left hand. The fork and knife should remain in your hands at all times.

Europeans tend to be more strict about table manners than Americans are. Do not rest your elbows on the table, but keep both hands above the table at all times. Accomplish this by resting your wrists on the edge of the table.

Never tilt your chair back on two legs. Never push food onto a fork with your finger.

European breakfasts are usually buffets with meats, cheese, and hard rolls. You may also find soft boiled eggs served in an egg cup.

When it comes to table manners, there are a lot of rules that strongly evolved due to practice. Here are some strange table manners around the world.

Tanzania

In Tanzania, it is impolite to get in time to dinner. It is preferable to be late 15 –30 minutes. If you eat while sitting down on the carpet or mat, it is not polite to keep your soles at sight. The oldest person at the table will be served first, while the host eats the last. Besides, in Tanzania it is rude to smell the food.

Russia

Everyone knows that Russian people are extremely famous for their hospitality. When in Russia, leave a bit of food on your plate to show the host that there was plenty to eat. Moreover, never refuse an offer of vodka or other alcoholic beverages as it is considered rude. When leaving the table, don't do it until you are invited to. The guest of honor is usually the first to get up. In order to show their respect for food, throwing it or being disrespectful to bread is considered a sin in Russia.

Afghanistan

In Afghanistan, the guests are placed far from the door. They are the first to be served and they have to eat the most, while the hosts eat at the end and less. A good host has to ask at least three times if the guests want another serving, and these have to refuse at least three times also. If someone drops bread on the floor, this should be lifted, kissed and only after put somewhere else. Food is traditionally eaten with bare hands and only the right hand should be used.

Japan

If you are ever invited to have dinner in Japan, you need to wait for the host to invite you three times before you start eating. When eating noodles, slurping noise is a tradition, unless you want to be taken as a weird person. Besides, it is polite to lift small bowls of rice or soup. Japanese people say that inhaling air while eating noodles improves their taste. Remember that in the Japanese restaurants one cannot leave tip.

France

It is almost rude to be punctual, since Frenchmen rarely are "on schedule", i. e., they almost invariably need an additional 15 – 20 minutes to get things squared away before the guests begin to appear.

Chile

Dishes should be served from the left and removed from the right. Guests should be served first. Do not answer the phone at the dinner table. Always chew with your mouth closed, and do not talk until it is empty. Eat quietly and do not slurp your food.

Eat only one helping of food, unless the host specifically encourages you to take seconds.

(http://www.etiquettescholar.com/dining_etiquette/international_dining_etiquette.html)

Answer the following question:

What are the strange table manners around the world?

Project Nine
Business Gift-Giving Etiquette

Learning Objectives

After completing this project, you will be able to:

* follow the proper business etiquette for gift giving;
* identify cultural differences in gift-giving practices.

Warming-Up

Please answer the following questions.

❑ Did you give gifts to your friends or relatives? When and what did you give?

❑ Why do we give gifts?

Listening

http://www.unsv.com/voanews/business-etiquette/lessons/178/

Listen to the dialogue and fill in the blanks.

Souvenir Shopping

公司副总裁 Jason 到上海出差,由 Gina 接待。Jason 让 Gina 帮忙选礼物。

J: Hey! You know what might be good gifts for my ________________? Chinese antiques?

G: ____
____.

J: Oh, I see. That makes sense. You have to preserve your heritage.

G: ____.

J: You mean fakes?

G: ____

____.

J: Yeah! That would look cool. ____________________.

G: Good idea. ______________________________________.

And ... they might even bring you luck!

J: You can't beat that! But what about the kids?

G: Humm ... that's a bit trickier. There are, of course, lots of __________.
available like software or music, but buying them isn't recommended.

J: No, I don't buy counterfeits. Besides ... my sons have loads of computer games and CDs.

G: Hey! I know. ______________________________________.
They can go around looking like little Chinese emperors! I know a great tailor!

J: Ha! Perfect! They'd like that for sure. Wow Gina. You're full of great ideas.
____.

G: But you are my boss!

J: (*Chuckle*) Right! Then I'll make a note to myself! Really though ... I can't thank you enough for all your help.

G: Not at all. ______________________________________.

▶ Reading

Task One

International Business Gift Giving Overview

Gifts serve many purposes in business, they are used to build and maintain relationships, to show respect and appreciation, or to enhance the image or reputation of a company. Gift giving is a time-honored way of expressing gratitude or appreciation. Cultural norms, however, can make giving gifts to people from other countries a challenge. A gift is a social gesture that may be expected in some countries, and could be considered a bribe in others. Not knowing the appropriate guidelines can lead to embarrassment and problems with business relationships.

Some multi-national companies and some governments have very strict policies regarding their employees accepting gifts. To avoid creating a problem, it's imperative you learn the policies for the companies you do business with.

Countries like Malaysia and Paraguay, concerned with corruption, frown upon any gift that could be construed as a bribe. In Malaysia you wouldn't give a gift until you had established a relationship with the person. In Singapore, government employees are not allowed to accept gifts, and the United States limits the acceptable dollar value to $25.

However, in some countries like Japan, Indonesia and the Philippines, exchanging gifts is strongly rooted in tradition. Part of the tradition is the gracious style used to present and receive them. It's important to plan time and focus on the process.

It's very important in Asia and the Middle East to only use your right hand, or both hands, to offer or accept a gift. In Japan and China's Hong Kong, people use both hands.

In Singapore a recipient may "graciously refuse three times" before accepting your gift. But in Chile, gifts are accepted and opened immediately. And in Indonesia, small gifts are given on a frequent basis.

Always be cognizant of religious laws when selecting gifts. For instance, pork is prohibited in the Jewish and Muslim religions, so you wouldn't select a gift made from pigskin. As in India, don't offer a gift made from cowhide. Another prohibition for the Muslim faith is alcohol.

A standard to keep in mind for any gift you select is quality. Choose quality items that are not ostentatious. If you have gifts with your company logo, it's better if the logo is discreet. And don't give company logo gifts in Greece, Spain and Portugal.

Hosting a meal at a nice restaurant is always a good business practice. A fine dinner is a wonderful way to give a "gift to your hosts", to show your guests you appreciate the business relationship you have with them, and an opportunity to build rapport. People in Brazil, England, Panama, and Peru enjoy being invited guests for a meal, and the Greeks look forward to an evening filled with dining. In China, plan a banquet, especially if you are being honored with one.

New Words and Expressions

overview	[ˈəuvəvjuː]	*n.*	概述;概观
bribe	[braib]	*vt.*	贿赂,收买
		vi.	行贿
		n.	贿赂
imperative	[imˈperətiv]	*adj.*	必要的,势在必行的;命令的;紧急的
		n.	需要;命令;祈使语气;规则
Malaysia	[məˈleiʒə]	*n.*	马来西亚;马来群岛
Paraguay	[ˈpærəgwai]	*n.*	巴拉圭
construe	[kənˈstruː]	*vt.*	分析;解释;翻译
		vi.	作文法性的分析
recipient	[riˈsipiənt]	*n.*	接受者;容纳者;容器
		adj.	容易接受的,感受性强的
Chile	[ˈtʃili]	*n.*	智利
cognizant	[ˈkɔgnizənt]	*adj.*	认识的,认知的;知晓的,觉察到的
pork	[pɔːk]	*n.*	猪肉
prohibit	[prəuˈhibit]	*vt.*	阻止,禁止
Jewish	[ˈdʒuːiʃ]	*adj.*	犹太人的;犹太族的
Muslim	[ˈmuzlim]	*adj.*	伊斯兰教的
		n.	穆斯林;穆罕默德信徒
cowhide	[ˈkauˌhaid]	*n.*	牛皮,牛皮鞭;母牛皮,母牛皮革
		vt.	用牛皮鞭抽打
ostentatious	[ˌɔstenˈteiʃəs]	*adj.*	招摇的;卖弄的;夸耀的;铺张的;惹人注目的

discreet	[dis'kri:t]	*adj.*	不显眼的,不起眼的;不矫揉造作的;谨慎的;小心的
Spain	[spein]	*n.*	西班牙
Portugal	['pɔ:tjugəl]	*n.*	葡萄牙
Panama	['pænəmɑ:]	*n.*	巴拿马;巴拿马城
Peru	[pə'ru]	*n.*	秘鲁

Task Two

International Business Gift Giving—Detailed

If a country isn't listed in a category, it means gifts may or may not be exchanged. Should you receive a gift, and don't have one to offer in return, you will not create a crisis. However, this is a good reason for planning to host a meal. It becomes your reciprocal gesture.

Countries and areas in which a gift is expected:

- Europe—Czech Republic, Poland, Russia, Ukraine
- Latin American—Bolivia, Columbia, Costa Rica
- Pacific Rim-China, China's Hong Kong, Indonesia, Japan, Korea, China's Taiwan, Malaysia, Philippines, and Thailand

Countries in which a gift is not expected on the first visit, but would be expected on a subsequent visit:

- Europe—Portugal, Spain
- Latin American—Brazil, Chile, Guatemala, Nicaragua, Panama, Peru, Venezuela
- Pacific Rim—Malaysia, Singapore
- Scandinavia—Finland, Norway

Countries in which a gift is not expected or gifts are less frequent exchanged:

- Africa
- Australia
- Europe—England, France, Hungary, Italy
- Latin America—Uruguay

- Scandinavia—Denmark
- Middle East—Pakistan, Saudi Arabia
- United States

The information below will give you more details regarding cultural and religious traditions surrounding gifts, some of the reasoning behind the symbolism, and most important, helping you make the right decisions when it comes to business gift giving.

Cultures with detailed rituals for the ceremony of gift giving are the Japanese and the Chinese. And Nomadic cultures in the Middle East have a tradition of hospitality to travelers, while Latin cultures consider all relationships as personal. So any country with a population from these cultural backgrounds will exchange gifts as a normal part of building relationships and doing business.

Gifts are a symbolic way to show appreciation and further relationships and in European cultures they are given, but not as frequently. And there isn't the detailed protocol for presenting a gift, except avoiding colors or flowers traditionally used for funerals, or romance. Australia, Canada, New Zealand, United Kingdom, United States, etc fall into this category.

In today's world, with global companies, as well as countries populated and influenced by different religions and cultures, it's important to develop good business relationships by taking the time to learn more about the person you're doing business with. This knowledge will give you insight into choosing more meaningful gifts that the recipient will know was specifically selected for him or her, and be more appreciated.

The following details on different cultures and religions are guidelines to follow when selecting and giving gifts.

Chinese business gift giving culture

Countries in the world with a Chinese cultural influence, a collectivist attitude, accept gifts with a reserved demeanor. In order not to appear greedy, a gift will not be immediately taken, but refused three times before finally being accepted. Each time it's refused, you as the giver must graciously continue to offer the gift. And once it's taken, tell the person you're happy it's been accepted. Do not brag about your gift in front of the recipient.

The gift is offered using both hands and must be gift-wrapped; though it won't be opened in front of you. It will be set aside and opened later. This tradition eliminates any concern that the recipient's face might show any disappointment with the gift.

If you're presented a gift, follow the same process of refusing it three times then accept it with both hands. You'll also not open it, but wait until later.

In China, official business policy considers gifts as bribes, which are illegal. Though the policy is softening, there may be times when a gift you offer will absolutely not be accepted. Should you find yourself in this situation, graciously say you understand and withdraw it. The gift should only be given after all business has been concluded so as to avoid the appearance of trying to influence the outcome and to eliminate the appearance of bribery.

A good guideline if there's a concern is to offer a gift, saying you're giving it on behalf of your company. It's important to always honor the most senior person, so he will be the individual you actually present with the gift, stating you want him to accept it on behalf of his company. This gesture, company to company, will usually circumvent any problem regarding undue influence. If you have several gifts to present, never give the same item to people of different rank or stature. The more senior the person, the more expensive the gift. Acceptable gifts for a company include items from your country or city, such as handicrafts, or an illustrated book. Be sure to bring a supply of these items with you, so that you can reciprocate if it happens that you are presented with a gift.

Typically one person is not singled out to receive a special gift, especially in front of a group. If you've established a good working relationship with someone and want to give a gift, arrange a time when the two of you are alone to present it. Then when you do give it, be sure to say it's being offered as a gesture of your friendship, not business.

A gift's value should be commensurate with the level of the business dealings. This applies both to an individual's gift and a corporate gift. There are times when an expensive gift fits the occasion and circumstance, but an overly extravagant one could create complications or embarrassment, as the recipient may not be able to reciprocate.

In Chinese culture symbolism is important, with colors and numbers having special meaning. For instance, at Chinese New Year, money may be given in a red envelope; it must be even amount, using an even number of new bills.

Red is a lucky color; pink and yellow represent happiness; and the number 8 is the luckiest number, while the number six is considered a blessing. The colors black, white and blue and the #4, or four of anything, are negatively associated with death or funerals. Also included in this category are clocks, handkerchiefs, and straw sandals, because they are associated with funeral ceremonies.

Another example of the importance of color is if a man wears a green hat it indicates his wife has been unfaithful to him.

Sharp objects like knives or scissors represent a "severing of a friendship or relationship" —include a business relationship. Avoid giving gifts in odd numbers.

You don't want to inadvertently select a gift that has a negative or unlucky association. And because of the symbolism, it can happen. For instance, a fine writing pen would be a good gift, unless it has red ink, which signals the end of a relationship.

Early in your business relationships, you may want to make your gift selections from a local store where you'll be given the proper information and direction. At least it's wise to have items gift wrapped once you've arrived in the country, to eliminate incorrect choices for colors and types of paper. Avoid giving gifts wrapped in yellow with black writing; that combination is reserved for giving gifts to the dead. Some regions may vary in their color meanings, so when in doubt, consult a hotel or gift shop for the appropriate color paper.

Japanese business gift giving culture

In Japan gift giving is an art form, representing friendship, respect, and gratitude. The ceremony is important; the gift is always in a gift box, or beautifully wrapped in quality paper, and given with great respect. Because the symbolism is what's important, frequently the actual gift may be very modest.

There's an expectation a gift will be offered at the first meeting, and gifts will continue to be part of your business dealings. Come prepared to that first meeting with a beautifully wrapped, quality gift that's not extravagant. It's a gesture that you're looking forward to a long lasting relationship.

One custom is to reciprocate with a gift that's half the value of a gift received. If your gift is too expensive, it could create an awkward situation, even at half the value.

Don't be surprised, however, especially if you're a high level executive, to receive a lavish gift. The Japanese executive will consider your status and the business relationship when selecting your gift. As I said, it's an art form.

If you have a gift to present, don't pop up at the end of the meeting with it. You don't want to surprise your Japanese associate. The proper procedure is to tell him or her sometime during the meeting that you have a small gift, or gifts you'll want to present at the end of the meeting. This verbal cue respects the protocol, and allows the opportunity to make arrangements for any additional people who may need to come into the meeting for the presentation.

When you offer your gift, hold it in both hands and bow, saying words that let the person know, "this gift is insignificant in comparison to the importance of the relationship". Saying it's "a small thing", even if the gift is expensive, conveys this sentiment.

The Japanese will politely refuse a gift once or twice before accepting it. And it will not be opened in your presence. When a gift is offered to you, follow this same ceremony. Politely refuse once or twice, and then accept it with both hands, saving it to open later.

In addition to gifts being routinely given for various occasions or meetings, there are two "gift giving" seasons each year. One is mid-summer (O-Chugen) and the other at the end of the year (O-Seibo). A gift should be given during each of these seasons.

Gifts of food or liquor (cookies, expensive candy, and fruit) are always good choices especially for modest gifts. If you're bringing a gift from your home country, make sure it's not "made in Japan". And don't select company items with your logo that may be a promotional item and look cheap.

Because of the long held traditions, you may choose to shop for, or at least have your gifts wrapped by a store, after you arrive in Japan. This way you'll know your gift will be correct.

In Japan symbolism is important. A gift with a pair of items is considered lucky, but sets of four or nine are unlucky.

Plus, the number 4 also means death; and the color red is associated with funerals, so don't give a pen with red ink, and don't write out a card using red. Books aren't appropriate; and sharp objects like knives, scissors, and letter openers symbolize "severing a relationship".

Rather than looking at the ceremony and symbolism as obstacles, learn about them so you're comfortable. Then this wonderful tradition of exchanging gifts will add to the enjoyment of your business relationships.

Latin business gift giving culture

Latin cultures don't have formal or traditional ceremonies surrounding gift giving. However, business relationships are developed as personal relationships. And in order to build a strong and lasting friendship, gifts are a thoughtful way to make a good first impression, and socially continue showing generosity, appreciation, and kindness.

Because relationships become personal, find out about your Latin counterpart or client's lifestyle. Then using these details, select insightful gifts that will reflect how important this person is. Always have the gift wrapped in a quality paper, as this is a subtle detail that can express the value of the relationship.

If you're a man giving a business gift to a female, in order for the gift not to be construed as a romantic overture, tell her you're delivering the gift to her on behalf of your wife, or your secretary.

Symbolism in this culture will also influence the choices you make for gifts and wrapping paper. Black or purple paper isn't used because it's used during Holy Week.

Items associated with death or funerals that wouldn't be used include handkerchiefs, and yellow, red or white flowers.

As in other cultures, sharp objects such as knives or scissors should never be given, since they represent a "severing of a relationship".

Jewish business gift giving culture

Orthodox Jews are not allowed to eat pork and shellfish. The dietary laws are very specific regarding which foods are acceptable to eat, and their processing and preparation. The foods that meet these stringent regulations are called kosher foods and have kosher labels.

Because wine is used in religious ceremonies, it's required to be kosher even for social drinking. So all wine and wine-based drinks consumed must be kosher, prepared and bottled by Jews.

Unlike wine, other types of alcohol are not required to be kosher. Therefore, you can select a fine bottle of liquor to give to a Jewish client or associate if he drinks.

If you want to buy a gift of food or wine, it's best to shop at a kosher store to guarantee you'll be giving an acceptable gift to your Jewish business associate. Even fruit should be purchased there to insure it's been properly inspected.

Muslim business gift giving culture

In the Muslim culture, the Koran forbids alcohol. Gifts of liquor or any product that contains alcohol, such as perfume, would never be selected to give. Also, forbidden are products or foods from scavengers, which includes pork, birds, and shellfish. So a leather item made from pig skin or ostrich could not be given, nor any food from these groups.

Other categories are also not appropriate for gifts. These include personal clothing items, which are far too personal to give as gifts. Dogs are considered unclean, so any dog item, even something with a picture of a dog would not be given. And knives because they have a sharp edge—severing relationships—are not appropriate.

Artwork that consisted of sculptures, drawings or photos showing the human body, especially a nude or partially nude female body, is not acceptable as a gift. And although nicotine is discouraged, it's frequently used in the Arabic and Middle Eastern countries.

A good gift for a devout Muslim is a compass. Each day he must face Mecca for prayers. With a compass, no matter where in the world he happens to be, he can easily find the correct direction.

If you're in a country that's not predominantly Muslim, and you'll be entertaining Muslim business associates, select a restaurant that serves halal food. And don't have alcohol served, especially if any government or religious officials are attending, even if you know your guests may drink in private. It's far better to stay more conservative when entertaining.

Gifts are presented using the right hand, or both hands. The left hand is never used alone to hand someone a gift, as it's considered unclean.

Hindu business gift giving culture

In the Hindu culture the cow is sacred, plus fish and all animal products except milk or butter are shunned. Therefore, you would never select any leather or food product from these categories.

Most Hindus also don't drink alcohol. Though some will, especially if Westernized, don't ever offer a gift of liquor unless you know the person drinks, and you've verified with him that it would be an acceptable gift. In some cases, the person may drink when traveling abroad or in private, but will not drink in public when in his home country.

Gifts are given and accepted using your right hand, or both hands; never only your left hand, as the left is considered unclean since it's used for personal hygiene. And gifts are not opened at the time they're received.

European business gift giving culture

Cultures without strong gift giving traditions, European cultures and countries influenced by these cultures, don't use gifts as an integral component of a business relationship. This doesn't mean an occasional and appropriate gift is not appreciated. It means a person is not expected to present a gift on the first meeting, or on a routine basis.

No matter which culture you may be doing business with, it's always professional to be attuned to opportunities for developing a more comfortable business relationship by hosting a meal, an evening at the theater or a sporting event. These opportunities may present themselves when you travel to the other person's home country, when the other person comes to your country, or when the two of you are attending a meeting or an international conference in a third locale.

New Words and Expressions

reciprocal	[ri'siprəkəl]	*adj.*	互惠的;相互的;相互补偿的;有来有往的
Czech Republic			捷克共和国
Poland	['pəulənd]	*n.*	波兰
Ukraine	[ju:'krein]	*n.*	乌克兰
Bolivia	[bə'liviə]	*n.*	玻利维亚
Costa Rica			哥斯达黎加
Pacific Rim			太平洋沿岸地区;泛太平洋
Brazil	[brə'zil]	*n.*	巴西
Guatemala	[ˌgwæti'mɑ:lə]	*n.*	危地马拉
Nicaragua	[ˌnikə'rægjuə]	*n.*	尼加拉瓜
Venezuela	[ˌveni'zweilə]	*n.*	委内瑞拉
Scandinavia	[ˌskændi'neiviə]	*n.*	斯堪的纳维亚
Finland	['finlənd]	*n.*	芬兰
Norway	['nɔ:wei]	*n.*	挪威
Pakistan	['pækistæn]	*n.*	巴基斯坦
Saudi Arabia			沙特阿拉伯
nomadic	[nəu'mædik]	*adj.*	游牧的,游牧生活的;流浪的
funeral	['fju:nərəl]	*n.*	丧葬,葬礼,丧礼
collectivist	[kə'lektivist]	*n.*	集体主义者
		adj.	集体主义的
demeanor	[di'mi:nə]	*n.*	风度;举止;行为

greedy	[gri:di]	*adj.*	贪婪的;贪吃的;渴望的
circumvent	[ˌsə:kəmˈvent]	*vt.*	用计谋取胜,智胜;(巧妙地)避开,规避;包围
undue	[ˌʌnˈdju:]	*adj.*	过度的,过分的;不适当的;未到期的
stature	[ˈstætʃə]	*n.*	身高,身材;(精神、道德等的)高度
single out			挑出;挑选
commensurate	[kəˈmenʃərit]	*adj.*	同量的;同大小的;相称的,相当的;适当的
inadvertently	[ˈinədˈvətntli]	*adv.*	非故意地;不注意地
extravagant	[ikˈstrævəgənt]	*adj.*	奢侈的;浪费的;过度的;放纵的
lavish	[ˈlæviʃ]	*adj.*	浪费的;丰富的;大方的
		vt.	浪费;慷慨给予;滥用
pop up			突然出现
overture	[ˈəuvətjuə]	*n.*	前奏曲;提案;序幕
		vt.	提议;为……奏前奏曲
stringent	[ˈstrindʒənt]	*adj.*	严格的,严厉的;严重的;迫切的,有说服力的
regulation	[ˌregjuˈleiʃən]	*n.*	管理;规则;校准
kosher	[ˈkəuʃə]	*adj.*	(食物等)按犹太教规制成的;供应符合犹太教规的洁净食物的;按犹太传统烹饪法制作的;[美国口语]真的,真正的;合适的;正确的;合法的
Koran	[kɔˈrɑ:n]	*n.*	可兰经,古兰经
scavenger	[ˈskævindʒə]	*n.*	食腐动物;清道夫;[助剂]清除剂;拾荒者
ostrich	[ˈɔ:stritʃ]	*n.*	鸵鸟;鸵鸟般的人[复数 ostriches 或 ostrich]
sculpture	[ˈskʌlptʃə]	*vt. /n.*	雕塑;雕刻;刻蚀
nude	[nju:d]	*adj.*	裸的,裸体的;无装饰的;与生俱有的
		n.	裸体;裸体画
nicotine	[ˈnikəti:n]	*n.*	[化学]烟碱,尼古丁
devout	[diˈvaut]	*adj.*	虔诚的;衷心的
predominant	[ˌpriˈdɔminənt]	*adj.*	主要的;卓越的;支配的;有影响的

halal	[həˈlɑ:l]	*vt.*	按伊斯兰教律法屠宰牲畜
		n.	伊斯兰教律法的合法食物
Hindu	[ˈhindu:]	*adj.*	印度教的；印度的
		n.	印度人；印度教教徒
sacred	[ˈseikrid]	*adj.*	神的；神圣的；宗教的；庄严的
shun	[ʃʌn]	*vt.*	避开，避免；回避
integral	[ˈintigrəl]	*adj.*	构成整体所需的；必不可少的；基本的；主要的
attune	[əˈtju:n]	*vt.*	使协调；使合拍；为……调音；调合波长

Task Three

General World Wide Gift Categories

There are some countries in which a small gift is expected at the first meeting. These include Japan, Indonesia, Philippines, South Korea, Bolivia, Columbia, Costa Rica, Russia, Poland, and Ukraine.

And in other countries you don't want to give an item with your company logo. These are Belgium, France, Greece, Italy, Portugal, and Spain.

Sharp objects

In many cultures, items with a sharp edge symbolize the severing of a friendship or relationship. In these cases, you wouldn't select a knife, pair of scissors, or a letter opener for a gift. Because of this common symbolism, it's better to select a gift from another category, rather than risk making a bad choice.

Locally produced product

If you're doing business in a country known for producing a particular product, local pride and quality dictate that you wouldn't offer that item as a gift, especially if it was manufactured elsewhere.

Good examples are: leather and wine in Argentina; leather in Brazil and Uruguay; beer and wine in Germany; wine in France and Italy; vodka in Russia and Poland; scissors in Finland; and silver in Mexico, because it's considered too common.

Electronic gadgets and office accessories

Business gifts that are useful for a businessperson, whether an executive or a staff member, are electronic items such as laser pointers, PDAs, calculators, and address books.

Desk and office accessories that make good gifts include fine quality pens, or pen and pencil sets, business card holders, good leather briefcases or leather organizers for use in the office or in a briefcase.

If the person smokes cigarettes, a nice cigarette lighter could be given.

Liquor

A quality bottle of liquor or wine always makes a good gift for someone who drinks alcohol, unless the person lives in a region noted for producing the product.

Chocolate

Universally, this is a good choice. There are many fine quality chocolates that make exquisite gifts for a business meeting, for taking with you to someone's home as a hostess gift, or for a thank you to a staff person who's helped you on a project. Because it can be boxed in various sizes, it also works if you need a gift for a large group.

There's even kosher chocolate for you to give to your Jewish business associates and clients.

Flowers

Flowers can be frequently used as a gift, especially if you've been invited to someone's home. You may want to bring flowers with you to the house, send them prior to the dinner party, or have them sent the following day as a "thank you". It's best to advise the florist that the bouquet is to be a gift, and the reason for the occasion, so an appropriate selection can be made.

In Europe, the old European tradition of always giving an odd number of flowers is still followed today (all except 13 which is considered unlucky).

In some cultures a particular color or type of flower is associated with romance or funerals, and would not be chosen to give a hostess. Red roses are frequently considered romantic. Funeral associations frequently occur with lilies or calla lilies, chrysanthemums, Frangipani, white roses, marigolds, carnations, heather, and white or purple flowers. In some Latin countries, yellow flowers symbolize contempt.

New Words and Expressions

Gadget	[ˈgædʒit]	*n.*	小玩意;小器具;小配件;诡计
electronic	[ˌilekˈtrɔnik]	*adj.*	电子的
laser pointer			激光教鞭,激光棒;激光指示器
PDA (abbr.)			个人数字助理(等于 Personal Digital Assistant)
lighter	[ˈlaitə]	*n.*	打火机;驳船;点火者
exquisite	[ˈekskwizit]	*adj.*	精致的;细腻的;优美的,高雅的
florist	[ˈflɔrist]	*n.*	花商,种花人;花卉研究者
calla lily			马蹄莲;水芋
chrysanthemum	[kriˈsænθəməm]	*n.*	菊花
frangipani	[ˌfrændʒiˈpæni]	*n.*	[植物]鸡蛋花属(Plumeria)植物,鸡蛋花
marigold	[ˈmærigəuld]	*n.*	万寿菊;金盏花
carnation	[kɑːˈneiʃən]	*n.*	[园艺] 康乃馨;肉色;粉红色
heather	[ˈheðə]	*n.*	[植物]欧石南;[植物]杜鹃花科(Ericaceae)植物;灰暗的淡紫红色
contempt	[kənˈtempt]	*n.*	轻视,蔑视;耻辱

Exercises

I. Fill in the blanks with the words in the form and tell whether they are fit for gifts or entertaining guests.

sculpture cowhide belt frangipani chrysanthemum marigold alcohol
compass carnation calla lily shellfish pork laser pointer

1.________

2.________

3.________

4.________

5.________

6.________

7.________

8.________

9.________

10.________

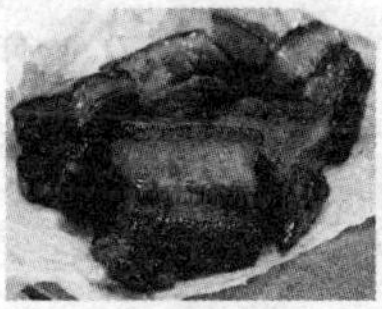
11.________

12.________

II. Read the statements below and decide whether the statements are true or false. Write T for true and F for false.

1. You may think that the beautifully wrapped box you're about to present to your host is a thoughtful gesture.
2. Chinese people usually open a gift in front of the giver.
3. If you're giving a pen, or signing a card, red ink is the best choice.
4. The number eight is considered unlucky, so giving or receiving eight items isn't a good thing. Just avoid the number four, which in Cantonese, is a lot like the word for death.
5. Wrap the gift well. Remember to leave the gift in the store's bag. Use colored ribbons to wrap a gift.
6. Chinese people who have had contact with Americans or other Westerners might expect you to follow the American custom of opening the gift in front of the giver. To avoid confusion, you can always ask, "Would you like me to open this now?"
7. When giving a "visiting" gift, find something the whole family can use. For example, give food or tea. Or, give something that is important in your home

country or community.

8. A bottle of wine is usually all right if you know host drinks wine, especially hard liquor (whisky, scotch, etc.) should be given as gifts.
9. Although workplace gift-giving should not be considered mandatory, many people and business do not exchange gifts, especially during holidays.
10. Flowers are good, but remember: roses are for personal relationship. Do not give roses.
11. America is a card-giving country. Americans tend to express their friendship through the process itself rather than the value of a gift.
12. Give gifts to co-workers in front of others; include a gift receipt so the recipient can easily exchange the item if necessary.
13. Don't assume the people in your office share your tastes.
14. You should be careful in the giving of gifts. You'd better give a gift in a job interview or prior to a business meeting.
15. Don't consider gifts that can be shared (with co-workers or family members), such as gourmet food items—especially those in festive tins or boxes.

Ⅲ. Read the statements below and choose the right answer.

When giving or receiving this holiday season, there's a right and wrong way to go about it. For example, is it okay to re-gift? Do you know how to handle an unexpected present? Is an email thank-you note acceptable?

1. Do you have to give a gift that has the same monetary value as a gift someone gave you?

   A. Yes, you don't want to look cheap.

   B. Yes. In fact, you should spend more.

   C. No. Find the nicest thing you can give in your means.

2. Someone gives you a gift, but you weren't planning on giving that person one. Do you have to reciprocate?

   A. Yes and make up an excuse for why you don't have her gift yet.

   B. Yes, but don't offer an excuse for not having one at the time.

C. No. Just say: Thank you.

3. When you give a gift, should you include the gift receipt?

A. Definitely.

B. Only for close friends and relatives.

C. No. It's a sign you didn't really know what to get.

4. Are thank-you notes necessary if you thanked the giver in person when you opened the gift?

A. Yes, in all cases.

B. Only for people who aren't close friends or relatives.

C. No.

5. Is it okay to give gifts to people who don't celebrate the same holidays you do?

A. No, it might be offensive.

B. Yes, as long as it's not a religious gift.

6. Should you give your boss a gift?

A. Yes, to show your appreciation.

B. No, it might look like you're kissing up.

7. Gift cards are popular, but are they a cop-out?

A. Yes, you'll be breaking etiquette rules if you give one.

B. Not necessarily. They're acceptable now.

8. If you are hosting a party, are you required to serve the wine, chocolate or other gifts your guests bring?

A. No, if you didn't ask them to bring anything.

B. Yes, it would be rude not to.

9. Which gift would not be appropriate to give to an acquaintance?

A. Cologne or perfume. B. Lingerie or underwear.

C. Alcohol. D. All of the above.

10. Is it okay to re-gift?

A. Yes, as long as you know the receiver won't find out it's a recycled gift.

B. Yes, as long as the item is in its original packaging.

C. No, it's dishonest.

IV. Put the following sentences into Chinese.

1. Japanese people may express their gratitude and friendship directly through the gift they have carefully chosen and given to the person they love and respect.
2. As a matter of fact, your gift to them would be appreciated all the more if you made it yourself instead of buying it from a store.
3. People's attitudes towards gift giving may vary from country to country, even though the desire to convey a feeling of friendship is often universal.
4. In general, American people don't care very much whether the gift is expensive or not.
5. In contrast, you are likely to get more cards than gifts in the United States.
6. Gift giving is different in different countries. In Japan, special gifts are sometimes given but not opened. Later, those gifts may be given to someone else. Many people have enough things and don't want too many gifts themselves. In Canada, many people will not give big gifts to someone else. They will pay for a park bench or a tree to help remember a person. In Sweden, doing something for someone is the best gift, people don't need to spend too much money, instead making a meal is enough.
7. This gift will help to improve the quality of our production.
8. But the fact you choose it and bring it all the way from China to America with you makes it very special.
9. You could bring some post cards of Chinese scenery or bookmarks or things like that.
10. You are very thoughtful. Chocolates are my favorite, you are so sweet.

▶ Speaking

1. Read the following paragraphs loudly and try to recite them.

If you receive a birth announcement from your friend or co-workers, this doesn't mean that you have to send a gift. It is not compulsory. If you wish to, you may give one. The best gift for babies is baby blankets, clothes or toys.

For a "Bon Voyage"(送别) gift, it is better to send your present in advance and not at the last minute. For most foreigners, flowers and things like magazines, cosmetics and drinks are preferable. Fruit is not a good idea. Nowadays, many people have quit smoking, so perhaps it's better not to send cigarettes.

For a close friend you may give something lasting and of high quality, such as a set of books or a wallet (with a dollar bill in it). If it is for a high school graduate, a dictionary or a pen set will do.

If you are a frequent weekend guest of a certain family, you may give some small gifts to their children. Things like jigsaw puzzles, a game, a book, candy and chocolate are proper for such occasions.

2. Read and practice the following dialogue in pairs and try to choose the correct answer.

Meeting with an Advisor: Giving a Gift

A: Hi Amy, do you think I could ask you a question? I am a bit confused.

B: Sure, what is it?

A: I met my academic advisor yesterday for the first time and I bought him a present, but he looked confused when I gave it to him. What did I do wrong?

B: Oh, he probably was confused because he wasn't expecting a gift from you. In US it is not necessary to bring your advisors or professors presents because they might get uncomfortable because they might think you want special treatment from it.

A: Oh, I didn't realize it wasn't normal.

B: I'm sure it wasn't a big deal, I'm sure he wasn't offended by it.

A: I will remember not to do that again, but that's different from my country.

B: Oh really? When do you give gifts in your country?

A: For example, in the new year when we meet for the first time and other festivals.

Quiz

1) The student gives her advisor a gift because ________.

A. she expects him to treat her differently

B. they are good friends

C. it is acceptable in her culture to do so

2) In which of the following occasions do people in the student's culture give gifts?

A. When they meet for the first time.

B. When they celebrate cultural festivals.

C. When they bid farewell to one another.

▶ Acting

Watch the videos and act out.

* Expressing Thanks

http://v.youku.com/v_show/id_XMzMzNzk5NDUy.html? firsttime=7

* You Really Shouldn't Have

http://v.youku.com/v_show/id_XMzM2MTk5Njky.html

* The Right Gift for Dad

http://v.youku.com/v_show/id_XMzMzNzk4ODUy.html

* Red Envelope

http://v.youku.com/v_show/id_XMzM4MzE3Mzky.html

▶ Supplementary Listening

* Business Etiquette (Christmas in America 1,2,3)

http://www.51voa.com/Business_Etiquette_1.html

▶ Supplementary Reading

Essential Elements for Purchasing Corporate Gifts

Purchasing corporate gifts is simple these days, thanks to the variety of products available online and through retail stores. Online shopping stores, e.g., Amazon, have a wonderful range of gifts at affordable prices. Through online shops you can even send presents to those who stay in another country. However, finding the right one still remains a challenge to many, especially with the vast selection of corporate gift ideas on the market. Below are the essentials of purchasing corporate gifts for either your employees or clients that will guide your every move in the corporate market.

According to OPEN from American Express (SM) Semi-Annual Small Business Monitor, the top corporate gifts are:

- cards or calendars (49%)
- gift certificates for retail or restaurants (26%)
- company branded items (23%)
- fruit/food basket or charity donation (both 18%)
- flowers/plants and wine/liquor (tied at 10%)

Before you run out and buy the "tried and true" corporate gift, consider when it is appropriate to give a business gift. Timing is everything! Here are some occasions when gift giving would be appropriate.

- When a client or staff member does a good job on a difficult training project.
- When you want to strengthen your business relationship with a client.
- To celebrate a business associate or employee's promotion or retirement.
- To celebrate a personal event of an employee, such as marriage or the birth of a child.
- When a holiday comes around.

Next, you may do as follows:

Check corporate policies: Many companies and government offices will have a gift policy limiting the dollar value of a gift or prohibiting gifts, which you must adhere to either while giving to clients or to your own employees. Be sure to check with your recipients to determine the limitations of gift giving so they don't have to return the item.

Determine wants: You may find it difficult to determine the kind of gift your clients really want. It is true that personalized gifts are always the best, but you may never have had the opportunity to know your clients on a personal level. If this is the case and you really want to make a difference with your gift, guessing will not help you to accomplish that. The best bet is to call your customers and ask them what they like, their hobbies, etc., to give you a great idea of what to buy.

Consider cultural differences: Each country and culture will have their own rules for corporate gift buying. It is your role to understand and respect these views so you don't offend them. For instance, in China, a gift should never be wrapped in white since it symbolizes death.

Go for quality: Any business gift you send reflects on the image of your company. Avoid lower quality gifts that can impair your image. Purchase quality products without breaking your budget.

Do use logo's sparingly: If you decide to put your logo on a client gift, make sure the gift is in the best taste and of the best quality. Your logo should be understated, not look like an advertisement.

Use hand written cards: A hand written note always makes a personal touch. You can attach one to your gift to show your client how much you care about him. Do double check spelling of names on outgoing gifts.

Spend on packaging: As important as choosing the right corporate gift for your client is the packaging of the gift itself. Spend the time and money on the wrapping to reflect your value on client relationships. If you lack the talent for gift-wrapping or have no time, use the gift-wrapping services available from retailers and shopping malls.

Deliver personally: If your business gift list isn't too large, consider personally delivering the gift to the intended party. A personally delivered gift will keep you at the top-of-the-mind with your clients, they will get to understand that you really care.

Know IRS deductions: Business gifts in US are tax deductible up to $25 per person for the tax year. This doesn't include incidentals such as packaging or mailing the gift. The type of business structure (i. e., partnership) you have can be subject to different rules. Be sure to review the IRS Publication 463.

Corporate gift giving is an opportunity to connect with your clients, strengthen ties, and share your holiday cheer. Adopting an attitude of giving will make the act of corporate gift buying less stressful and more fun.

Some examples of gift giving Etiquette

In order to highlight some of the different aspects of cross-cultural gift giving etiquette a few examples shall be presented.

Gift Giving Etiquette—Saudi Arabia

- Gifts should only be given to the most intimate of friends.
- Gifts should be of the highest quality.
- Never buy gold or silk as a present for men.
- Sliver is acceptable.
- Always give/receive gifts with the right hand.
- Saudis enjoy wearing scent-"itr". The most popular is "oud" which can cost as much as £ 1,000 an ounce.
- It is not bad etiquette to open gifts when received.

Gift Giving Etiquette—America

- Small gifts such as pens, business diaries and mementos with company logos are usually sufficient.
- Gifts are normally opened when received.
- When visiting the home, it is normally appropriate to present a gift to the hostess.
- A gift can be something small but elaborate for a person with whom you are close.
- It is important to avoid highly personal gifts.

Gift Giving Etiquette—Germany

- Gifts are expected for social events, especially to express your thanks after you have been invited to a dinner party at a home.

- Avoid selecting anything obviously expensive, as this may take the other person feel "obligated" to your generosity.
- A lovely bouquet of flowers (though not red roses) for the lady of the house is a typical gift. When purchasing this at the flower shop, ask the florist to wrap it up as a gift.
- For the company you are visiting, quality pens, tasteful office items with your company logo, or imported liquor are usually safe choices.
- Fine chocolates can also be an appropriate gift when you are invited to a home.
- An elegant, tasteful silk scarf can be an acceptable gift for the lady of the house.
- Avoiding bringing beer as a gift, since many of the finest brands in the world are already produced and widely available here.
- A small gift is polite, especially when contacts are made for the first time.
- Substantial gifts are not usual, and certainly not before a deal has been reached if you don't want your intentions to be misinterpreted.
- Clothing, perfumes, and other toiletries are considered far too personal to be appropriate gifts. Scarves, however, are acceptance gifts according to German business protocol.

Gift Giving Etiquette—France

- Do give a gift that shows that you are intellectual, such a gift of books or music.
- Do bring a gift for the hostess if invited to a French person's house. Good host gift ideas include flowers and wine. Bear in mind that France is known for its wine, so do your research and bring a nice bottle of wine! If you are invited to dinner, a dessert or cheese previously decided on also makes a nice gift.
- Don'T give an even number of flowers as a gift. Flowers should always be given in odd numbers, except for thirteen, as that is an unlucky number.
- Do be very careful when picking out flowers as a gift. There are a few taboos when it comes to giving a French person flowers. White flowers are typically only used during weddings, white lilies and chrysanthemums are flowers for

funerals, and red carnations stand for bad will.

Gift Giving Etiquette—Australia

Generally, gift-giving is not part of Australian business culture.

But, if you are invited to a home for dinner, it's permissible to bring a token gift of flowers, chocolates, a craft from your home region, or wine.

An illustrated book from your home region can be another welcome gift.

A preserved food product unique to your home region can also be a good choice; preserves must be canned or bottled, however, or they will be confiscated by Australian customs.

Bear in mind that your thoughtful choice is considered more important than the actual cost of the gift.

The above are a few of many examples about cross-cultural differences in gift giving etiquette. It is advisable to try and ascertain some facts about the gift giving etiquette of any country plan to visit a country on business. By doing so, you maximize the potential of your cross-cultural encounter.

Answer the following questions:

1. What are the essentials of purchasing corporate gifts for either your employees or clients that will guide your every move in the corporate market?
2. Please say something about gift giving etiquette in Saudi Arabia, America, Germany, France and Australia.

Project Ten

Business Travel Etiquette

Learning Objectives

After completing this project, you will be able to:

* plan a business trip;
* behave appropriately on a business trip;
* know different ways of check-in and their pros and cons.

Warming-Up

Discuss the following questions with your peers.

- ❑ Have you ever traveled to some places in China? Have you ever traveled abroad? If so, please say something about your travel experience.
- ❑ Can you give some business travel etiquette tips that every person should know before traveling?
- ❑ Do you know how to check in at the airport?

Listening

http://www.unsv.com/voanews/business-etiquette/lessons/149/

Listen to the recording and fill in the blanks.

Jet Lag

Mike 出差刚回来,遇到同事 Larry。

L: Hey, Mike! Good to have you back! ______________________________.

M: Hi, Larry. Yeah, ____.

L: Was it a rough trip?

M: ____.

L: Ah, jet lag ... the scourge of business travelers.

M: Yep. I flew from Beijing to Boston for a meeting, and then hopped back on a plane for a flight to the trade fair in Frankfurt. Then turned to Beijing before catching a train back here to Shanghai.

L: Wow! That's a lot of traveling! No wonder you're exhausted!

M: ____
____.

L: Yeah, it's hard. You know jet lag only hits if you travel east-west or west-east. You could fly from Germany to Cape Town in South Africa and you wouldn't feel anything.

M: Right ... because it's all in the same time zone. Unfortunately for me ... all my travel was between different time zones. I've gotta say: I'm really suffering! Why is jet lag so nasty?

L: ____.

M: So when you travel between time zones your body is thrown off its cycle?

L: ____
____.

M: Wow, that's a long time. I'm going to need a few weeks off!

L: (*Chuckle*) That would be best, but unfortunately our boss isn't quite that generous.

M: Is there anything I can do to make my jet lag less severe the next time I make an international trip?

▶ Reading

Task One

Planning a Business Trip

This is an age of globalization and nations all round the world have come very close. Multinational corporations have their offices in almost all countries and to carry on operations smoothly, they need some employees to move for some time and work at their foreign offices. When traveling to a different state or a different country, it's imperative to be fully prepared. From packing your suitcase to booking a hotel room to making sure you arrive at your meeting on time, there are plenty of factors to consider in planning your business trip. By making just a few sensible preparations before you board that plane, you can be less stressed and more comfortable.

Clarify objectives, budget and create your list of tasks for the trip

Clearly define your objective on why you are going on a business trip. Find out what your established budget is for the trip. Your task list is a clear, concise summary of all that you hope to accomplish in the target market. This may include meeting prospective customers, identifying potential partners, such as agents or distributors, obtaining information on competitors, regulations, legal issues and marketing and promotion strategies suitable for the local audiences.

Research

Confirm meetings and reservations. If you're traveling out of the country, learn about the local customs and culture and figure out exchange rates. If you happen to be visiting an unstable country, have contacts with representatives with your country of origin at the Embassy or Consulate to inform them of your business trip and objectives. Do research on the weather to help you figure out what you should pack, aside from business attire. Having a well thought-out agenda is key when going on a business trip. Research maps to see what the closest restaurants, banks, hospitals and other vital locations that are within proximity of your hotel and/or meeting place. If you have free time, consider visiting tourist spots.

Double-check documents requirements

You will always need identification at the airport, coming and going. You will almost always need a passport (learn about China passport rules). Although Hong Kong and Macau are parts of the People's Republic of China (PRC), as Special Administrative Regions (SAR), each has its own visa entry regulations. This also means that you might need a visa to the HKSAR or Macau from the Chinese mainland and one to enter the Chinese mainland from Hong Kong or Macau. You will probably need a travel visa (you may be given a blank form on the plane). You may need to show a work visa to enter a country for work. You will seldom need, but may want to carry, travel immunization records. You may want, but may not need if you are renting a car at an airport abroad, an international driver's license. Learn about all the travel documents you may want in the course of air travel and make copies! Some countries—like Chile, Kenya, and India—require a visa for entry; others, like South Africa, won't allow entrance unless a traveler's passport contains at least two blank, unstamped pages. You need to be aware of those requirements before you make your flight reservations.

Book your trip

Book a trip online or call a travel agent if you'd like to speak to a live person. You can find the most affordable deals on flight, hotel, and transportation all on one website. Know the difference between "direct" and "nonstop" flights, and always opt for the latter. Unlike nonstops, direct flights can touch down at other airports on the way to their ultimate destinations. And while stops are built in to the total travel time, the potential delays they can cause aren't; therefore, whenever possible, fly nonstop. Purchase refundable travel tickets whenever possible, as business arrangements and travel specifics can often change unexpectedly. Secure your travel tickets with a credit card to provide yourself with more purchasing power. Credit cards often provide travel insurance, warranties and other protection when used for travel. Make sure you purchase your ticket under the exact name that appears on your ID.

Pack for a trip

Purchase a suitcase in an unusual color or pattern so it stands out from the crowd and is less likely to be mistaken for someone else's. If your bag is black like so many bags are today, do something to make it unique to prevent someone in a hurry from grabbing yours off the carousel instead of their own. Tie colorful ribbons to handles and attach a sturdy identification tag to the outside of your bag, and include a copy of your travel itinerary and your destination address inside the bag on top of your belongings so that if it gets misdirected, a simple search will turn up information on where to find you.

Make a checklist of every item you plan to take on your trip. This will include toothbrush/toothpaste, clothing, socks, shoes, toiletries, pajamas, razor, deodorant and paperwork and possibly also maps, guidebooks, reading material, and hotel or rental car information. Bring empty plastic bags for dirty items. Place heavy items at the bottom of your bag. Pack clothing using the time-honored "roll" technique. Place breakable items, like jewelry or glass, wrapped in socks and tucked into shoes inside your luggage. Never pack expensive items in your checked bag. When you are packing things into a backpack, place the lighter items at the bottom and the heavier ones on top. Your bag will feel lighter this way as the pack rests on your lower back. It is also smart to place the things you use the most on top. Dirty clothes are perfect to pack at the bottom of a backpack.

Check the airline website for rules and restrictions about checked and carry-on baggage, and weigh your bags before you travel. Going over the limits often costs extra, and carrying items you shouldn't will cause problems at security. Safety restrictions vary between countries but include obvious safety hazards (knives in your carry-on, flammable liquids in any of your luggage), not-so-obvious hazards (nail clippers or files in your carry-on), and a few seemingly inexplicable items (an unopened bottle of water on US flights—unless you purchased it after going through security). Weight and size restrictions depend on the airline, so check their website ahead of time for more information. Most medium duffel bags and hand luggage marketed as carry-on will be accepted into the cabin. Avoid bringing peanuts on planes. These can cause allergic reactions in other passengers. If crossing international borders, don't bring agricultural items (fruits, vegetables, seeds), meats, or dairy products. Though you may be able to get away with it in some countries, many regulate these items to reduce the spread of nonnative species and disease. In the US, there are very specific liquid and gel allowances: You are allowed to bring a maximum of 3.4 ounces of a liquid/gel per container (not total). For example, a 2-ounce bottle of shampoo, a 2-ounce bottle of toothpaste, and a 3.4-ounce bottle of face wash would be okay. Better take solid shampoo bars and tooth powder, some places bar all liquids in carry-on bags.

Each first class passenger can carry on two pieces of baggage (each baggage is no more than 5kg); each passenger of business class, premium economy class or economy class can carry on one baggage (no more than 5kg). Each piece of checked baggage may not exceed 50kg in weight and 40 * 60 * 100cm in dimension. If you have the possibility, fly via the US as airlines will allow you 64kg (two 32kg bags) instead of the 20kg in the rest of the world. Even if it is just a stopover in the US, you will be allowed to carry the extra weight.

Be sure to pack medications and other important items in your hand carry, not your check-in baggage. If your luggage gets misrouted, you will still have them. If you take a laptop computer through airport security in the US or Canada, you will need to take it out of its case and place it by itself in a plastic bin for X-ray screening. Keep small electronics, such as MP3 players, digital camera, e-readers and iPads in a briefcase or backpack with their chargers and batteries in the same compartment when possible. They can remain in your carry-on bag throughout the screening process. You should not have to take them out as you would a full-size laptop.

Make a photocopy of your passport and store it separately from the original. If you lose your real passport, having a copy will speed the replacement process.

Scan your passport, passport photos and paper tickets (if not the e type) in. Store this (in an email for example) in your web based email account. You can also store the details of your emergency "lost card" telephone numbers in your web based email account so you know who to contact if your credit card or ATM card is lost or stolen. This way, even if you lose everything, you have immediate access to your all important information. You can even email the details page of your passport to the embassy or consulate when applying for a new one. Also consider writing your home and destination address (and mobile number if you have one) on a self-adhesive sticky label to stick INSIDE your luggage in a visible place. If your luggage is lost and the baggage label has come off, at least the airline can still figure out whose luggage it is.

Split up your bank cards, cash, travelers' cheques and credit cards as much as possible in different pockets, your bags and wallet when packing. In case you do get robbed, at least you won't be strapped for cash (unless you have all your bags AND your wallet stolen of course!).

Punctuality

Get to the airport at least two hours prior to your plane's departure. This may seem like too much time, but it will be just enough time if you encounter long lines, security issues or traffic.

New Words and Expressions

pack	[pæk]	*vt.*	打点（行装）；包装；捆扎；挑选；塞满
sensible	[ˈsensəbl]	*adj.*	有判断力的，有头脑的；明智的；意识到的
accomplish	[əˈkʌmpliʃ]	*vt.*	完成；实现；达到
distributor	[diˈstribjutə]	*n.*	经销商；[电] 分配器；分配者；散布者
customs	[ˈkʌstəmz]	*n.*	风俗（custom 的复数）；海关；习惯；关税
unstable	[ˌʌnˈsteibl]	*adj.*	不稳定的；动荡的；易变的
consulate	[ˈkɔnsjuleit]	*n.*	领事；领事馆；领事任期；领事职位
visa	[ˈvi:zə]	*n.*	签证
		vt.	签发签证
immunization	[ˌimju:naiˈzeiʃən]	*n.*	免疫
opt for			选择
refundable	[riˈfʌndəbl]	*adj.*	可退还的；可偿还的
carousel	[ˌkærəˈsel]	*n.*	（机场的）行李传送带；旋转木马
itinerary	[aiˈtinərəri]	*n.*	旅程；路线；旅行日程；旅行计划；预定行程
pajamas	[pəˈdʒɑ:məz]	*n.*	睡衣；宽长裤
razor	[ˈreizə]	*n.*	剃刀

		vt.	剃,用剃刀刮
backpack	[ˈbækpæk]	n.	双肩背包,背包;远足用的背包
		vt.	把……放入背包
carry-on baggage			随身行李,随身携带行李
flammable	[ˈflæməb(ə)l]	adj.	易燃的;可燃的;可燃性的
nail clipper			指甲钳;指甲夹;指甲刀
file	[aiɪ]	n.	锉刀;文件;档案;文件夹
duffel	[ˈdʌfəl]	n.	粗呢;露营用具
allergic	[əˈlə:dʒik]	adj.	对……过敏的;对……极讨厌的
species	[ˈspi:ʃi:z]	n.	[生物] 物种;种类
gel	[dʒel]	n.	[物化] 凝胶,胶体
		vi.	胶化
allowance	[əˈlauəns]	n.	允许;限额;津贴,零用钱
premium	[ˈpri:miəm]	adj.	高级的;优质的;高价的;售高价的
		n.	保险费;额外费用
medication	[ˌmediˈkeiʃən]	n.	药物;药物治疗;药物处理
charger	[ˈtʃɑ:dʒə]	n.	充电器;委托者;控诉者
battery	[ˈbætərɪ]	n.	电池,蓄电池
original	[əˈridʒinəl]	n.	原件;原作;原物;原型
		adj.	原始的;最初的;独创的
split	[split]	vt.	分离;使分离;劈开;离开
travelers cheque			旅行支票
prior to			在……之前;居先

Task Two

Travel Etiquette Tips

Travel etiquette helps us to make our traveling experience even more pleasant, so it's utmost important to follow certain travel etiquette during the journey. Helpful, cooperative and well mannered behavior reflects your background. Your decent attitude and calm composure counts a lot in travel etiquette yardstick.

Look good and presentable

Being presentable and looking decent is important. Make sure that you are wearing ironed, clean and good clothes. Wear the necktie and suit properly to look like a sincere professional. Wear comfortable and warm clothes. Have good posture while walking and sitting and a smile on your face. Maintain eye contact with people while talking. Be cooperative and helpful with your fellow passengers. Be cordial with travel personals. Your attitude should reflect courtesy and politeness. If you are traveling in a group, make sure the fun and enjoyment doesn't intrude the privacy of your co-travelers. Converse softly while traveling with others.

Follow rules

There are always a set of rules set by the travel agencies. Airlines have their own set of rules while railway, buses, etc. have their own. Go through the guidelines and abide by them. Do not make any effort to disrespect the rules or violate them.

Don't hog seats in the boarding area

Planes are full, airports are busy, and space is tight on board and in the gate area. Be kind and leave the seat next to you open so someone else can sit there. Don't place your luggage or newspapers on empty seats. You must know your spatial boundaries and do not occupy your fellow passenger's seat. Do not lean or rest your legs in front or behind. Try to remain confined to your own seat. Make sure your gestures don't create discomfort to your fellow passengers.

Get your documents ready

Give yourself time to check in if all the necessary documents are ready. Tickets, identity proof, passports, boarding passes, etc. must be produced immediately when asked for. Make sure you do not take long time searching the important documents inside your bag. Remember other people are waiting in the line.

Use the space under the seat in front of you

Small purses, backpacks, and other items may fit under the seat instead of putting in the overhead bins. Many times you'll have easier access to your items, your fellow passengers will appreciate having space for larger carry-ons.

Check before you recline

Anyone who has ever flown has encountered the frustration of the person in front of you reclining the seat into your space. Yes, you have a right to recline. If you're flying somewhere in economy class, you might want to think twice before reclining—or at least ask for permission before you do. Give that traveler behind you who is working on a computer a chance to close his laptop before your seat crushes it.

Let people in front of you off the plane first

The plane pulls up to the gate and every person on board wants to be the first off the plane. Clearly that can't happen, and we are a civilized society, so a simple rule will help keep people from being trampled upon arrival. If you are standing in the aisle, make sure the people in the row in front of you have a chance to exit before you start walking forward.

Middle seats get the armrests

Give those unlucky travelers a break and at least let them use both armrests. If you're seated at the window or the aisle, survive with the one armrest that's dedicated to you.

Don't slam the hotel room door

Once the business traveler survives the stressful flight experience, she is almost home-free when she gets to the hotel. But there's one big thing that can ruin a hotel stay: noise. Few hotels are soundproofed enough to keep loud noises from penetrating the sanctum of your room, and the worst offender here is the slamming door. When you enter and exit your room, close it gently.

Be courteous in respect to your technology use

A great tip for both the business and the pleasure traveler, always remember to be respectful when using technology. Other travelers don't want to listen to your phone call or hear your ring tone for each email received. Talk as quietly as possible and always put your phone on vibrate!

Always clean up after yourself

Be it by plane, car or train that you're traveling, everyone has trash that they need to dispose of at some point. Make it a point to throw away the trash in an appropriate location, rather than leaving it for an employee or future traveler to dispose of!

Keep the volume down

Continuing with noise-in-the-hotel theme, loud TVs and phone conversations can also drive your neighbors crazy. It's easy to feel like you are safe and sound in your room and forget that sound travels. Especially late at night, turn it down so others can make the best of their precious hours of sleep.

Practise good elevator etiquette

There are three separate components to elevator etiquette: boarding, riding the elevator, and disembarking. Before hopping on an elevator, you should also think about whether or not you should really be in the elevator. If you are only traveling one or two floors, taking the stairs is more polite, unless you are disabled or you are carrying heavy packages. Boarding etiquette dictates that you should wait until everyone who is getting off has left the elevator before you step inside. You should not attempt to block the doors of the elevator to hold them open, because this is rude and potentially dangerous. If you are running to greet the elevator, you can politely ask that someone press the "door open" button, but be aware that the occupants of the elevator may decline. Always face the door of the elevator, stand as close to a wall or corner as possible to make room for other riders. You should move to the back of the elevator if you are going a long way, and stay in the front if you plan to get off soon. If you decide to stand in front of the elevator buttons, be prepared to be asked to push buttons for other elevator riders. While in an elevator, you shouldn't eat, smoke, or talk on your cell phone. Don't enter a crowded elevator and stare at the previous elevator inhabitants like a weirdo.

Practise good escalators and moving walkways etiquette

Escalators and moving walkways (or moving sidewalks) are a convenient way to travel from floor to floor, go up and down slopes and comfortably cover flat distances.

When entering or riding escalators and moving walkways, grasp the handrail as you step promptly onto the moving step or walkway; stationary passengers should stay to the right and let those walking pass on the left. Always walk on the left, stand on the right. Frequent travelers are busy and every minute counts, people should not straddle the entire width with their luggage and just stand on the moving sidewalk or escalator in an airport, step aside and let them get by.

In business trips, failure to maintain a high standard can sometimes be too humiliating. Therefore, whatever location or commodity you are accessing, you must do so with a good sense of travel etiquette. If you are into a foreign business trip, try to get accustomed to the culture to some extent. This will help you to overcome difficulties especially with language. Maintain a smart polished outlook while on trip. Be careful with your conversations, talk sense and try to be confidential with your boss or colleagues. Follow business entertaining etiquette after the tour is over. This gives a professional impression.

New Words and Expressions

utmost	[ˈʌtməust]	*adj.*	极度的;最大的;最高的;最远的
composure	[kəmˈpouʒə]	*n.*	镇静,沉着,泰然自若
count	[kaunt]	*vi.*	有价值;有重要意义;计数
		vt.	计算;认为
yardstick	[ˈjɑːdstik]	*n.*	准绳,评价的标准,衡量;码尺(直尺)
cordial	[ˈkɔːdiəl]	*adj.*	热忱的,诚恳的
intrude	[inˈtruːd]	*vt.*	把……强加;把……硬挤
		vi.	闯入;侵入;侵扰
recline	[riˈklain]	*vi.*	使向后倾斜;向后倾斜;靠;斜倚
		vt.	使躺下;使斜倚
frustration	[ˌfrʌsˈtreiʃən]	*n.*	失望,失意,泄气;挫败;挫折

crush	[krʌʃ]	*vt.*	压碎;弄皱,变形
trample	[ˈtræmpl]	*vt.*	践踏;蔑视,伤害
aisle	[ail]	*n.*	通道,走道;侧廊
armrest	[ˈɑ:rmˈrest]	*n.*	扶手;靠手
be dedicated to			奉献给,献身于
penetrate	[ˈpenitreit]	*vt.*	渗透;穿透;洞察
		vi.	渗透;刺入;看透
sanctum	[ˈsæŋktəm]	*n.*	圣所;密室;私室
dispose of			处理;转让;解决;吃光;除掉;卖掉
disembark	[ˌdisimˈbɑ:k]	*vi.*	出电梯,登陆,下车;上岸
		vt.	使……上岸
disabled	[disˈeibld]	*adj.*	残废的,有缺陷的
block	[blɔk]	*vt.*	阻止;阻塞;限制
		n.	块;街区;大厦;障碍物
		adj.	大块的
escalator	[ˈeskəleitə]	*n.*	[美]自动扶梯;电动扶梯
slope	[sləup]	*n.*	斜坡;倾斜;斜率
handrail	[ˈhændreil]	*n.*	扶手;(楼梯等的)栏杆
stationary	[ˈsteiʃənəri]	*adj.*	固定的;静止的;定居的;常备军的
straddle	[ˈstrædl]	*vi.*	跨坐;两腿叉开坐
get accustomed to			变得习惯于,习惯于
polish	[ˈpɔliʃ]	*vt.*	使变得优雅;磨光;擦亮
confidential	[ˌkɔnfiˈdenʃəl]	*adj.*	机密的;表示信任的;获信任的

Task Three

Choose the Check-In Option That's Right for You

Long gone are the days of arriving at the airport three hours early to stand in line at the airline check-in desk. With so many different check-in options available, you don't always have to spend time in line. But with options come decisions. This guide to checking-in should help you decide which method is right for you.

Online check-in

Online check-in allows you to complete the process yourself on the airline's website if you have an electronic ticket (or "e-ticket"). Typically, this can be done between 24 hours and 90 minutes before the flight is due to depart. When you check in online, you'll need to verify all your flight details, choose a seat if you have not already selected one, choose meals if applicable and confirm that you are planning to take the flight. Some airlines will then allow you to print out your boarding pass using your own printer while others will require you to pick up your boarding pass from a self-service kiosk at the airport. If you have bags to check in there is usually a bag drop-off point in the airport. Bags will need to be dropped off at least an hour before departure.

Pros: This is the quickest and easiest way to check in. You can do it from the privacy of your own home or office, avoid lines at the airport, and save time before you fly.

Cons: If the airline expects you to print the ticket yourself, you need access to a printer. Faxes or photocopies of boarding passes are not accepted. If traveling in a group, each passenger needs to check in individually. Some airlines will not accept online check in for passengers under 16 years old or for those over 65 traveling with a senior discount.

Self-service kiosks

Self-service kiosks are available for most airlines in most large airports. Though you still have to check in at the airport, the self-service check-in lines are normally shorter and the process is much quicker. Luggage can be dropped at designated baggage drop points for your airline. You normally need to have an e-ticket or a paper ticket with a magnetic strip to use the kiosks. The machine will read your ticket, credit card or passport and ask you to select the destination of your flight. It should then bring up the correct details of your flight and ask you to confirm. Kiosks are typically open between 24 hours and 90 minutes before a flight departs.

Pros: This is an efficient way to check in at the airport. As kiosks open for flights many hours before check-in desks, lines are almost always shorter. If you live close to the airport, it's also possible to check in up to a day before your flight leaves. This can be particularly useful if you have a very early morning flight.

Cons: Not all airlines or airports operate self-service kiosks, and those that do may have restrictions. It is important to check with the airline before you plan on using this method, and check that it is available for your specific route. Some airlines will only let you use self-service kiosks if you are traveling with no checked luggage or traveling domestically. Children traveling as unaccompanied minors are normally not allowed to use self-service check in.

Phone check-in

Some airlines still offer telephone check-in. The process is similar to arriving at an airline desk at the airport, except that you'll be asked to give all the details that you would usually show on a ticket. You'll need to provide your name, flight number, destination, date of travel, class of service and often your reservation number. It is normally possible to check in by telephone from around 48 hours up to about 90 minutes before the flight departs. Times vary by airline, so check before you fly.

Pros: Phone check-in is a straightforward service that you can manage from your home before you leave—or even from a cell phone on the way to the airport if you're running late. You'll also have someone at the end of the phone to talk you through everything you need to do, and sometimes that personal touch is necessary.

Cons: Many airlines are phasing out or no longer use telephone check-in services, making it the least available method. Phone check-in may not be available 24 hours, so if you're on a very early morning or late night flight, make sure you call during normal business hours. You will still need to pick up your boarding pass at the airport, so you generally need to be there an hour before scheduled departure—more if you are also dropping off luggage.

Check-in desk

The traditional method of check-in still exists and is widely used. Travelers arrive at the airport between three hours and one hour before the flight, and then stand in line at the airline desk to receive boarding passes and hand over any luggage. Check-in times for flights vary depending on your destination. For cheap international flights, travelers are required to check in between two and three hours prior to the scheduled departure. Domestic flights require check-in at least one hour before departure.

Pros: Human contact at the desk means this is the least confusing option. If you have any special requirements, like a wheelchair or assistance from airline personnel, you'll need to check in at the desk. There's also a (very slight) chance that you may get an upgrade if you're there in person. If you want to get bumped from your flight, then you'll need to check in at the desk. If there are any problems with your flight, the airline agent at the check in desk can reissue tickets or rebook you on another flight.

Cons: This can be the slowest and most tiresome way to check in. If you're unlucky, lines can be long, and there's no option of arriving just before the flight leaves.

Other check-in options

Some airlines offer very attractive options for check-in from certain resorts. Virgin Atlantic, for example, will let you check in at some hotels in the Caribbean, from Downtown Disney at Disney World or at the airport train station in Hong Kong. Staff can check you in, give you a boarding pass and even take your bags to the airport. This is perfect if you want to spend a bit more time on the beach ... Check with the individual airlines for details regarding other no-hassle check-in choices

New Words and Expressions

electronic ticket			电子客票
verify	[ˈverifai]	*vt.*	核实;查证
kiosk	[ˈkiːɔsk]	*n.*	(售票、茶点、问询等用的)小亭;公用电话亭
self-service kiosks			电子机票、自助式资讯便利站

drop-off point			递送物品的场所；（拐骗等）放置赃物的地方
designated	[ˈdezigneitid]	*adj.*	指定的；特指的
magnetic strip			磁片，[材] 磁条
domestically	[dəˈmestikli]	*adv.*	国内地；家庭式地；适合国内地
unaccompanied	[ˌʌnəˈkʌmpənid]	*adj.*	无伴随的；无伴侣的；无伴奏的
straightforward	[streitˈfɔ:wəd]	*adj.*	简单的；坦率的；明确的；径直的
		adv.	直截了当地；坦率地
phase out			使逐步淘汰；逐渐停止；分阶段结束（或停止）……的使用
drop off			[口语]把……从车上卸下；（让……）下车，从（交通工具）上下来；把……放下
pro	[prəu]	*n.*	赞成者；赞成的意见
con	[kɔn]	*n.*	反对票；反对论
in person			亲身；外貌上；身体上
reissue	[ˌri:ˈiʃu:]	*vt./vi.*	重新发行；再发出
resort	[riˈzɔ:t]	*n.*	度假胜地；常去之地；凭借，手段
hassle	[ˈhæs(ə)l]	*n.*	困难，麻烦；烦扰
		vt.	找麻烦，搅扰；与……争辩；使……烦恼

Exercises

I. Complete the sentences with the words below and change the form where necessary:

Airplane travel is one of the most common forms of transportation to get to overseas destinations, but making plane reservations and buying plane tickets are only the first steps. You need to know what to do and what to say once you arrive at the airport. Read the words below and consult a dictionary if you need a definition.

aisle	aisle seat	baggage claim area
boarding area	boarding pass	carry-on luggage
cockpit	emergency exit	flight attendant
gate	lavatory	life jacket
metal detector	overhead compartment	oxygen mask
pilot	seat belt	security checkpoint
security officer	terminal	ticket counter
tray table	window seat	X-ray machine
shuttle bus	available	transfer
departure	destination	customs

1. The _______ will be serving food and beverages after the plane reaches its cruising altitude.
2. After the plane lands, you can pick up your luggage at the _______.
3. If the cabin loses pressure during flight, you should put on your _______ so you can breathe comfortably.
4. Are there any seats _______ on an earlier flight?
5. What is your _______ on this trip?
6. I'll be taking their _______ from the airport.
7. Be sure to be at the gate at least 30 minutes before _______.
8. You will need to _______ to a different plane in Miami.
9. Please ensure your _______ is securely fastened, your seat back is upright, and your tray table is folded away.
10. All carry-on baggage must be placed underneath the seat in front of you or in the _______.
11. To pass across the border, one must go through _______.
12. I want an _______ seat.
13. A gate agent or airline service-counter staffer can replace the lost _______ when you show valid ID.
14. You must arrive at the air _______ before 8:40 a. m.
15. That means there's plenty of time before we have to go to the _______ and put our baggage through the X-ray machine.

Ⅱ. Read the statements below and decide whether the statements are true or false. Write T for true and F for false.

In America, tipping helps compensate those who provide a service that are not paid very well. But, where does it begin and where does it end? Do you know? Take our 6*-question quiz to make sure you're not stiffing anyone on the tip!*

1. When you drop off your car, you should tip a car valet attendant.
2. Your cleaning lady owns her own business, you should tip her every other time she comes to clean.
3. A "service charge" on your catering contract covers taxes. A tip is extra.
4. When dining at a restaurant, you leave a 10% tip, indicating: the service was basic.
5. If you're just getting a drink, the "norm" for tipping bartenders is $1 per drink.
6. You should tip the concierge at your hotel when they take your bags to the room or hold the door open for you.

Ⅲ. Read the statements below and choose the right answer.

On an airplane, passengers want to be courteous and accommodating, but aren't afraid to speak up if someone is being rude. "What would you do?" If you encounter with the following occasions:

1. "If another airline passenger seated near you won't turn off his/her cell phone while in flight, what would you do?"

   A. Say something directly to the person. B. Call a flight attendant.

   C. Sit quietly and say nothing. D. Not sure.

2. "If another airline passenger seated near you is using headphones to listen to music or a movie and the sound is so loud that everyone around him/her can also hear, what would you do?"

   A. Ask them to turn it down. B. Call a flight attendant.

   C. Sit quietly and say nothing D. Not sure.

3. "If a child was seated behind you on an airplane and constantly kicked your

seat, what would you do?"

A. Call a flight attendant.

B. Sit quietly and say nothing, hoping the parent will stop their child.

C. Say something directly to the parent or child.

D. Ignore it, children will be children.

4. "If you were flying alone and a couple asked you to switch seats so that they could sit togethor, what would you do?"

A. Gladly move regardless of what kind of seat it was.

B. Move only if it was not a middle seat.

C. Move only if new seat was an aisle seat.

D. Move only if it were closer to the front of the plane.

5. "If you were traveling with a companion on vacation and you received an upgrade to first class, What would you do?"

A. I would say "see you after the flight" and head to the front of the plane.

B. It depends on who I'm traveling with.

C. It depends on the length of the flight.

D. I would pass up the opportunity so we could continue to sit together.

6. "If you placed a small bag in the overhead bin and were asked to place it under the seat in front of you so someone else could put a very large roller bag above, What would you do?"

A. Do so without a second thought.

B. Do so, but grudgingly. I believe the other passenger should've checked their bag.

C. Politely decline offering one or several reasons why your bag should stay where it is.

D. Politely decline offering no explanation.

7. "While passing through a TSA security checkpoint, if a traveler in front of you is taking too long removing shoes, laptop, etc. What would you do?"

A. Wait, but be frustrated that they don't have their act together.

B. Patiently wait.

C. Jump in front of them.

D. Tell them to move faster.

IV. Put the following sentences into English or vice versa.

1. 给多少小费取决于服务程度的好坏。
2. When you go to different parts of the world, it's very important to understand local etiquettes.
3. 晚上好，我有预订房间，名字是汤姆森。
4. Your room is 502 on the fifth floor. Breakfast is served between 6:30 a. m. and 9 a. m. Enjoy your stay.
5. 我能用您的信用卡划账押金吗？
6. If you have any, please just leave it in the laundry bag behind the bathroom door.
7. 这件毛衣要用冷水手洗。
8. Please tell us or notify in the list whether you need your clothes ironed, washed, dry-cleaned or mended and also what time you want to get them back.
9. 所有的客户都要求在起飞前打印出他们的登机牌。
10. Can I have your passport, your immigration form, and your customs declaration form, please?

▶ Speaking

1. Read the text loudly, and try to recite the following paragraph.

Hotel tipping guide

Upscale hotels will likely have numerous hospitality-workers including a valet, a bellman, a doorman, and the concierge to assist you. These kind people are here to make your stay a pleasant one, so make sure to show your appreciation. Tipping is certainly a personal preference, but if you choose to tip keep in mind the following guidelines:

Valet: \$2 – \$3, weather depending.

Shuttle service: \$2 per person (including bags per person).

Doorman: \$2- \$3, depending on level of service.

Bellman: The general rule is \$1 per bag, but if you're alone and only have one bag you might want to add a few dollars to the tip.

Concierge: Some high-class hotels have full-service concierge staff available to help guests with everything from restaurant reservations to theater tickets. Depending on the level of service you received from the concierge, consider tipping anywhere from \$5 – \$25.

Room service: \$2 – \$4, depending on the total bill.

Housekeeping: More hotels are looking to conserve energy by limiting room service. The general rule is for \$2 per day your room is cleaned and sheets are changed. If you request sheet changes on a daily basis, you might consider tipping a little more.

2. Read and practise the following dialogues in pairs.

Dialogue A

Explaining How to Get the Service

(A: *Room Attendant* B: *Guest*)

A: Excuse me. Have you any laundry? The laundry man is here to collect it.

B: No, not now, thank you.

A: If you have any, please just leave it in the laundry bag behind the bathroom door. The laundry man comes over to collect it every morning.

B: Thank you.

A: Please tell us or notify in the list whether you need your clothes ironed, washed, dry-cleaned or mended and also what time you want to get them back.

B: I see. What if there is any laundry damage? I wonder if your hotel has a policy on dealing with it.

A: In such a case, the hotel should certainly pay for it. The indemnity shall not exceed ten times the laundry

B: That sounds quite reasonable. I hope there's no damage at all.

A: Don't worry, sir. The Laundry Department has wide experience in their work.

B: All right. Thank you for your information.

A: Not at all.

Dialogue B

Express Service

(*A: Laundry clerk B: Mrs. Bell*)

A: What can I do for you?

B: Could you send someone up for my laundry, please? Room 908, Bell.

A: Certainly, Mrs. Bell. A valet will be up in a few minutes.

B: Good. I also have a silk dress which I don't think is color-fast. Will the color run in the wash?

A: We'll dry-clean the dress. Then the color won't run.

B: You're sure? Good! And the lining of my husband's jacket has come unstitched. It might tear over further while washing.

A: Don't worry, madam. We'll stitch it before washing.

B: That's fine. Now, when can I have my laundry back?

A: Usually it takes about two days to have laundry done. But would you like express service or same-day?

B: What is the difference in price?

A: We charge 50% more for express, but it only takes 5 hours.

B: And for same-day, will I get the dress and skirt back this evening?

A: Yes, madam. All deliveries will be made before six o'clock.

B: I'll have express then.

▶ Acting

1. Watch the video: Checking into a hotel at the front desk and role play.

http://v.youku.com/v_show/id_XMzMyNzg0MjI0.html

2. Online Investigations

Imagine that you are have received $3,000 to take a three-week vacation to one or more of these cities: Las Vegas, Hawaii, or Paris, and one city of your choice. Use the Internet to determine the cost of airfare and train/subway travel to get there from your current location. Compare prices offered by different travel companies.

▶ Supplementary Listening

* Business Etiquette (Traveling with the Senior Executive; Airport Hassles (1,2), Jet Lag(2), etc.)

  http://www.voanews.cn/voaet/17705.htm

Listen to the dialogues and dictate down the important points.

* Checking In at a Hotel Conversation

  http://v.youku.com/v_show/id_XMzMyNzg2MzE2.html

Watch the videos and dictate down the important points.

▶ Supplementary Reading

Tips for Finding Cheap Airfares Online

Unfortunately for weary travelers, there's no real shortcut to finding cheap airfare. As with any purchase, you need to shop around to get the best deal—by trying different booking sites, altering your dates and waiting until just the right time to purchase. But if you're willing to put in a little time and effort, you could save big on your next flight.

1. Buy early. Especially during peak travel periods, making reservations late in the game can cost you a lot of money. Airline ticket prices typically go up in the last two weeks before flying, so if you're planning ahead, try to make the call before this deadline. And if you're traveling internationally, you'll want to book even earlier—from three to six months in advance—for the best deals.

2. Buy late. Often you can buy tickets at the very last minute for a great price, if the airlines have failed to fill their planes. Many airlines offer weekly newsletters that feature their best last-minute deals.

3. Shop around. Check several of the on-line agencies.

4. Try to make your departure and return dates on Tuesdays, Wednesdays, and/or Thursdays. These days of the week are usually cheaper.

5. Test alternate departure and return dates to see if arriving/departing on one day is cheaper than another.

6. If you live near more than one airport, try each airport to see if departing from one is cheaper than the others. Alternately, if your destination city has more than one airport, check each of it's airports for the cheapest price.

7. If you have a flexible itinerary, test to see if one destination city is cheaper to travel to than others (i. e. London vs. Paris).

8. Avoid arriving in one city and departing from another (i. e. arriving in London and departing from Paris). This almost always costs more. If you are short on time, however, getting a open jaw (multi-city) ticket can save travel time and aggravation.

9. Sign up for the "Fare Watcher" programs that many of the on-line agencies offer. They will notify you when a price change for a destination occurs.

10. Start looking at air fares as soon as possible. Purchase tickets a minimum of 21 days before departure to find the best prices. The cheapest available fares are usually made available by airlines 90 – 60 days prior to flight departure.

11. Look for tickets on the Internet after midnight. Apparently the best deals are out there for night owls!

http://www.backpackeurope.com/trans/air/

http://www.independenttraveler.com/travel-tips/air-travel/tips-for-finding-cheap-airfare

Body Language

You step over someone's legs in Nepal and don't even realize you've committed a grave social taboo! Although most locals will excuse breaches in etiquette, wouldn't you rather be informed? Read below for a list of etiquette tips, taken from our various guidebooks, to help you navigate different parts of the world.

1. In Asia, never touch any part of someone else's body with your foot, which is considered the "lowest" part of the body. If you accidentally do this, apologize by

touching your hand to the person's arm and then touching your own head. Don't point at objects or people with your feet, don't prop your feet on chairs or tables while sitting. —From the *Lonely Planet Thailand* travel guide (and other Asia guidebooks)

2. Also in Asia, refrain from touching people on the head or ruffling their hair. The head is spiritually the "highest" part of the body. Don't sit on pillows meant as headrests, as it is a variant on this taboo. —From the *Lonely planet China* travel guide

3. Shaking hands was introduced to Fiji in the 19th century by way of Tonga, and quickly became the established custom. An affectionate handshake can be very long, and may even last throughout an entire conversation. —From the *Lonely Planet South Pacific Phrasebook*

4. In Nepal, it's bad manners to step over someone's outstretched legs, so avoid doing that, and move your own legs when someone wants to pass. Also do not step over or sit on a monk's cushions in or near a temple, even if no one is sitting on them. Always walk around stupas and chortens (Tibetan-style stupas) in a clockwise direction. —From the *Lonely Planet Nepal* travel guide

5. In Japanese baths, called onsen, always wash first before entering the water. The water is considered fouled if someone does not do this, kind of the American equivalent of peeing in a pool. Also, use a wash cloth to cover your private bits and pieces. —From the *Lonely Planet Japan* travel guide. (Also see: Top 10 hot springs in Japan)

6. The people of Italy are emotionally demonstrative, so expect to see lots of cheek kissing among acquaintances, embraces between men who are good friends and lingering handshakes. Italian men may walk arm-in-arm, as may women. Pushing and shoving in busy places is not considered rude, so don't be offended by it. Try to hold your ground. The Italian body language vocabulary is is quite extensive, but the following six may prove useful when traveling.

7. Shaking hands across a threshold is considered unlucky in Russia. An interesting feature of this is that some pizza delivery guys refuse to conduct a transaction across a threshold; you either have to go out to the hall or invite them just inside the door. —

From the *Lonely Planet Russia* travel guide

8. In India it is possible to pay a tremendous compliment with body language alone. When somebody approaches a person with their tongue between their teeth and gathers the air around the person's head with their hands to draw it into their own personal space, it means they find the person either unbearably beautiful or extraordinarily intelligent. —From *Lonely Planet*'s Indian English Language & Culture

9. Don't stick your index finger and middle finger up with the palm of your hand facing towards you in the UK ... it's the equivalent of giving someone the finger. Tip: Don't order two beers in this fashion in UK bars. Doing it palm facing out is OK (i. e., the peace sign)—From a *Lonely Planet* staffer in the UK

10. Moroccan greetings can last up to 10 minutes. Shake with your right hand then touch your hand to your heart, to indicate that you're taking the meeting to heart. Good friends may tack on up to four air kisses, accompanied by a stream of well wishes: "How are you? Everything's good with you? I hope your parents are well? Baraka (blessings) upon them!"—From *Alison Bing*, *Lonely Planet Morocco* author

(http://www.lonelyplanet.com/india/travel-tips-and-articles/76514)

Answer the following question:

What are the tips for finding cheap airfares online? Say the different body languages of each country mentioned above?

Project Eleven

Interview Etiquette

Learning Objectives

After completing this project, you will be able to:

* prepare for a job interview;
* behave properly during the interview;
* answer interview questions tactfully;
* apply phone interview tips and techniques into practice;
* write a thank-you email.

Warming-Up

Discuss the following questions with your peers.

- ❑ Have you ever been to a job interview?
- ❑ What preparations should a candidate make before an interview?
- ❑ What makes up a whole job interview and how should candidates behave during it?

Listening

http://www. unsv. com/voanews/business-etiquette/lessons/111/

Listen to the recording and fill in the blanks.

Job Interview

The manager of *Players Magazine* Fred Dixon is interviewing David Tang.

(*Office ambience*)

F: OK ... what do you think are your biggest weaknesses?

D: Hmm ... I'd say that my biggest weakness is ____________________. Sometimes I get too close to the project and need to step back to get the whole picture.

F: All right. ____?

D: I've had to make a lot of major adjustments in my life such as moving to a new country, learning a new language and making new friends. I'd say it was all quite stressful but I faced each challenge as it came and step-by-step things got better. For me I think the key is not to let things pile up but ________________.

F: OK. So what you would say is the thing that's most important to you in your job?

D: ____.
____. I need guidance, but I don't want my creativity to be stifled.

F: Can you tell me why you left your last job?

D: Well, I needed a challenge. ______________________________.
____. I enjoyed my time at my last job, but I feel like I'm ready for the major leagues.

F: I noticed that you have recommendation letters from each of your previous supervisors.
____.

D: I'm honored that they value my work. I've found that I generally get along well with co-workers. I'm just not really into drama and I'm pretty easy-going.

F: Well ... thanks for coming in today, David. ______________________________.
____.

D: Great! And thanks for your time, Fred. I'll be looking forward to your call.

▶ Reading

Task One

In-Person Job Interview Etiquette

Knowing proper job interview etiquette is an important part of successful interview. How you dress, what you bring to a job interview, how you greet the interviewer, and how you communicate can all make a big difference in the outcome of the interview.

Before the interview

Before you head into the interview there are few preparatory steps to take.

Do your research. Gather as much information as you can about the company or organization that has invited you for the interview. This will give you a clear idea about the mission, future plans, work environment and reputation of the company. At minimum, review the company's website and Google its key players. Find out who you'll be interviewing with and learn something about them, such as when they were last quoted in a publication or if they've recently received an award or if the company has expanded into several new markets over the past year.

Rehearse. Read the job description carefully as to what they expect from you. Evaluate your qualifications, experience, and core competences, areas of strength and accordingly draw up a questionnaire along with your replies to the expected questions. Questions that you're pretty much guaranteed to be asked during an interview are: "Can you tell me something about yourself?" "Why do you want to work for this company?" "Why should I hire you?" "What are your strengths and weaknesses?" "Where do you see yourself in five years? Or what are your goals for the next 5 years?" "Why did you leave your previous employer, or why are you leaving your present job?" "What salary are you expecting?" "Do you have any questions to ask me?" So be prepared with insightful answers for these classics. Practise looking in the mirror and answering the questions out loud. This prep work will help you clarify your thoughts, brush up your communication skills and make you much more comfortable during the interview.

Get the materials ready for a job interview. Organize your resume and any other materials you are taking with. Put together in advance copies of your resume/the application form and the original interview letter along with all your testimonials. Also, bring a list of questions to ask the interviewer. If you're interviewing for a tech or web job and you want to show examples of your work, it's fine to bring your laptop or iPad to show the interviewer what you have accomplished.

Don't walk into a job interview with a coffee cup or bottle of soda or water or anything else to eat or drink. Don't chew gum.

Your cell phone should be turned off and out of sight. Do not put your cell phone on vibrate. You don't want to be the applicant whose text messages or calls disrupted the interview.

Dress accordingly. When you are dressing for a job interview, the image you present is really important. Your image is what makes the first impression on the interviewer. First impressions are lasting impressions, so it's important to dress appropriately when interviewing. First you should brush your teeth and use a mouthwash; your hair should be clean and combed; nails should be clean and trimmed. Dress up smartly but a little conservatively. No jeans, floaters or funky shirts. A plain white or light colored shirt is most ideal to wear. A dark colored suit brings out the personality and adds grace. Use good footwear (black or brown) and color coordinate with your dress. The tie for gents and accessories for the lady should not be loud. Keep them understated. Men can look their professional best wearing one of the many men suits available to you in today's stores. Shirts should be clean and ironed. If in doubt, wear a classic, conservative tie. Women can look their professional best with business attire. Wear dress shoes and shoes should be clean and/or shined. A dark suit (jacket and pants or skirt) and a crisp white shirt, simple make-up, and clean, professional shoes will be perfect in most cases. And definitely avoid dangling earrings, too much perfume, and multiple, clanking bracelets. Carry a folder for your papers and avoid use of a briefcase. If the company does not have a dress code, remember that it's better to overdress than underdress.

Be punctual. Do not forget to confirm the date and venue before you head for the interview. Sometimes the interview schedule can get changed or cancelled. Although the companies do inform the candidates before hand but it is good to double—check in case you have somehow missed the communication. It's important to arrive a few minutes early, or on time, at the latest, for a job interview. Know where you're going, how much travel time you need, and how to get to the interview location. Give yourself an extra 20 minutes, which will give you an opportunity to stop in the restroom and freshen up, if need be, to make sure you don't have any hair, make-up or wardrobe malfunctions. A few extra minutes will also give you an opportunity to catch your breath and stay calm. An interview is even more stressful than normal if you're rushing to get there on time. Whatever you do, do not be late.

During the interview

Though you may cringe at the thought, you need to sell yourself during the interview. You have a product (yourself) to offer this organization, and you must make sure that the interviewer understands what you have to offer.

When you arrive at a job interview, introduce yourself to the receptionist, if there is one. Let him or her know who you are and who you are scheduled to meet with. Greet politely "Good morning/afternoon/evening" depending upon time of the day. Greet your interviewer by name, with a dry, firm handshake and a smile. Addressing each interviewer by name as he or she is introduced, use the more formal "Mr. (Smith)" or "Ms. (Johnson)". Wait for the interviewer to sit down or invite you to sit down before seating yourself. If you are left to choose a place yourself, choose a place from where you can clearly see all the interview participants, and from where they can also see you.

Demonstrate your interest in the job and in the company. Enthusiasm is vital! Be conscious of the body language you're displaying through your face, arms, hands, torso, feet and legs.

Smile a lot. Smiling naturally (without pursing your lips tightly together) will make you appear confident, friendly, and approachable. Even if you're not feeling it, fake it. A smile conveys that you're someone who can get along with fellow employees, wow the boss, and impress the clients.

Keep eye contact with your interviewer. If you are speaking, or the interviewer is asking you something, raise your head and make regular eye contact to show that you are actively involved. With panel interviews it is best to look at and direct your answer to the person asking the question, with a glance periodically at the other interviewers. Hold eye contact for periods of about 10 seconds before looking away briefly and then re-establishing eye contact. Eye contact is important in making your look sincere and truthful. Not making eye contact makes the interviewer feel disconnected from you. Overusing direct eye contact when you are speaking can come across as lecturing or challenging the interviewer. Looking constantly downwards makes you appear insincere or submissive.

As you sit across the interviewer(s), look confident and relaxed. Sit upright but not too stiffly in your chair. This indicates that you are comfortable and feeling confident. Hunching down in your chair gives the impression of nervousness and low self-esteem. A slouching posture indicates a careless attitude and a lack of energy. Sitting on the edge of your chair can come across as being nervous and tense. Relax and lean slightly forward, about 10 degrees, towards your interviewer. This gives the message that you are both interested and involved. Leaning back makes you appear too relaxed and casual. Leaning to the side can be perceived as not feeling comfortable with the interviewer. Tilting your head very slightly to one side comes across as friendly and open. Keeping it straight comes across as self-assured and authoritative. Don't twirl your hair, which makes you look nervous or juvenile.

If you are unsure of what to do with your hands, rest them, loosely clasped in your lap or on the table. If you keep your hands in your lap the entire interview, you could signal that you lack self-confidence. Having your hands above the neck, fiddling with your face, is unprofessional and conveys nervousness and anxiety. Keep your hands away from your face. Interview body language experts will tell you that touching the nose or lips can indicate that the candidate is lying. Holding a hand behind your head is often a sign that you are annoyed or uncertain.

Folding your arms across your chest suggests a closed and defensive attitude. Waving your hands and arms around can be perceived as uncertainty and a lack of professionalism. Common wisdom is that the less you move your arms and hands about the more confident and in control you are.

Be aware of the interview body language message your legs are giving. A lot of leg movement is both distracting and indicates nervousness. Resting one leg or ankle on top of your other knee makes you look too casual and comes across as arrogant. Crossing your legs high up conveys a defensive attitude in the one-on-one context of a job interview. Crossing them at the ankles or placing both feet flat on the floor conveys a confident and professional look during the job interview.

Be prepared for a little small talk, but don't overdo it. Follow the interviewer's lead and let them guide the direction of the conversation. Listen carefully to what the interviewer is saying. Nod your head to show that you are listening, interjecting appropriately with "Yes sir/madam", "absolutely", "definitely", etc. Reinforce your professionalism and your ability to communicate effectively by speaking clearly and avoiding "uhs", "you knows", and slang. If you don't listen well during the interview, you are telling the interviewer that you may not listen well to your co-workers and managers. Take a few seconds to think about a difficult question before responding. Responding quickly may convey that you're impulsive. Be brief and speak in concise terms about relevant experiences that reflect positively on your skills and your character. Don't ramble when you respond. Do be sure that your responses are focused, and highlight the skills you have that are relevant to the job. Keep in mind that your responses are your sales pitch. You're selling the interviewer on yourself as the best candidate for the job, so be sure you focus on your relevancy, i. e. why you are a good candidate, how you can do the job, what you can contribute, and how you will benefit the company if you're hired. The employers are always interested in knowing how your skills, experience and expertise will add value to the job in question. Your answers should be built around their expectations. Don't make up answers to questions you don't know. Your interviewer will conclude that you will do the same thing in the work place. Don't display defensiveness when a tough question has you stumped. Ensure that your voice tone is not apologetic or defensive. Speaking in a clear and controlled voice conveys confidence. Maintain a pitch that is comfortably audible to the person(s) around. Avoid erupting into laughter on your own; laughing along with the interviewer is far more acceptable.

If the question seems ambiguous or you need more clarification, you may ask the interviewer to elaborate or restate the question. Where appropriate, ask questions that will provide information about the job and the interviewer.

Take the water. If your interviewer offers you a glass of water, take it, even if you're not thirsty. This little prop can help buy you time to formulate an answer to a difficult question or just give you a moment to center yourself.

Focus on the positives of former employers. Badmouthing a previous employer or supervisor is the quickest way to lose a job offer. If you have experienced a bad employer or an inept manager, find the positives in your relationship and focus on those. If there were no positives and you must talk about the job, focus as much as possible on your successes in that job and not on the conflicts.

Say goodbye gracefully. Close the interview on a positive note: indicate that the job looks like a good fit and that you are very interested in the job and you feel you can make a contribution to the organization; ask about any needed follow-up and when you can expect to next hear from the company or ask when would be the right time to call; and always thank the interviewer for his or her time as you leave. Be sure you have the interviewer's business card or at least the proper spelling of their name, their title and their address and phone number. Even if the interview is not going as you had planned or you get negative vibes, do not show your disappointment and disinterest. Maintain your poise till the end. Whether you get the job or not, at least you went into the interview with style and grace, and communicated your intentions with confidence and professionalism. With a bit of luck, your body language will have been the icing on the cake. Your interviewer will remember you as a confident, assertive, friendly, and honest applicant—all the important things that get you the job.

At the end of the interview, offer the recruiter at the end of the interview a list of three references, including contact information for each reference, gather your belongings calmly, rise smoothly, smile and nod your head. If shaking hands with everyone in the room isn't convenient, at least shake hands with the hiring manager and the person who brought you to the interview space.

After the interview

Interviewing for a job is a long, complicated and complex process. Basically, when a person is interviewed for a job, there are several aspects that one should keep in mind when each interview round is over and also after the entire job application process is completed.

Continue your job search. The quote "Don't put all your eggs in one basket" is appropriate here—your odds are not 100% clear. Logically, you should not put a freeze on your job search efforts until the moment you sign the job contract.

Retrospect. Once the interview is over and you have left the interview location, you should reassess/reevaluate how the interview went and how you could improve the experience. This is the right time to evaluate your interviewing performance. With your new gained experience, you have the necessary tools to prepare yourself for the next job interview.

Do not tweet or blog. No matter how badly you may want to update your social media status, do not share details of your interview on the Internet. Your interviewer may be checking up on you online.

Write thank-you emails and notes. One of the first things that you should keep in mind after the interview is networking. After you have given the job interview, make sure that you send a thoughtful thank-you letter or email. Sending a thank-you note or an email promptly (within 2 business days) will only emphasize your professionalism and will serve in making a good impression on the interviewer and the other people involved. The purpose of this letter is to show appreciation for the employer's interest in you, to demonstrate that you have good manners and know to write a thank-you letter, to reiterate your interest in the position and in the organization and to review or remind the employer about your qualifications for the position. If you thought of something you forgot to mention in the interview, mention it in your follow-up/thank-you letter, or follow up with any information the employer may have asked you to provide after the interview.

Follow up an phone call. Another aspect to remember is to continue with the right type of networking and contacting. The best way to keep in contact is by calling up the people concerned on a regular basis. This helps in keeping your picture in their mind as well as creating an idea that you are genuinely interested in the job opportunity.

The time to call the interviewer or company is also quite important. Usually, people are too rushed in the mornings and would not have time to have a calm conversation with you. However, after lunch and an hour before the day ends is a good time to catch the interviewer with some time on his or her hands.

Inform your references. Nowadays, most interviews require references to be given at the very beginning of the interview, if you have given references to the interviewer, make sure that you call up the reference people and inform them that you have given their names and contact details as references. You may also direct your references as to what to say when asked. This depends on the closeness of your relationship.

In case you do not receive any communication from the company, it is all right to call up after about ten days to find out regarding the outcome of your interview.

You can be optimistic: if your interview lasts more than 45 minutes. Also if there is a detailed discussion about your salary and preferred location. If you are asked to wait or an indication about the second interview has been given, you do stand a chance. All this means that things have gone well and you have left a favorable impression on the interviewers.

Even if you are not hired, try to get some feedback from the company. That may be of great help for the future interviews. Sometimes not getting hired has no reflection on your capabilities—so do not lose heart; keep your spirits up, because tomorrow is another day.

Review these job interview etiquette tips for before, during and after a job interview, to ensure that your job interview etiquette is up to speed and you're making the best impression on the interviewer.

New Words and Expressions

outcome	[ˈautkʌm]	*n.*	结果,结局;成果
head	[hed]	*vi.*	向……方向移动
mission	[ˈmiʃən]	*n.*	使命,任务;代表团
reputation	[ˌrepjuˈteiʃən]	*n.*	名声,名誉;声望
guarantee	[ˌgærənˈtiː]	*vt.*	保证;担保
		n.	保证;担保;保证人;抵押品
prep	[prep]	*n.*	预备;预习;准备功课;(abbr.)准备(preparation);预备的(preparatory)
brush up			复习;提高;擦光
testimonial	[ˌtestiˈməuniəl]	*n.*	证明书;推荐书
laptop	[ˈlæptɔp]	*n.*	膝上型轻便电脑;笔记本电脑
vibrate	[vaiˈbreit]	*vi.*	振动;颤动;摇摆;踌躇
		vt.	使振动;使颤动
conservatively	[kənˈsəːvətivli]	*adv.*	谨慎地;保存地;适当地
floater	[ˈfləutə]	*n.*	沙滩凉鞋
funky	[ˈfʌŋki]	*adj.*	时髦的;时髦别致的
coordinate	[kəuˈɔːdineit]	*vt.*	使协调,使调和;调节;整理
loud	[laud]	*adj*	[口语](颜色、服饰等)刺眼的;俗艳的;过分花哨的
understated	[ˌʌndəˈsteitid]	*adj.*	(服装等)朴素的;不惹眼的;轻描淡写的;低调的
business attire			工作服,职业装;正式商务着装
clank	[klæŋk]	*vi.*	发叮当声;发铿锵声
		vt.	使铿然作响

		n.	叮当声;当啷声
bracelet	[ˈbreislit]	*n.*	手镯
folder	[ˈfəuldə]	*n.*	文件夹;活页夹
overdress	[ˈəuvədres]	*vi.*	穿得过分讲究
underdress	[ˈʌndədres]	*vi.*	穿得过于朴素(或过于随便)
malfunction	[mælˈfʌŋkʃən]	*vi.*	发生故障;不起作用
		n.	故障;失灵;疾病
cringe	[krindʒ]	*vi.*	感到局促不安;畏缩;奉承;阿谀
		n.	畏缩;奉承
torso	[ˈtɔ:səu]	*n.*	(人体的)躯干
purse	[pə:s]	*vt.*	使缩拢,使皱起;噘起
		n.	钱包,小钱袋;金钱,财源
panel interview			专门小组会谈;小组面试
submissive	[səbˈmisiv]	*adj.*	顺从的;服从的;柔顺的
stiffly	[ˈstifli]	*adv.*	直挺挺地,生硬地;顽固地;呆板地;拘谨地
hunch	[hʌntʃ]	*vt.*	(人)耸肩弓身,弯腰驼背,弓身坐着
slouch	[slautʃ]	*vi.*	没精打采地坐着(或站立)
twirl	[twə:l]	*vt.*	使快速转动,使快速旋转;捻弄;盘绕,卷
juvenile	[ˈdʒu:vənail]	*adj.*	青少年的;幼稚的
		n.	青少年;少年读物
fiddle	[ˈfidl]	*vi.*	用手无目的地摸弄(某物),随便摆弄(常与 with 连用)
defensive	[diˈfensiv]	*adj.*	自卫的;防御用的
interject	[ˌintəˈdʒekt]	*vt.*	打断;插(话); 突然插入
ramble	[ˈræmbl]	*vt.*	闲聊,瞎扯;漫谈;漫步;漫游
stump	[stʌmp]	*vt.*	[美国口语]把……难倒,使惶惑;使挫败
prop	[prɔp]	*n.*	支柱;支持物;撑材
formulate	[ˈfɔ:mjuleit]	*vt.*	构想出 (计划或提案);明确地表达

inept	[iˈnept]	*adj.*	无能的,不称职的,笨拙的;愚昧的,愚蠢的,不理智的
vibe	[vaib]	*n.*	气氛,氛围
assertive	[əˈsə:tiv]	*adj.*	坚定而自信的;肯定的;独断的
recruiter	[riˈkru:tə]	*n.*	招聘人员;(学校的)招生人员;征兵人员
reference	[ˈrefərəns]	*n.*	证明人;介绍信;证明书;参考,参照,参看;查阅
retrospect	[ˈretrəuspekt]	*vt./vi/n.*	回顾,追溯;回想
professionalism	[prəuˈfeʃənəlizəm]	*n.*	职业特性;职业作风;职业精神;专业化
reiterate	[ri:ˈitəreit]	*vt.*	重申,反复讲;重做,反复做

Task Two

Phone Interview Etiquette

Phone interview etiquette is just as important as in-person job interview etiquette when it comes to getting hired. Today, many companies conduct initial phone interviews to help determine the best qualified candidates for job opportunities. Given this, it is important to make a great impression that leads you to an in-person interview and one step closer to landing the job. Here are several phone interviewing tips to get you going:

Pre-contact

When you provide phone numbers in your CV or application letter, it's important to list the number(s) at which you can be reached, indicating whether or not it is acceptable to be contacted at your current position. Also include your email address if you check it often.

Prepare for the interview by compiling a list of your strengths and weaknesses, accomplishments and answers to typical questions. Have your resume and notes in front of you to refer to when you are to speak about your work experience. Have a pen and paper available to take notes. Be in a quiet place alone—turn off the radio, television and any other background noise that might be distracting and that you will be able to concentrate. Make sure that your phone battery will not run out.

When you miss the contact

If the hiring staff leaves a message for you, return the call as soon as you can. As you are returning the call, remember that the recruiter may have called 10 other people that day about the same or a different position. When you return the call, give your full first name and last name and indicate that you are returning the recruiter's call regarding the × × × position.

When you're there for the contact

The phone rings, and you are there to answer! The common standard recruiting rap goes something like this "Hi Aurora, this is Bridget calling from the New England Aquarium in Boston. I'm calling regarding our water-quality position and would like to spend about 10 minutes on the phone with you asking some preliminary questions. Is this a good time to talk, or could I arrange a time to call you back?" Many interviewers like to make sure that interviewing now is convenient for the candidate. Most recruiting professionals will give candidates this courtesy, particularly when calling a candidate at her current place of employment.

Many recruiters want you to talk to them when they call, and may not want to call again later. They may have only one or two clarifying questions that would take just a few minutes. Or they may want to do the full 10 –60 minute phone interview with you. Other recruiters want the candidate to feel composed and settled and have a quiet place to talk and think, and may not mind making a later appointment. If you are good on the phone and quick on your feet, you may want to go ahead with the interview. If you are in the middle of something, running out the door, or can't remember what the job is, it may be best to suggest another time. A good phrase is "I'm so happy you called. I have about 10 minutes before I have to run out the door. Is that enough time, or can I call you back later this afternoon?" This way, you are expressing your interest, being clear about the time you have, and suggesting a time to connect later.

Take notes. If the entire hiring committee is on the other end in a conference call, you will want to write down each person's name/role down so that you can refer to it later.

It's important that you are clear about whether or not you can hear the interviewer clearly. Don't say, "Can you speak up?" Do say, "I'm having trouble hearing you. Can you hear me clearly?" The latter is more polite and clarifies whether the connection between you is bad or if the problem is on the recruiter's end.

Answer the phone in a professional and friendly manner. As with any interview, you are to be asked questions at the end. Take a moment to think about the question, and then respond. Speak slowly and clearly and concisely. Make an extra effort to sound enthusiastic and confident. Smile during the phone interview to project a positive tone in your voice and your image. We have heard it before that smile can be heard through the phone! You will sound more pleasant and more confident. Make sure to build rapport with the interviewer. This can be done by using the interviewer's name throughout the call or by asking the interviewer about his/her experience with the company, etc. End on a positive note: always thank the interviewer for his/her time and let the person know how interested you are in pursuing the job. Remember your goal is to set up a face-to-face interview. After you thank the interviewer ask if it would be possible to meet in person.

During the phone interview, don't smoke, eat, drink or chew gum or candy. Don't ramble—make sure that your answers are direct and to the point. Don't interrupt the interviewer when he or she is speaking. Don't provide too much information—keep your answers short and to the point; however, make sure to fully answer the questions. Don't badmouth former employers.

After the call

Immediately after the call, write a short thank-you note to reiterate your interest in the position. It often goes something like "Thank you for spending time with me on the phone today talking about the enrollment-management position. I enjoyed the conversation and have a better understanding of the job. I'd be interested in an on-site interview, and would welcome the opportunity to further discuss my candidacy."

A chance to test the waters

During a phone interview, interviewers can check out whether you are as good as you sound on paper, if you are articulate and if you'd be a good person to have joined the firm. Most importantly, a phone interview serves a way to narrow down the pool to finalists and semifinalists. The phone interview is a way for both the candidate and the interviewer to test the waters. So, relax, be professional, and be yourself!

New Words and Expressions

given	[ˈgivən]	*prep.*	考虑到
		v.	给予(give 的过去分词)
land a job			得到一份工作
CV	[ˌsi:ˈvi:]	(*abbr.*)	简历(Curriculum Vitae [kəˈrikjuləmˈvaiti:])
compile	[kəmˈpail]	*vt.*	编制;编译;汇集;编辑; 汇编
distract	[disˈtrækt]	*vt.*	转移;分心
rap	[ræp]	*n.*	[美国俚语]谈话,交谈,聊天
courtesy	[ˈkə:tisi]	*n.*	礼貌;好意;恩惠
composed	[kəmˈpəuzd]	*adj.*	镇静的;沉着的
settled	[ˈsetld]	*adj.*	稳定的;固定的
enrollment	[inˈrəulmənt]	*n.*	[英国英语](enrolment)招收;加入;入伍;入会;入学
candidacy	[ˈkændidəsi]	*n.*	候选资格;候选状态
test the waters			试水;市场测试;投石问路
narrow down			缩小;限制;减少;变窄
pool	[pu:l]	*n.*	一拨面试的人;人才库;(人员、商品等的)储备

Exercises

I. Job-Hunting Etiquette Quiz. Instructions: Answer true or false to the following statements. Write T for true and F for false.

1. When greeting someone for the first time, a cupped handshake (in which

your left hand covers the normal handshake) is a good way to show my sincerity and interest.

2. At an interview or meeting, it is generally necessary for me to stand only when a women walks into the room (regardless of my gender).
3. At job fairs—and other professional settings—when I receive a business card from someone, I should take the time to really read the card before sticking it in my pocket or briefcase.
4. I should always turn off (or silence) my cell phone and beeper before heading into any interview or business meeting.
5. In dining situations, my drinks are on my right and my bread plate is on my left.
6. On an on-site interview, if I get a parking ticket while at the interview, I can add the cost of the ticket to the expense reimbursement form I submit to the company.
7. After a job interview, regardless of whether I am still interested in the job or not, I should always follow up with a thank-you note.
8. A few days after a job interview, I begin calling the employer every day to see when a hiring decision will be made.
9. When introducing myself at job fairs or other business settings, I should avoid saying anything except my name until the other person responds in kind.
10. When I know a company I am interviewing with is having a casual day on the day I am interviewing, it is best to dress down for the interview.
11. During an on-site interview, it's okay to order a cocktail before the meal or wine with my meal when everyone else is drinking.
12. I have a great sense of humor, so it's perfectly fine to have a humorous greeting on my voicemail (or answering machine) when job-hunting.
13. At meetings at where people are wearing name tags, the best place to put your name tag is on your right chest/shoulder area.
14. When I place telephone calls to potential employers, I use a clear and

confident voice and always first identify who I am and why I am calling.

15. At job and career fairs it's okay for me to walk up to a group of people engaged in conversation and interrupt by introducing myself.
16. When talking on the phone with a potential employer or other business contact, it's okay for me to put them on hold while I answer another phone call.
17. I always avoid asking questions at an interview because it is rude to interrupt the interviewer by asking questions.
18. During an on-site interview, when dining out, I always rest my soup spoon and butter knife on the saucer or plate rather than on the table.
19. The rules of etiquette aren't as important in businesses that have a "laid back" corporate culture.
20. No matter what type or level of job I am applying for, I always go out of my way to greet the receptionists and secretaries with sincerity.

II. Read the statements below and decide whether the statements are true or false. Write T for true and F for false.

1. If you apply for a position of assistant in a store or restaurant, you don't have to make yourself neat, tidy, and well-groomed for the interview.
2. There is no need arriving early for the job interview so long as you can get there on time.
3. You don't have to prepare questions to ask the interviewer because the interviewer wouldn't allow that.
4. You could bring your laptop or iPad to show the interviewer what you have accomplished if you are going for an interview for a tech or web job.
5. At job interviews, you can carry with you a coffee cup or bottle of soda or water or anything else to drink in case they don't offer drinks.
6. On arrival at a job interview, if there is a receptionist, tell him or her who you are and who you are scheduled to meet with.
7. Never ask the interviewer to repeat the question even if you're not sure what

he or she is asking.

8. When responding to questions at job interviews, make sure your answers are focused and the skills relevant to the job are highlighted.
9. Extra copies of your resume are unnecessary for job interviews.
10. It is inappropriate to ask the interviewer when you might expect to learn the result towards the end of the interview.

III. Match each of the following words in Column A to the phrase or definition that is most closely related in Column B.

Column A	Column B
1. finalist	A. someone who supplies members or employees
2. on-site	B. the act of distracting; drawing someone's attention away from something
3. recruiter	C. a formal recommendation by a former employer to a potential future employer describing the person's qualifications and dependability
4. Curriculum Vitae	D. having your hair neatly brushed and combed
5. distraction	E. a contestant who reaches the final stages of a competition, e. g. a candidate on the shortlist for the job position
6. highlight	F. taking place or located at the site
7. reference	G. emphasize, give prominence to
8. well-groomed	H. a summary of your academic and work history
9. certificate	I. an unemployed person who is trying to get a job
10. job seeker	J. an official document that you receive when you have completed a course of study or training, or an official document stating that particular facts are true

IV. Put the following sentences into English or vice versa.

1. How you dress, what you bring to a job interview, how you greet the interviewer, and how you communicate can all make a big difference in the

outcome of the interview.

2. Bring extra copies of your resume with you, in case the interviewer needs a copy or you end up meeting with several people.

3. Phone interviews are terrifying to some job-seekers and absolutely painless to others.

4. 不管你感兴趣的是哪种工作,你都想给面试官一个良好的第一印象。

5. 关键是不能让问题积累起来,而是遇到一个解决一个,迎头痛击。

6. 回答面试问题,力求简洁切题,并且注意突出与应聘工作相关的技能。

▶ Speaking

1. Read the text loudly, and try to recite the following paragraph.

If you are in the middle of something, running out the door, or can't remember what the job is, it may be best to suggest another time. A good way phrase is "I'm so happy you called. I have about 10 minutes before I have to run out the door. Is that enough time, or can I call you back later this afternoon?" This way, you are expressing your interest, being clear about the time you have, and suggesting a time to connect later.

Immediately after the call, write a short thank-you note. It often goes something like "Thank you for spending time with me on the phone today talking about the enrollment—management position. I enjoyed the conversation and have a better understanding of the job. I'd be interested in an on-site interview, and would welcome the opportunity to further discuss my candidacy."

2. Read and practice the following dialogue in pairs.

(David Tang 到 Players 杂志社求职面试,考官是杂志社经理 Fred Dixon。)

F: Hello, Mr. Tang. Take a seat.

D: Thanks, Mr. Dixon. Call me David, please.

F: OK, David ... call me Fred. How are you this morning?

D: Very well, thanks. Actually, I'm quite excited.

F: Oh?

D: I've been a big fan of *Players Magazine* for many years now. I love what you do here. I love the witty writing, the clever features and even the layout.

F: Nice of you to say. We've been working hard to try to keep the magazine as current and relevant as possible. So... I've looked over your resume. You're bilingual, right?

D: Yes. Actually, technically Chinese is my mother tongue ... my parents immigrated to Canada when I was seven years old. Later on I went to school in the States and Europe as well.

F: Well, being bilingual is always a plus. We are thinking about expanding our operations and—of course—China is a huge market. Anyway ... let's see here ... can you tell me why you think you'd be a good fit for our organization?

F: That's good. OK ... here's a question that might seem kind of off the wall. If you were a car ... what kind of car would you be and why.

D: Hmmm ... interesting question. I'd say I'd be one of those Japanese sports cars. Not too big ... not too flashy on the outside, but lots of power under the hood. You're asking this to get a sense of my personality, right?

F: Yeah, that's the idea. So you're saying you are reliable and quietly powerful ... is that it?

D: Yeah ... that's a good way of putting it.

▶ Acting

Watch the video and role play.

Interview Sample in English

http://v.youku.com/v_show/id_XMzE4Nzk2Nzg0.html

▶ Supplementary Listening

* Business Etiquette (Lesson 019 – Identifying Yourself over the Phone, Lesson 110 – 111 Job Interview (1.2), Lesson 109 – 108 Prepare for Job Interview (1. 2), etc.)

http://www.voanews.cn/voaet/17705.htm

Listen to the dialogues and dictate down the important points.

* Job Interview
  http://v.youku.com/v_show/id_XMTM1MTIwMzY=.html
* Effective Interviewing
  http://video.about.com/jobsearch/Job-Interview-Tips.htm
* Interview Etiquette
  http://v.youku.com/v_show/id_XMzY3MDU2MTA4.html
* Putting Your Best Foot Forward
  http://v.youku.com/v_show/id_XMzY3MTMwMTA0.html
* Response Techniques
  http://v.youku.com/v_show/id_XMzY3MTU0MTIw.html
* Job interview
  http://v.youku.com/v_show/id_XMjU4MTgxMTEy.html

Watch the videos and dictate down the important points.

▶ Supplementary Reading

Tips for Job Seekers on Interview Questions

The process of interview preparation gives you the opportunity to mentally orient yourself as suitable for a job so that at interview you are already seeing yourself in the role. You can find out the most common interview questions and answers below.

Researching for interview questions

An important part of interview preparation is to find out as much as possible about the organization and the position. Find the company's website and learn about the organization. What does the company do? What is its structure? Are there any issues to be aware of? Being able to demonstrate your knowledge will show the interviewers that you have some understanding of the company's role and position in the market, its competitors and any challenges.

Having a good understanding of the position you applied for is just as important. This will help you identify your own suitability for the job vacancy and demonstrate this during the interview.

Self-awareness and interview preparation

Being aware of your strengths and challenges in an interview situation will help you present the best image of yourself. Try to prepare some examples of your work so that you can convince the interviewer of your skills and ability.

Practice makes perfect. Ask a friend or colleague to help you practice your job interview technique and give you helpful comments. Make sure you choose someone who knows your work and will give honest and constructive feedback.

Finally, if you are attending an interview at a company at which you already work, be careful not to undersell yourself. Never assume that the interviewers already know all about you; it can be helpful to try to forget you know them and answer interview questions accordingly.

Common interview questions and answers

Typically there are 3 types of job interview questions. General exploratory questions are often used at the start of an interview, aimed at relaxing you and getting to know you a little. Behavioral interview questions are designed to focus on how you function in a role and focus on your past approaches and look for how you might fit the company. Situational interview questions are typically designed around real or hypothetical situations applicable to the job vacancy. Following are the 5 most common interview questions and answers to help you in your interview preparation.

- **Tell us about yourself**

Often as the first question, this is a great opportunity to make a positive first impression. Make sure you mention your expertise and strengths, how your career has developed and where you want to head now—relating this to the job vacancy of course. Be brief and concise; don't get carried away and give them your life story.

- **Why have you applied for this job?**

Talk about why the company interests you—perhaps you're passionate about the services it provides—and how the role matches your professional interests and experience. Values are a big thing with organizations these days so make sure you've checked for a values statement on their website and can talk about how they fit with your own.

- **What is your understanding of the company?**

Use your interview question research to talk about what the company does, why it exists and where it sits in the market. Maybe the company is facing some challenges or might even be in the media; this interview question is a chance to demonstrate your knowledge.

- **What are your strengths and weaknesses?**

Your interview preparation will have given you an understanding of what the company is seeking, so make sure you are ready to match your skills and knowledge to their needs. A good way of describing a weakness is to talk about what you have done to manage it, e. g. you have had to learn when to step back from your tendency to be a perfectionist.

- **Where do you see yourself in 5 years?**

Most people dislike this interview question because often the real answer is "I don't know". One way of dealing with it is to talk about how you would like to be experiencing the workplace, i. e. feeling valued, making a real contribution, developing and using your skills and knowledge.

And finally …

When you are answering interview questions, keep in mind that you need to promote yourself for the position. Make sure that you tie each of your answers back to your skills and motivation and demonstrate how you are the right fit for the organization.

Answer the following question:

1. Is it appropriate for the interviewee to ask questions like "where is your company based" and "in which cities do you have branches"? And why?
2. If you are having a job interview for the position of a salesman in one of the Fortune 500 companies, how would you answer the question "Where do you see yourself in 5 years"?

Read more information about job interview:

* Sample Thank-You Letter After Interview
  http://www.buzzle.com/articles/sample-thank-you-letter-after-interview.html
* Dining Interview Etiquette
  http://jobsearch.about.com/cs/interviews/a/interviewdining.htm
* 10 Things Not to Say in a Job Interview
  http://jobs.guardian.co.uk/article/4459144/10-things-not-to-say-in-a-job-interview/
* What You Should Never Say in a Job Interview
  http://money.usnews.com/money/blogs/outside-voices-careers/2011/07/04/what-you-should-never-say-in-a-job-interview
* Top 10 Things You Should Never Say During a Job Interview
  http://pattyinglishms.hubpages.com/hub/5_things_you_should_NEVER_say